The Economic Transformation of America

The Economic Transformation of America

Robert L. Heilbroner
New School for Social Research

in collaboration with
Aaron Singer
Manhattan College

Harcourt Brace Jovanovich, Inc.

New York   Chicago   San Francisco   Atlanta

For Seymour Hammel

ISBN: 0-15-518800-3

Library of Congress Catalog Card Number: 76-024990

Printed in the United States of America

Maps and charts by Theodore R. Miller

Picture credits on page 259

Contents

Economic Transformation as a Theme of History

Preface

We are about to begin the study of American history from an unaccustomed perspective—the perspective of the economic transformation of American life. And we are going to open our examination of this perspective by asking an unaccustomed question: *What is history?*

What Is History?

This may seem a roundabout and pointless way to broach our subject. Why not proceed directly to the matter at hand? What is to be gained by asking so simple a question? Is history not the record of what has happened, the chronicle of what we know about the past?

The question is not so simple, however. For *which* among many pasts is our history? Is it the past that we learn when we memorize lists of presidents? Is it the past memorialized by the dates of wars? Is it the past reflected in the notebooks of explorers? Or is it all these pasts together, some immense volume in which we find presidents, wars, explorations, and all else?

Our inquiry brings us to a disconcerting recognition. There is no such immense volume. Indeed, none is possible. A history that included all the threads of our past would require us to know everything that had ever happened. That is more than we can know about our own lives, much less the lives of others. History in this all-encompassing sense can never be written.

We are left, then, with the need to write history from some perspective, highlighting one theme or another from our "total" history. There are innumerable such possibilities. We can write histories of American politics, art, social life, crime—each with its own cast of characters and plot. Needless to say, the same event may enter into more than one such history, and different histories may feature quite different events. The assassinations of Lincoln and Kennedy, for example, certainly bulk large in the history of politics, but they would figure as well in a history of American crime—although in that context they would be reduced to the insignificant status of mere homicides. The development of jazz figures large in American social history but not in American diplomatic history. *Thus the choice of a theme is a decisive determinant of what we will find in "history."*

These brief reflections help us when we now turn to the theme of this book. For the choice of economic transformation causes us to view events from a perspective different from that of the usual American history. Its cast of characters features business leaders, working men and women, inventors, not the usual presidents, generals, or patriots. Its plot ignores the great epic of American democratic development and dwells instead on the less familiar currents of economic expansion and conflict. Technical processes, such as steel-making, play a role as central as those usually accorded to political processes such as lawmaking. Enormous events like the Civil War appear only in the background; whereas matters that we ordinarily hardly bother to notice, such as J. P. Morgan's purchase of the Carnegie Steel Company, suddenly loom very large.

Why study the past from such an unusual angle? The answer is that our perspective has an extraordinary power of illumination. Not all themes of history shed equal light on other themes. It is the property of the theme of economic transformation that it touches on so many others. In fact, it is not too much to say that without a comprehension of the American economic transformation many other histories of American life remain unintelligible. Certainly the great drama of our democratic evolution loses most of its meaning unless we project it against the changeful backdrop of economic events. So, too, the histories of social change, of science or literature or even fashion —in short, most of the innumerable histories that can be written about America—require for their full understanding a grasp of the profound economic transformation through which America has passed.

The Economic Transformation

And so we arrive at our beginning and can put the question we have been waiting for: what has been the economic transformation of America?

Alas, there is no simple way to describe it, for the transformation has not been a simple process. One aspect of it has involved economic growth—the sheer increase in the quantity of our material output. Certainly anyone who compares American economic life in 1700, 1800, 1900, and today must be struck with the ever larger tonnages of steel and cement and wood and chemicals and organic products that enter into our collective lives at each successive date.

But sheer growth in itself is only a first approximation to the economic transformation. We could never comprehend the meaning of growth if we did not take into account the invasion of life by machinery. If we were to take snapshots of American life from 1700 to today, we would find that machines were ever more visible, no matter where we pointed the camera. On the farms, reapers and combines and mechanical pickers displace men; lathes and engines and conveyors crowd the factory floor; the railroad and the automobile take the place of the horse; ordinary living becomes inextricably involved with telephones, television, appliances.

Elsewhere the economic transformation takes on other aspects. Consider, for example, the way in which Americans have depended on one another. In 1700, well over three-quarters of all families grew the food they consumed, and probably as many wove the clothing they wore. Today 95 Americans out of 100 are unable to provide their own food; probably 99 out of 100 are unable to clothe themselves. In fact less than 10 percent of all employed persons even work for themselves today; in 1800 about 80 percent of Americans did so.

Thus another part of the economic transformation has been a gigantic uprooting, a massive rearrangement of economic relationships, a wholesale revision of the necessary skills and tasks of the population. Would our colonial forebears, magically transported to present-day America, manage to fend for themselves? Would present-day Americans, magically transported to colonial days, survive at all?

And even these changes do not fully describe the transforming process. Economic life today is dominated by powerful government, huge corporations, strong labor unions. These, too, are the products of the economic metamorphosis we must examine. Most of the government agencies with which we are familiar are not as old as our parents. The major labor unions did not arrive on the economic scene in full strength until the 1930s. Even the big corporations are new. The total value of the hundred largest companies in 1900, when the cry of "big business" was already being raised, was probably less than the value of the *single* largest company today, even after we allow for inflation.

Thus it must be clear that our theme is necessarily complex, for the economic transformation of America must be observed as a many-faceted process of change. We will not try to make the process simple or one-faceted, for that would do violence to the very meaning of the historical narrative we wish to recount. But we will approach the transformation in stages that will help us gain a surer footing in economic history.

In Part One of our book we primarily stress the role of *economic growth*, watching the expansive momentum of the young economy gather strength and gradually turn in the direction of manufacture. This part will set the stage for the main drama to follow. Part Two will pursue the theme of transformation into the *industrialization of life*. The invasion of machines, only dimly visible in Part One, will come to the fore as a major aspect of the overall transformation. Out of the industrial impetus we will see as well the rise of the new institutions of big business and labor unions and big government.

Part Three will concentrate on a different aspect of the transformation. We will be studying the convulsion of the Great Depression and its aftermath. Now the theme of economic transformation will focus mainly on *the change from a laissez faire to a mixed economy*—changes in work, in industrial processes, in institutional structures recede into the background, while developments in economic problems and policies come to the fore. And finally, in Part Four we reach modern times, to speculate on the nature of the economic transformation taking place in our own day, and in particular on *the challenges raised by the environment to a continuation of the trajectory of our economic growth.*

Thus we will trace the economic thread of change and growth and conflict from very early times down to the present and even into the future. As our narrative unfolds and the ramifications of the economic transformation become more apparent, we will see how useful the theme becomes as a way of organizing and understanding that unrecapturable universe of experience we call "history" and of defining our position in that equally vast and ungraspable universe we call "the present." Perhaps our theme will even give us a clearer sense of our possibilities in the face of that third unknowable universe, the future.

But all this lies ahead. First we must familiarize ourselves with our new perspective by turning back the pages to the early years of the American experience and searching for the roots of economic growth and development in those times.

**PART
ONE**

The Momentum
of Growth

Beginnings of
Economic Growth

1

When we look back on the past, the economic growth of America seems inevitable. Out of the extraordinary abundance and variety of resources, the generally benign and favoring climate, the vigorous people, some inherent impetus seems to have pushed America from the very beginning into the swift stream of economic development. Particularly in contrast to the backward regions of today, growth in America appears to have been effortless, the spontaneous outcome of natural forces.

Was Economic Growth Inevitable?

Certainly the prime indicator of economic expansion—the sheer capacity of a society to sustain human life—leaves no doubt as to the pace of early American economic growth. Take Virginia, for example,

Baltimore in 1752

where 350 settlers fought for existence in 1610. Within forty years, fed both by continuing immigration and a birth rate of 55 per thousand that puts to shame the highest birth rates of the tropics today, Virginia boasted a population of nearly 20,000; by 1700 the number was 60,000; within another seventy-five years, almost half a million. Forty percent of the population was black, for the slave trade was one of the funnels of human increase, but the sheer rapidity of the growth in numbers testifies to the equally rapid growth in the economic carrying-capacity of the land.

As with Virginia, so elsewhere. Baltimore, a hamlet of seven houses in the memory of Charles Carroll, a signer of the Declaration of Independence, grew within his lifetime to a city of 70,000; Philadelphia, with a population of 4,000 in 1690, numbered 35,000 in 1776, making it second only to London in the English-speaking world. If we take the colonies as a whole, what had been in 1650 only a thin sprinkling of 50,000 souls from Maine to Jamestown had virtually quintupled its numbers by 1700, and between 1700 and 1750, virtually quintupled again.

Meanwhile the face of the nation was changing in ways that also made evident the pace of economic growth. Within the span of life of a man and his son, the rude Plymouth plantations had given way to the solid substance of Boston, and the wilderness had made way for the cultivated countryside. In 1650 a trip from Boston to New York overland was an expedition; by 1705 a middle-aged schoolteacher

Seventy-five years later

could make the journey in two weeks, with only mild mishaps and some flutterings of trepidation concerning the "savage Indians" through whose territories she had to pass; by 1789 Indians were already a curiosity in the civilized parts of New England.

It is not only the growth of population and the taming of the wilderness that testify to the surge of economic growth in the colonial world. Through the colonial ports poured an ever-rising stream of American products destined for the English table (rice), taste (tobacco), mills (indigo), and navy (spars and timbers). Between the beginning of the eighteenth century and the outbreak of the Revolutionary War, the value of colonial shipments to England rose sevenfold, from $395,000 to $1.9 million. More striking, a colonial nucleus of manufactured production was also burgeoning, along with agriculture. By 1776 flour mills at the head of Chesapeake Bay reportedly had the finest equipment in the world, distilleries in Philadelphia exported well over 200,000 gallons of rum annually, and most surprising of all, the thirteen colonies possessed more forges and furnaces than all of England and Wales and exceeded them in the output of pig and bar iron. In fact American iron output totaled one-seventh of world output.

Clearly, an astonishing momentum of economic advance could be discerned in the colonial world almost from its inception. The economic transformation of the nation seems to have begun instantly and effortlessly. No wonder that in retrospect it seems "inevitable."

Men and Materials

Was it in fact inevitable? Let us look more deeply into the sources of America's economic growth and ask why it was so quick and powerful, unlike the experience of the underdeveloped nations in the Southern and Eastern Hemispheres of the world today.

No sooner do we ask this question than a crucial element of American development comes to the fore. It is that America never was an *underdeveloped* country, although it was, of course, an *undeveloped* one. The differences between the two are vast. Take the matter of land and resources. Much of the underdeveloped world today suffers from the retarding effects of debilitating climates, epidemic diseases, leached-out or unworkable "lateritic" soils that turn into brick once the grass cover is removed, hobbling shortages of many resources. America had none of these handicaps. The new continent offered the accustomed temperatures of Europe, a healthy environment, soils as good or better than those of the old country, and an abundance of timber and mineral wealth.

Even more important was the quality of the human resources. What quickly strikes the observer of the low-income nations today are the maddening antidevelopmental characteristics of so much of their populations—an inability to imagine change, a listless acceptance of general misery, a passive acquiescence in personal misfortune, all attitudes shaped by the social environment but acting to preserve that environment unaltered. In America no such apathy or acceptance of age-old ways ever posed their immense obstacles. On the contrary, the settlers of the New World were mainly products of an English culture that was itself intensely expansion-minded, and by their very presence in America they showed themselves to be risk-oriented, or were the offspring of individuals who had been willing to take on a great and dangerous adventure in hope of betterment.

The Puritan Ethic

Thus the original colonists brought with them a spirit of economic and political activism and a cultural liveliness that contrast sharply with the attitudes of the underdeveloped nations today. "Our ancestors," declared one Massachusetts fisherman, "came not here for religion. Their main end was to catch fish!"[1] Or as one historian has put it: "Capitalism came in the first ships."[2]

Part of that indispensable attitude of striving was no doubt the consequence of what we call the Puritan ethic, a fusion of spiritual and material views that encouraged busyness and worldly enterprise. Cotton Mather, the famous Puritan minister, stated the case vigorously in 1695:

> Would a Man *Rise* by his Business? I say, then, let him *Rise* to his Business. It was foretold (Prov. 22.29) *Seest thou a man Diligent in his Business? He shall stand before Kings.* . . . Yea, how can you ordinarily enjoy any rest at *Night*, if you have not been well at work in the Day? Let your *Business* ingross the most of your time.[3]

Perhaps the conjunction of the appetite for gain and the approval of industriousness reached its clearest expression in 1757 in Benjamin Franklin's famous *Almanack*, where "Poor Richard" tells his countrymen how to prosper:

> The Sleeping Fox catches no Poultry, and . . . there will be sleeping enough in the grave. . . . Let us then be up and doing. . . . Sloth makes all things difficult, but Industry makes all easy, so Poor Richard says. . . . [So] drive thy business, let not that drive thee; and Early to Bed, and early to rise, makes a man healthy, wealthy and wise.[4]

The Supply of English Capital

This emphasis on social predispositions to growth can lead us too easily to lose sight of other considerations, no less significant in explaining the meteoric rise of the American economy. One of them was the supply of capital, an essential ingredient of growth desperately lacking from the underdeveloped world, where the first thing that strikes our eyes is the absence of the machines, buildings, equipment, and power that drive the economic systems of the industrial world.

Here again special conditions helped the colonists over a barrier that has proved almost impassable for so much of the contemporary underdeveloped world. These special conditions lay in the relationship of the American settlements to England, a relationship very different from that which weighed upon the colonies of Asia and Africa and South America.

With no gold to plunder, the colonists had to bring over or build up their own capital. With no passive population to exploit—despite abortive efforts to enslave the Indians and an early encouragement to the African slave trade—the settlers did most of the labor of the colonies themselves.

Thus American colonial growth was in large measure English growth, transplanted to another land. To be sure, it would not be long

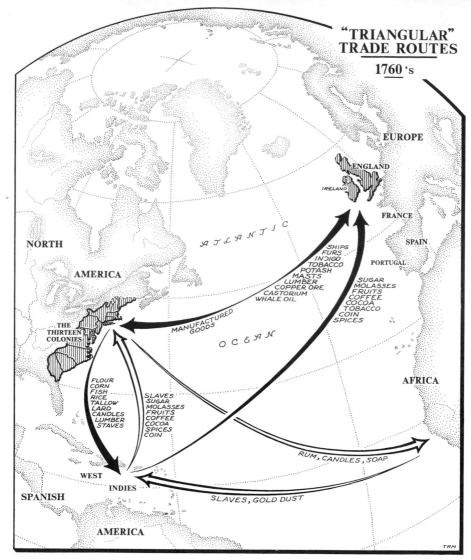

Triangular trade

before sharp divisions pitted colonists and home country against one
another. But for the first critical century, while the new country was
being gradually equipped with the necessities for a prosperous existence, there was a much greater feeling of coincidence than conflict of
interest. English men and women, with English ideas, speaking an
English tongue, using English technologies, and embracing many
English ideals, had in fact founded an extension of England across

the Atlantic. From this intimate connection there naturally arose an access to capital that was indispensable for America's progress.

The access began with the tools, supplies, and simple equipment that were transported in the first ships to provide the initial critical stock of capital goods. Thereafter, other capital was advanced by English promoters or invested directly by the Crown or brought along by middle-class or wealthy émigrés. Indeed, all through the eighteenth and even nineteenth centuries America lived on borrowed capital, some of it in the form of advances from English merchants, some in the form of a reliance on British shipping, in which, as late as 1771, four-fifths of all the Atlantic traffic was carried. On this easy and favored access to English money and English shipping the colonists built their thriving trade, including the famous "triangular trade" (see illustration) that poured rum into Africa, slaves into the West Indies, sugar and molasses (to make rum) into the colonies, and profits into pockets on both sides of the Atlantic.

"Born Free"

Was growth inevitable, then? Certainly climate, land, the self-selected individuals, the availability of capital and trade all combined to make the economy expansive, once growth had begun. Still, imponderables remain. How important, for example, was the spirit of freedom, the absence of a rigid social structure? Canada, with nearly all of the American blessings, did not "take off" on a steep gradient of growth. Hence we cannot assume that we have fully explained why the momentum of growth was attained so early simply by saying that America was never forced to surmount the physical and social and political obstacles of an underdeveloped land. As many historians have remarked, America was "born free." Perhaps that fortunate accident, more than any other single cause, contributed to its economic destiny.

Doubts, Misgivings, False Starts

No such destiny was apparent to many leading citizens of the colonies, however. They were not so much aware of the common culture they shared with their mother country as of their growing differences with it; not so much beckoned on by the fruitful continent as constrained and blocked by its wildness; not so much grateful for the bustle and striving of the common man as leery of or uneasy about it; not so grateful to England for its financial support but resentful of its superior competitive abilities. In a word, the outlook to many Americans appeared fraught with risk, and the growth of the national economy anything but assured.

Small Beginnings

Particularly was this true with respect to that small but strategic sector on which we now begin to focus our attention—manufacturing. "Sector" is undoubtedly too grand a term, for despite its iron forges and flour mills, manufacturing enterprise was still almost invisible to the observer. Even in 1800, after manufacturing had received the impetus of the Revolutionary War, it is doubtful if one person in thirteen worked in either trade or manufacturing (although we must bear in mind that many farmers were also artisans who produced much of their own "manufactures," such as woven cloth, simple tools, candles, soap, and the like).

Such "industry" as existed was largely centered in the cities and towns where owner-craftsmen, often with an apprentice or two, carried on a variety of trades for the local community. A survey in Philadelphia in 1787, for example, shows us some sixty kinds of manufacture—potash, woodworking, carriages, leather crafts, grain-milling, woolens, nails, clocks. What strikes us in surveying this incipient industry, however, is the tiny scale of its endeavor—paper-making in which each ream was an accomplishment; boot-making by the individual pair; wood-turning to order; the forging of axes and scythes and plowshares for the individual customer; the production of crockery in lots of a few dozen. Even when we turn to the most important industries we are still struck by the minuscule scale of production. The iron foundries of the colonies may have outproduced those of England, but they nonetheless turned out only 30,000 tons of iron a year—about twelve pounds per capita, or no more than the least-developed country today. Nails, for instance, were so scarce that pioneers burned their cabins to the ground to recover them before moving on. Similarly, the flour industry, for all the excellence of its equipment, exported only 250 tons in a good year, and the entire output of the shoemakers of New England was only 80,000 pairs, or one pair per forty (white) population.

Not only was production small, but the struggling enterprises in the nascent manufacturing sector had to contend with the deliberate efforts of their English competitors to stifle their growth. As early as

1699 Parliament had forbidden the export of woolens beyond the boundary of any colony, in an attempt to discourage an American industry that threatened to press too hard on English woolen manufacturers. In 1732, in response to loud complaints from the London hatters, another parliamentary act barred the colonial exportation of hats, and in 1750 Parliament prohibited the construction or continuance of any mill or engine for slitting or rolling iron, or any plating forge or furnace for making steel.

Had these acts been strictly enforced they might have dealt a fatal blow to the tiny nuclei of colonial industry. Fortunately, the restrictive legislation appears to have been largely ignored. New iron mills, for example, continued to be set up and even advertised, and American axes acquired such repute that some British firms actually passed off their own products as American.

Changing Attitudes Toward Manufacture

British hostility to American manufactures was to be expected. Perhaps more significant was the general colonial indifference to them. With the main exception of iron—no fewer than six signers of the Declaration of Independence were directly connected with the iron industry—businessmen shied away from manufacture in favor of trade or agriculture. The reasons are not difficult to understand. English competition was severe. American labor was expensive. Local capital was scarce—at the time of the Revolution there was not a single chartered bank in the new nation. And then, not least, the easiest path to money-making seemed to be in tobacco or grain or in the shipping trade.

Indeed, it is likely that had the Revolutionary War not broken out, manufactures might have been long delayed. But the advent of the war quickly revealed the strategic role of manufacturing, whatever its economic profitability. For the Revolution soon came to depend on America's small manufacturing capacity. The colonial iron industry assumed a critical importance—Washington located his winter camp at Valley Forge (note the significance of the name) to guard its essential metal-working shops. The tiny textile and leather industry was suddenly indispensable for providing the army with its issue of four shirts, two pairs of overalls, two pairs of shoes, breeches, coat, and cap.

Despite subsidies from the Continental Congress, the tiny industrial core was clearly unable to expand fast enough to support the war effort. Woolens were scarce and the army shivered for lack of adequate clothing. More telling, in the vital matter of arms, the scale of manufacture and delivery remained pitifully small. The largest Treasury payment of which we have record was $1,200, or roughly the price of a hundred muskets, and the average delivery was probably a dozen or two. Had it not been for the receipt of 80,000 muskets from France, the Revolutionary army would have been reduced to fighting with pitchforks.

Thus it was the war that first revealed the need for a strong manufacturing sector. But with the return of peace, the considerations of national self-sufficiency were relegated to second place behind those of immediate profit. With the conclusion of hostilities, old trade connections with England were gradually resumed. A backlog of orders existed for all the goods denied by the war—linens and silks and fancy materials, "good" tableware, household bric-a-brac of various sorts—and dealers in these wares turned naturally to the makers they knew in London rather than to untried possibilities of production in New Haven or Boston.

Further, as the war ended, the expansive thrust of American business again turned to the alluring prospects of trade and agriculture. Near the end of the war, John Ledyard, a young New Englander, returned from China where he had sold pelts, bought for a song on the Pacific coast of America, for $100. Soon thereafter the China trade became a source of lucrative profit and steady commerce; in 1801 fifteen American ships put in at Canton with 18,000 skins valued at over $500,000. In the face of such profits, the lure of manufacturing was small. "The brilliant prospects held out by commerce," reminisced an observer in 1818, "caused our citizens to neglect the mechanical and manufacturing branches of industry; fallacious views, founded on temporary circumstances, carried us from those pursuits which must ultimately constitute the resources, wealth and power of the nation."[5]

Thus it was not surprising that the wartime enthusiasm for manufactures waned. John Adams, Washington, Franklin, all partisans of manufacturing during the war, now regarded prospects as unpromising, while abroad the general opinion prevailed that American manufactures would not take firm root. Thomas Cooper, an English economist who wrote a book of advice for émigrés, opined that the prospects for American woolens, linens, cotton goods, and pottery were dim, although he took a more hopeful view of glass, gunpowder, paper, and iron. Lord Sheffield, surveying the outlook for English exports in 1783, wrote, "British manufactures will for ages ascend the great rivers of [the American] continent. . . . [I]t will be a long time before the Americans can manufacture for themselves. Their progress will be stopped by the high price of labor, and the more pleasing and profitable employment of agriculture. . . . If manufacturers [by which he meant workers in manufacturing] should emigrate from Europe to America, nine-tenths of them will become farmers; for they will not work at manufacturing when they can earn a greater profit at farming.''[6]

Technical Problems

If these were not enough discouragements for manufacturing, there was yet another—the difficulty of creating an efficient industry in a nation that was technologically behind England and severely short of capital-building facilities. Take for example the case of textiles, a prime candidate for manufacture in every nation that is commencing the development of its economy. As we have already seen, the colonial wool-manufacturers were early denied access to the British market. But this economic barrier was not as difficult to surmount as a *technical* problem. England was the home of a cluster of epochal inventions that had matured around the time of the Revolutionary War: Arkwright's and Hargreaves' spinning jennies, Crompton's mule, Cartwright's power loom.

The British government had no intention of sharing these breakthroughs with colonials or anyone else. It quickly prohibited the export of textile-making machinery and drawings and even forbade the emigration of skilled textile workmen—a policy continued until 1845. Thus for nearly a decade before the Revolution, American textile enthusiasts struggled to found an industry by smuggling in models and drawings of English mill machinery. The effort was of little avail. Some models were intercepted in transit and destroyed; others arrived only to prove inoperable or of antiquated design. Thus it is not surprising that most of the early textile ventures were unsuccessful; typically, a factory established in Beverly, Massachusetts, was operating at a deficit after four years, despite exemption from taxation and subsidies from the legislature.

When the textile industry finally became established, it was largely the result of the efforts of Samuel Slater, a former employee of Richard Arkwright, inventor of the jenny and cotton-manufacturer on a vast scale. Slater landed in New York in 1789 and quickly established contact with Moses Brown, a Rhode Island textile pioneer who had tried in vain to establish an efficient cotton mill. Slater persuaded Brown to allow him to build a machine with seventy-two spindles with the aid of the local blacksmith. In 1791 the machine was "done." Actually, it refused at first to work, but after some desperate last-minute repairs the machinery, tended by nine children, turned out its first yarn. The accomplishment was proudly announced in Alexander Hamilton's *Report on Manufactures*, of which we shall learn more shortly. By 1801 the mill was a solid success, with a work force of over 100 children and adult overseers.

The Jeffersonian View

Despite Slater's success, it was clear that the path to manufacturing profit was uphill. Twenty-seven mills were spawned within a few years by the Slater-Brown venture. Most of them failed within a short period. *A Society for Establishing Useful Manufactures*, founded in New Jersey with ambitious plans to produce hats, cloth, and other

The Slater mill at Pawtucket, R. I.

Jeffersonian visions and Jeffersonian fears

goods, foundered within five years, although it was promoted by no less skillful an organizer than Hamilton himself. The irrefutable fact confronting American businessmen was that powerful adverse market forces subjected all manufacturing ventures to the gravest perils. And finally, one last current of opposition had also to be faced. This was the widely held view that manufacturing was inherently corrupting and debasing—a view that claimed the introduction of the factory system into the United States would bring with it the horrors of the factory towns in England and Wales.

Of all the protagonists of this view, the most articulate was Thomas Jefferson. Although he personally delighted in inventions and extolled household crafts, Jefferson set himself squarely against the enlargement of manufacture beyond the modest role it played in sustaining an independent and self-sufficient *household*, and did not translate this idea into the scale of an independent and self-sufficient *economy*. At bottom his objection rested on two conceptions of the manufacturing process. One sprang from a classical estimation of farming and a correspondingly dark picture of nonagricultural toil: "Those who labor on the earth," he wrote in his *Notes on Virginia* (Query XIX), "are the chosen people of God, if ever He had a chosen people. . . . Generally speaking, the proportion which the aggregate of other classes of citizens bears in any state to that of its husbandmen, is the proportion of its unsound to its healthy parts, and is a good enough barometer to measure its corruption."

Jefferson's second objection was that manufactures were not really a national necessity but a luxury. In America, he felt, the immensity of the land allowed nearly everyone the possibility of becoming a husbandman, and should any manufactures be required they could be obtained by trading agricultural surpluses for the products of the grimy manufactory.

The Turn Toward Industry

Thus, however marvelously predisposed toward economic growth, it was not at all clear that America was equally well predisposed toward *industrial* growth. Indeed, the obstacles we have noted strongly imply the opposite. The powerful guidance of natural economic forces, the absence of the needed technology, and the inclinations of native sentiment in favor of agriculture all tended to direct American economic effort away from industry.

What changed the course of American economic growth? In retrospect we can discern three sources of the gradual shift in economic direction. The first was simply that by hard trial and numerous errors the young economy discovered a few nooks and crannies of manufacturing in which it could meet and better English competition. One such nook was a low grade of cotton goods, well suited to American needs. Another was the flour-milling industry, already well established by Revolutionary times and sheltered by transportation costs from effective competition from abroad. A third was the small-arms industry, favored and patronized by government; yet another was the domestic iron industry, also protected by the high costs of transportation against English competition. In these industries the first roots of an industrial economy were firmly planted.

Second was the slow growth of an articulate philosophy that could be used to rebut the Jeffersonian view. In the 1780s a small but determined group of manufacturing protagonists began to present the manufacturers' view: Was there, as the pro-agriculture side claimed, a shortage of labor that would impede the establishment of an expansive industry? The remedy for that was simple: women and children would work in the mills. As one mill owner put it:

> Teach little hands to ply mechanic toil
> Cause failing age o'er easy tasks to smile;
> • • •
> So shall the young find employ
> And hearts, late nigh to perish, leap for joy.[7]

Was the work of manufacturing degrading, as the agriculturalists claimed? On the contrary, asserted the proponents of manufacturing, it could be made the occasion of moral improvement by the incorporation of courses of religious instruction. Samuel Slater did in fact found a Sunday school for his child employees, and we shall see in our next chapter that the early mills tried at first to combine profitable employment with workers' uplift.

Finally, was there a shortage of necessary capital? That too could be remedied by assistance from the state—by extending bounties and grants to pioneer businessmen and by strengthening the general credit and currency of the nation.

Hamilton's Reports

All through the Revolutionary period these sentiments gathered strength. It was not until after the new government was established, however, that they found an effective and articulate spokesman on the national level in Alexander Hamilton. In the first of his three famous reports to Congress, the *Report on Public Credit* (1790), Hamilton argued that Congress should take the bold step of calling in all the old debts of the states and the Continental Congress and replacing them with new bonds issued and guaranteed by the new national government. This step, quickly taken, did indeed dramatically establish the creditworthiness of the government and thereby laid the groundwork for a climate of confidence needed to advance the shaky cause of manufacturing.

Second, Hamilton urged the creation of a national bank, not only as a repository for federal funds and an agent for tax collection but as a source of credit and loans for industrial and commercial enterprise. Despite the misgivings of Jefferson (who thought that the bank was an undesirable aggrandizement of government power as well as an exercise of power beyond that envisaged by the Constitution), the new institution was voted by Congress and signed into law by Washington. It soon helped to alleviate the problem of credit for would-be manufacturers.

Last, Hamilton's *Report on Manufactures* (1791) forcefully enunciated all the arguments we have already reviewed and pressed the case that a manufacturing sector was essential to the security and prosperity of the nation. What interests us here, however, is not merely Hamilton's vision of an economy in which manufactures existed side by side with agriculture. More striking are his proposals that *government itself should take an active hand in bringing this new partnership about.* Hamilton's *Report* urged tariffs to exclude foreign goods competitive with those made at home; controls to prevent the export of raw materials that might be needed by American manufacturers; bounties and subsidies for enterprising manufacturers; rewards for American inventions and embargoes to prevent American industrial secrets from leaking abroad; a national board to promote arts, agriculture, and manufacture. A strong believer in private enterprise, Hamilton was nonetheless the first proponent of a form of national "planning," in which the government sought to channel the energies of enterprise in directions that presumably served the national interest better than the unguided pull of the marketplace.

The Napoleonic Wars

Hamilton's *Report* languished in Congress; it was far ahead of its time. The proposed aids to manufacturing were ignored, and the country continued its easy dependence on Europe's manufactures, bought with the proceeds of its agricultural exports.

That situation came to a jolting halt with the Napoleonic Wars. Napoleon sought to close the Continent to British manufactures; Britain sought to weaken Napoleon by cutting off his sources of raw materials. As a result, both nations systemically searched and seized all vessels, including those of neutrals. In growing exasperation, President Jefferson sought to bring counterpressure by closing off American trade from both sides. The Embargo Act of 1807 prohibited all vessels in the United States from leaving for foreign ports and required special bonds for those engaged in coastal trade.

The results were extremely painful for many. American exports fell from $108 million in 1807 to $22 million in 1808, with devastating effects on anyone engaged in exporting. Yet if the embargo ruined the export trade, it brought sudden profits to anyone who could make the articles that were no longer available from abroad. As a result, whereas only fifteen cotton mills had been built prior to 1808, eighty-seven mills were erected in 1809, and the textile industry continued its expansion, albeit at a slower pace, until 1812.

No less important than the stimulus given to industry, and the consequent diversion of capital and talent from shipping into manufacture, was a gradual change in national views about the proper place of manufacturing. The ultimate conversion was that of Jefferson himself. In a letter written to Benjamin Astin in 1816 Jefferson admitted that he had originally been opposed to the spread of manufactures. But that had been before the economic hardships of war. "We have experienced," he wrote, "what we did not then believe . . . : that to be independent for the comforts of life we must fabricate them ourselves. We must now place the manufacturer by the side of the agriculturalist."[8]

Jefferson's conversion came *after*, not during, the war. Its late date was symptomatic of a persisting national reluctance to admit the necessity of founding a strong manufacturing sector. For with the conclusion of the Napoleonic Wars, as previously with the end of the Revolutionary War, English manufactures again came flooding into the country, bringing bankruptcy to those new industries that could not meet English competition or had not found a niche of their own.

Thus the actual implementation of Hamilton's *Report on Manufactures*, with its belated Jeffersonian endorsement, would not come for some time. An outright protectionist tariff was not passed until 1828, and then it was labeled the "Tariff of Abominations" by the Southern interests who remained adamantly opposed to the Hamiltonian vision. Indeed, the setting of an industrial course would not be fully made until the terrible gantlet of the Civil War had been run and the contest between the industrializing North and the agricultural South had been bloodily resolved once and for all.

But the process of change was only recognized and endorsed, not begun, by these later events. Economic growth, so strongly evident from the earliest days of the colonies, had to be diverted away from agriculture and trade toward manufacturing by a lengthy experience during which the nation gradually came to understand the need for, and the requirements of, a strong manufacturing capacity. The early lessons, blows, and growing convictions from which the nation made up its mind have been the main subject of this chapter. Now we must look into some of the supporting changes in economic and social institutions that were necessary to give effect to the change of heart.

NOTES

[1] Quoted in Samuel Eliot Morison, *The Maritime History of Massachusetts* (1961), p. 13.

[2] Carl Degler, *Out of Our Past* (rev. ed., 1970), p. 1.

[3] *Two Brief Discourses* (1695), p. 48.

[4] Quoted in Leonard W. Labaree (ed.), *The Papers of Benjamin Franklin*, vol. VII (1963), pp. 341–42.

[5] Quoted in Douglass C. North, *The Economic Growth of the United States* (1961), pp. 47–48.

[6] *Observations on the Commerce of the United States*, pp. 101, 105.

[7] Quoted in Samuel Rezneck, "Rise and Early Development of Industrial Consciousness in the United States," *Journal of Economic and Business History* (August 1932), p. 373.

[8] Paul Leicester Ford (ed.), *The Writings of Thomas Jefferson*, vol. X (1899), p. 10.

Preparations
for the Age
of Manufacture

2

An observer in 1815 would have been pardoned if he had failed to understand the country's new ambitions for manufacture. The nation was still overwhelmingly rural in aspect and agricultural in occupation. Even in its most densely populated Northeastern areas, barely 10 percent of the population lived in "urban" concentrations of 2500 or more, while in the South the ratio was only half that. Moreover, even in the cities, "industry" was an unusual calling. The great bulk of the city workers were employed in mercantile businesses, in seafaring, or in the handicraft and service trades that catered to city life. The number found in mills or manufactories was negligible— throughout the entire nation probably only 15,000 persons, perhaps 1 percent of the gainfully employed, were engaged in iron or textiles, the two most promising candidates for industrial growth.

Lacks and Requirements

There were, moreover, serious problems that hindered the growth of the tiny nuclei of industry—the flour mills, sawmills, paper mills, woolen "factories," and artisan establishments that dotted the countryside. One of them was the marked isolation of the average American establishment. A comparison with England is useful here. In England, thanks to the smallness of the nation and to its peculiarly indented coast, a network of transportation bound the parts of the country into a more or less unified market. With no town more than 70 miles from the sea and with at least 20,000 miles of turnpike-highway (much of it admittedly execrable), England was knit together into an economic whole.

By contrast, America was fragmented into unconnected economic parts. When the British cut off coastal traffic during the War of 1812, transportation costs on a barrel of flour from New York to Boston shot from seventy-five cents to five dollars. In those days it took two yoke of oxen three days to make a 35-mile round trip, so that it cost more to drag a ton of iron 10 miles through the Pennsylvania hills than to bring it across the ocean, and the inland freight on corn was so high it was unmarketable outside a radius of a few miles from its origin.

A lack of adequate transportation was not the only handicap facing American industrial aspirations. Equally serious was the absence of a supply of labor to man its hoped-for mills. Here too England had a decided edge. The long, slow growth of English population, combined with the steady expulsion of poor "cotters" from the land, brought a steady stream of men, women, and children into the English mill towns. In America, population was booming, but the easy availability of land offered farm employment—and better, farm ownership—to the growing population.

Finally, America was technologically backward. Already by the early nineteenth century, as we shall see, the country had produced more than its share of individual technical brilliance, but it lacked the sheer scale of capital to enable it to build the machinery it needed. Significantly, when Robert Fulton designed the engine that was to propel the *Clermont* up the Hudson in 1807, he had to write to James Watt and Matthew Boulton's factory in England to make the contraption, because there was no place in America that could produce so complicated a piece of machinery.

Thus the foundation, the infrastructure, of an industrial economy had to be laid down. The country had to be unified physically as well

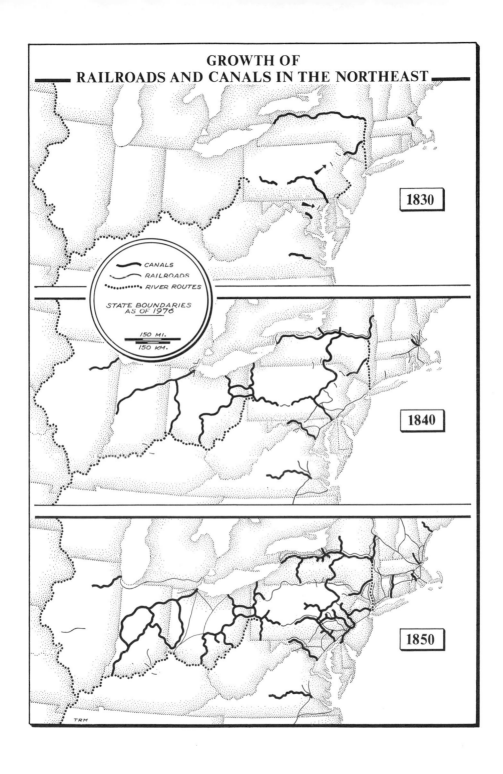

GROWTH OF
RAILROADS AND CANALS IN THE NORTHEAST

1830

CANALS
RAILROADS
RIVER ROUTES

STATE BOUNDARIES
AS OF 1976

150 MI.
150 KM.

1840

1850

as politically. A labor force had to be freed from the land and made available to the mills. A core of industrial expertise and capacity had to be developed. Until those tasks were complete—and that would not be until the very eve of the Civil War—an all-important aspect of the economic transformation of the country would be incomplete, and a full-scale entrance into the manufacturing age could not commence.

THE WEB OF TRANSPORTATION

The first need was transportation. Already in 1808, Albert Gallatin, Jefferson's brilliant Secretary of the Treasury, had proposed a broad and far-reaching system of "internal improvements" by which the nation would be tied together from north to south and east to west by a net of federally sponsored turnpikes and canals. Unfortunately, the plan perished in a flood of bickering, not so much over the principle of federal aid (although there was doubt as to the constitutionality of Gallatin's proposals) as from intense sectional jealousies and the fear that one state might get ahead of another. Of Gallatin's ambitious network, only one road was actually built—the great westward-leading pike from Cumberland, Maryland, to Wheeling on the Ohio River, and then later to Columbus and Vandalia, Ohio. Over it streamed an endless caravan of Conestoga wagons carrying population westward. Its sturdy stone bridges still carry traffic today.

In the absence of a national plan to create arteries of commerce, there grew up a kind of capillary system under private or state sponsorship. By 1800 there were already 72 profit-seeking turnpike companies in the Northeast, and ten years later the number had multiplied into the thousands: in New York alone there were 400 toll roads, though most of them were barely passable. Since the cost of construction rather than speed of travel or convenience was the main factor, the pikes were built as straight as possible, marching resolutely over hill and dale rather than seeking a more level, but longer, route through the valleys. We can judge their quality by an Ohio law of 1804 prohibiting the leaving of stumps over a foot high in *state* roads, and from the appellation "mudboats" given to the sledges that pulled cotton in the South during the rainy season.

Nevertheless the pikes were the first effective answer to the transportation challenge. They provided not only a slow circulation of commerce and travel but an economic boom of considerable dimensions. In New England alone, by 1840 over $6.5 million of private funds had been invested in turnpikes, much of it in small companies with capitals of less than $100,000; in Pennsylvania another $6 million, two-thirds private, one-third public, had also been spent. Indeed, not many years after the Revolution, a sum as great as the total domestic debt at the close of the Revolution had been invested in roads, thus providing a valuable economic as well as a physical stimulus.

The Erie Canal

Not surprisingly, many of the turnpikes failed. They were built with high expectations, little or no planning, and poor execution; by 1835 more than half of the turnpike ventures in the country had been either partially or wholly abandoned. Moreover, their demise was hastened by the coming of a new and much more efficient means of transportation, the canal.

Canals were not of course a new invention. In 1761 the Duke of Bridgewater built a famous canal in England to carry coal barges—a canal that actually crossed over streams on elevated waterways (an etching of the time shows a boat being towed by horses crossing over another sailing by the wind), and Gallatin had proposed ambitious canal-digging along with his plans for national roads. The problem was that whereas turnpikes cost $5,000 to $10,000 a mile, canals cost $25,000 to $80,000 a mile, and they took not a year or two to build but eight or ten. With the nation's sparseness of population and the long distances between cities, canals thus seemed impossibly costly for the United States. By 1816 barely more than one hundred miles of canals had been dug, most of them only two to three miles in length.

The event that moved canal construction off dead center was the tremendous adventure of the Erie Canal, in the words of one historian "the most decisive single event in the history of American transportation."[1] The idea of such a canal, linking the Great Lakes and the Atlantic, had appealed to a few imaginative persons since the early 1800s, and in 1809 a delegation actually went to visit Jefferson to interest him in the scheme: Jefferson observed that it was a fine project and might be realizable in a hundred years.*

That the canal was built was largely owing to the fortunate

* It was typical of Jefferson that, after the canal was opened, he was quick to admit his mistaken judgment and mused on the motivations that made such a bold venture possible.

Locks on the Erie Canal

endorsement of the Erie project by Dewitt Clinton, who was then casting about for an effective program for his campaign as Governor of New York. Voyaging with a few companions, Clinton surveyed the route and returned bursting with confidence that the immense undertaking could be done with funds and labor available within New York State alone.

By 1817 the legislature had been convinced as well, and on July 4th of the next year the work of digging "Clinton's Big Ditch" was actually commenced. Within a year 3,000 workers, largely immigrants, were digging; by the end of 1819 a middle section of some seventy-five miles was opened to traffic. By 1825 the canal was completed, an overnight wonder of the world.

And it *was* a wonder of the world. In parts it ran along embankments high enough for the barge-travelers to look down upon the tops of trees; at one point it went through seven miles of rock, sometimes to a depth of twenty-five feet; it sailed for miles through flat country crossed by light and airy bridges that stitched together the bisected land and forced the passengers to duck or go below deck. At a speed of four miles an hour and for a fare of four cents a mile, with "excellent provisions and comfortable lodgings on board," the barges brought their travelers on a romantic 363-mile journey and, more important, conveyed their cargoes on an incredibly economical basis.

For the canal worked a veritable revolution in the economic relationships of the area. Before the opening of Erie, the cost of bringing grain from the western regions of the state to New York City was three times the value of wheat, six times that of corn, ten times that of oats. Now, overnight, this stifling weight of transportation costs disappeared, as freight rates fell by 90 percent. In 1817 freight moved from Buffalo to New York via wagon at just under twenty cents a ton-mile; in the mid 1850s it was moving at less than a cent a ton-mile.

As a result, the volume of goods entering into commerce soared. Tonnage on the canal amounted to 58,000 tons by 1836; by 1860 it had reached 1.8 million tons. Moreover, as early as 1840 it was apparent that the canal was imparting a visible stimulus to the development of manufacturing, now that lowered freight rates greatly reduced the cost of raw materials and vastly extended the possibilities of marketing the output.

The Canal Boom

The success of the Erie Canal touched off an era of canal-building even more important for the economic integration of the country than the turnpikes. Within a year after Erie there were a hundred major projects for canals; by 1840 the combined length of completed canals exceeded the distance across the continent. Penetrating as far to the west as the far side of Indiana, with some fingers going even farther—the Illinois and Michigan Canal linked Chicago with the Illinois River and thus with the Mississippi—the canals provided a skein of broad water highways that did indeed unite East and West and (to a lesser extent) North and South.

The magnitude of the financial effort also far exceeded that demanded by the turnpikes. The decades of the 1820s and 1830s saw the huge sum of $125 million spent on canals. Unlike the financing of the turnpikes, most of this spending was state-financed, often with private participation. Reviewing the role played by government in these pre–Civil War years, Robert A. Lively has described what he called "the American System":

> . . . the elected public official replaced the individual enterpriser as the key figure in the release of capitalist energy; the public treasury, rather than private saving, became the main source of venture capital; and community purpose outweighed personal ambition in the selection of large goals for local economies. "Mixed" enterprise was the customary organization for important innovations, and government everywhere undertook the role put on it by the people, that of planner, promoter, investor and regulator.[2]

This is not to say that the government was a generally successful investor, either in the era of canal-building or later when it helped underwrite the railroads. In the canal era, financial failures outweighed financial successes by far; more than one state courted bankruptcy by overambitious building.

Yet even with the unsuccessful ventures came benefits. The vigorous spending served to stimulate economic activity at large. And when canals were themselves financial losers, they nonetheless brought business opportunities and profits to the enterprises they served. In similar fashion, our present-day road system would not be adjudged an economic failure simply because toll revenues failed to cover its costs: we measure the benefits of the road to the larger economy. So it was with the pikes and the canals. By 1859 the ton-mileage on the canals (already adversely affected by the railroads) totaled 1.6 *billion*. The canals had opened up the interior so that Ohio and Indiana grain could be sold in Europe and European or New England wares could be sold in Ohio. Moreover the canals (and to a lesser degree, the turnpikes) made possible an astonishing redistribution of population. Between 1790 and 1840, before any rail line breached the Appalachians, the percentage of the national population on the far side of that barrier increased from next to nothing to an astonishing 40 percent.

The Railroad Age

Thus when the railroads came, they appeared not as the main agents of the necessary transportation infrastructure, but as its capstone.* The Baltimore and Ohio, the first operating steam railway in

---

* We have not mentioned a special chapter of the transportation revolution dealing with the steamboat—the extraordinary invention that made it possible to transport people and material economically *upstream*. Steamers and paddle wheels were not

America, did not commence operations over its thirteen miles of track until 1828. In the next two years, while canal building was booming, only seventy-three miles of track were laid down. The general opinion was that railroads would not amount to much.

The doubts were understandable. Rails were generally made of flat strips of iron fastened to wood with spikes. Frequently the spikes would loosen and the rail would curl up around the wheels of the engine or even pierce the floor of the cars. Some lines laid their rails directly on stone and suffered their equipment literally to be pounded to pieces. Sparks from the engines set fields afire; engines jumped their tracks; railroads were said to run at unhealthy (as well as unsafe) speeds.

But by the 1840s it was clear that doubts had been ill-founded. During the ten years following 1830, while 3,326 miles of canals were dug, 3,328 miles of track were laid, and a rapidly improving technology had already put to rest many of the fears of the past. In the next ten years almost 9,000 miles of track were laid down; in the 1850s, 22,000 more would be put into place. During the 1840s alone over $200 million was spent on railroad building—a sum larger than the entire investment of the previous four decades in turnpikes, canals, and steamboats. By the eve of the Civil War railroads had become the first billion-dollar industry in America.

The Effect of the Industry

The impact of railroadization, as these figures show, was profound and pervasive, although our inquiry into the canals makes it plain that railroads were merely an advance in the transportation revolution and did not in themselves initiate the nation's industrial or agricultural growth.

Yet, in some ways the railroads imparted a different stimulus to the nation's economic transformation. Like the canals, the rails cheapened rates and quickened the pace of activity, but unlike the canals, they never froze over. Hence economic activity became less tied to the seasons. Much more than the canals, the railroads served as stimuli for the development of such crucial industries as iron and later steel, locomotive manufacture, and metalworking in general. Again unlike the canals, they mobilized the industrial imagination of

---

only picturesque but economically efficient, serving to reduce carrying charges and thereby to impart an additional momentum to economic growth in general and the development of manufactures in particular.

the country: Frederika Bremer, a Swedish novelist visiting the nation before the Civil War, noted that boys in school amused themselves by drawing locomotives (or steamboats)—always in motion, always smoking. She concluded that "interest in locomotive machinery had a profound connection with life in [this] country."[3]

Not least, the development of the railroads was even more effective than the canals in stimulating the flow of capital into the economy. A good portion of this, as with the canals, was government capital. By 1860 at least 60 percent of the railway costs in the South and nearly 50 percent of those in the North had been borne by public investment. In addition, the lure of the railroad tempted capital from private pockets. As early as 1838 the Eastern Railroad of Massachusetts had 2,331 stockholders, and the original Pennsylvania Railroad was financed almost entirely by house-to-house sales of stock. In the West, farmers often mortgaged their properties to help finance a short line through their region, and many manufacturers underwrote all or part of the spurs or short lines to their places of business.

Some of these investments turned out very badly. The first great depredations of finance made their appearance in these years as the president of the New York and New Haven Railway sold 20,000 shares of unauthorized stock, the proceeds of which went entirely into his own pocket. And the president of the Vermont Central dispersed 10,000 shares of illegal stock so skillfully that the legislature had to increase the authorized capital of the firm to save the unidentifiable victims from being fleeced.

Despite these harbingers of much larger depredations to come, the railroads never lacked for investors eager to put their money to work through rails and engines and cars. In particular, European investors rushed to buy American railway bonds and shares. By 1853 more than one-quarter of all American railroad bonds were foreign-owned. As a machine for siphoning European wealth into American capital equipment, the railroads were as effective as they were in completing the network of transportation indispensable for the industrial development of the nation.*

---

* Like all large-scale technological change, the advent of the railroads brought gain to some, loss to others. In *Life on the Mississippi*, Mark Twain vividly described the impact of the railroad on the previously flourishing steamboat trade:

> These railroads have made havoc with the steamboat commerce. The clerk of our boat was a steamboat clerk before these roads were built. In that day the influx of population was so great, and the freight business so heavy, that the boats were not able to keep up with the demands made upon their carrying capacity; consequently

FORGING A LABOR FORCE

Self-employed America

It is an illuminating commentary on early nineteenth-century America that whereas nearly everyone worked—on a farm a child was useful for small chores as soon as he or she was ready to carry things—yet in 1800 only 10 percent of the labor force were "employees." *Self*-employed farmers, *self*-employed "mechanics" or artisans, small *independent* tradesmen made up the bulk of the white working force. What was lacking was the personage we associate with the very essence of the industrial process—the factory worker, selling his or her labor power to the factory owner.

There were several reasons for this absence. One, to which we have already referred, was the easy availability of land. A second was the organization of manufacture on what is called a "putting-out" basis, in which a merchant capitalist distributed yarn to be woven, or straw to be plaited, or leather to be sewn, to workers *in their homes*, returning later to pick up the finished work. A third reason, with which we are already acquainted, was the general distaste, even horror, in which "mill work" or factory work was held. As one author put it:

> Cotton mills! In England the very words are synonymous with misery, disease, destitution, squalor, profligacy and crime! The buildings themselves are huge edifices which loom like gigantic shadows in a smoky dense atmosphere. Around them are wretched houses and places of the most infamous resort; and blasphemies and curses are the common language of those who frequent them.[4]

---

the captains were very independent and airy—pretty "biggity." . . . The clerk nutshelled the contrast between the former time and the present one, thus:

"Boat used to land—captain on hurricane-roof—mighty stiff and straight—iron ramrod for a spine—kid gloves, plug tile [hat], hair parted behind—man on shore takes off hat and says:

"'Got twenty-eight tons of wheat, cap'n—be great favor if you can take them.'

"Captain says:

"'I'll take two of them'—and doesn't even condescend to look at him.

"But nowadays the captain takes off his old slouch [hat], and smiles all the way around to the back of his ears, and gets off a bow which hasn't any ramrod to interfere with, and says:

"'Glad to see you Smith, glad to see you—you're looking well—haven't seen you looking so well for years—what you got for us?'

"'Nuth'n,' says Smith; and keeps his hat on, and just turns his back and goes to talking with somebody else."

A consequence of this ubiquitous self-employment was that the organizers of the first mills and large plants had difficulty in rounding up a work force. One of Samuel Slater's original child employees, risen to become a textile-mill owner himself, wrote to the Secretary of the Treasury in 1833 that "our greatest difficulty at present is a want of females, women and children; and from the great number of factories now building, have my fears we shall not be able to operate all our machinery another year."[5]

The complaint summed up a real difficulty. Men preferred not to work in the mill when they could find work on the farm. Women and children were the preferred employees, but they could be attached to a mill only if the mill owner managed to house the family nearby. That was manageable when the required labor force was only a few dozen hands. It became unmanageable when technology made it possible to design mills that could employ hundreds, even thousands. To staff the bigger mills, a new system was needed.

The Lowell System

That system was the creation of an American businessman of considerable talents, Francis Cabot Lowell, son of a comfortable Boston family, and a successful merchant himself. In 1810 he took his family abroad for their health and while in England became interested in cotton manufacture. We can make some measure of his capacities from the fact that he *memorized* enough of the equipment and layout of the mills he visited to be able to reproduce them in New England on his return.

Together with Nathan Appleton, Lowell founded The Boston Manufacturing Company in 1813, an instant success and a longtime dominant firm in the textile business. What interests us here, however, is the manner in which Lowell provided himself with the necessary help to put his new plant into motion. Determined not to have a mill village of poor, dependent families, he set out to revolutionize the labor supply by attracting intelligent young farm girls of good character to his mills. He did so by building dormitories and rooming houses, staffing them with housemistresses of unimpeachable respectability, and then scouring the countryside for young girls who would accept two or three years' employment as a means of gathering a small dowry or bettering themselves. Every effort was made to disassociate the mills from their English reputation of looseness and moral depravity and to create a spirit of earnestness, moral uplift, and financial self-improvement.

Inside a cotton mill

The Boston associates succeeded so well that within a short while they were "more puzzled to get rid of hands than to employ them." In addition, the mill town of Lowell became something of a preindustrial Mecca for sociologically minded sightseers. Michel Chevalier, a French traveler, noted that "Lowell is not amusing, but Lowell is clean, decent, peaceful, wise."[6] Charles Dickens came in 1842; after scrutinizing the factory girls he wrote that "from all the crowd I saw in the different factories that day, I cannot recall or separate one young face that gave me a painful impression; not one young girl whom, assuming it to be a matter of necessity that she should gain her daily bread by the labour of her hands, I would have removed from those works if I had had the power."[7]

Immigration Begins

The Lowell System was undoubtedly a remarkable chapter in the process of economic transformation, but it did not last very long. For one thing, the system was considerably less benign beneath the surface than it appeared. Hours were very long and pay low: the girls put in a twelve-hour day six days a week, for which they were paid $2.50 a week *before* the deduction of $1.25 for room and board. Typically, the factory owners manipulated their clocks to squeeze out a few minutes of extra working time; in 1831 the girl operatives struck against a factory that was cheating them of an extra half-hour a day; in Pawtucket, Rhode Island, public outrage forced the mills to set their clocks by the sun.

Meanwhile the mill owners were discovering another, more docile source of labor. At the very time that the supply of young girls was nearing exhaustion, a growing pool of Irish and English (and some German and Canadian) workers began streaming into Boston, desperate for work, willing to take anything. The names on the factory lists in Chicopee, Massachusetts, changed from Lucinda Pease and Wealthy Snow to Bridget Murphy and Patrick Moriarty. In Fall River in 1826 only 26 out of 612 operatives were foreign, but by 1846 the majority of the plant was Irish. "By 1850," writes one historian who has studied this period in depth, "[t]he white gowned girls who marched to welcome Presidents, who talked so intelligently to foreign visitors, who write poetry and stories filled with classical allusions, were no longer to be found in the factory mills."[8]

Elsewhere in the country, employers had long since turned to immigrant labor as a means of supplementing the labor force available to them. As early as 1828 the Chesapeake and Ohio Canal Company sent agents abroad to recruit workers from Cork and Belfast at rates well below prevailing American levels. The immigrant accepted work on the canals under hideous conditions that broke 5 percent of the labor force each year from fever and disease. Many of them stumbled into factory towns where they formed the first permanent urban proletariat in America. It would not be long before urban reformers would be describing with shock the conditions in the cellars and garrets and hovels that housed the urban poor.

Yet it is a telling commentary on the comparative standards of Europe and America that immigration—"that great referendum on American conditions," as historian E. C. Kirkland has dubbed it[9]—rapidly swelled to vast proportions. Between 1820 and 1840 immigration rose from roughly 10,000 to 90,000 a year; by 1850 it had jumped to over 300,000; by 1854, to nearly 500,000. Nearly half the increase in the nonslave working force between 1830 and 1850 was supplied by foreign labor.

The swelling tide of immigrants was not merely a continuation of the initial immigration that had founded the colonies. Those earlier arrivals had been on the whole literate, often skilled, fired to get ahead. The new wave, by and large, was illiterate, unskilled, easily exploited. We catch a glimpse of the prevailing managerial spirit in this excerpt from the report of a mill agent visiting Fall River in 1855:

> I inquired of the agent of a principal factory whether it was the custom of the manufacturers to do anything for the physical, intellectual, and moral welfare of their work people. 'We never do,' he said. 'As for myself, I regard people just as I regard my machinery. So long as they can do my work for what I choose to pay them, I keep them, getting out of them all I can. What they do or how they fare outside my wall I don't know, nor do I consider it my business to know. They must look out for themselves as I do for myself. When my machines get old and useless, I reject them and get new, and these people are part of my machinery.'[10]

We will look again at the role played by the immigrant worker, but here it is useful to reflect on the broader problem that the issue raises. Not only Karl Marx but the conservative German sociologist Max Weber has held that capitalism could not function without a property-less proletariat—a mass of workers who had no choice but to sell their labor on the market, accepting whatever terms and conditions the "market" offered. Certainly the industrial system in America could not find its needed workers as long as land was cheap and easily available. In the Lowell System, and then in the army of immigration, we find efforts to *create* a work force willing to perform harsh work for low wages. Thus the same economic transformation that created the industrial framework of the nation also brought into being a new class that would irreversibly alter the original aspect of America as a nation of independent working men and women.

TECHNOLOGY AND GROWTH

The network of transportation undergirded the growing American economy; the new labor force gave it its necessary factory hands; but for the emerging economy to "take off," there was required yet another factor—the creation of an industrial "know-how," a general expertise, a native technology.

Yankee Ingenuity

At the outset of the nineteenth century, and certainly in the eighteenth and seventeenth centuries, America lagged far behind Great Britain in technology. There were good reasons for this. By 1850, for every two Englishmen who worked the land, three worked in some kind of industry, broadly defined. By way of contrast, in America in 1850 not even 15 percent of the labor force was in manufacturing. Thus England had a far greater weight and variety of industry, a finer specialization of labor, and a more massive concentration of business talents in the area in which America was now beginning to seek its fortune.

Yet from the beginning, some advantages were to be found on the American side. One of them was a widely admired American propensity to innovate and experiment. A parliamentary committee, touring America in 1854, reported that every workman seemed to be continually devising mechanical aids to his work. In the same vein, James Nasmyth, the famed British inventor of many machine tools, told a parliamentary committee that English workmen and manufacturers were hampered by a "certain degree of timidity resulting from traditional notions and attachment to old systems, even among the most talented persons."[11] Typically, inventions spread more rapidly in America for the same reason: in 1859, fifteen years after the sewing machine had been invented, America had fifteen times as many sewing machines as England.

Whence this "Yankee ingenuity"? In part it was the product of farmer-mechanics, trained in country mills and blacksmithing shops, who apparently achieved an extraordinary self-reliance and versatility. From an early date, many tools, such as the hatchet, were altered by these craftsmen so that American axes and hammers early acquired a reputation abroad. In a society freed from the heavy hand of traditional class barriers and guild rules and regulations, such inventiveness found a natural outlet.

Add to this an economic incentive to invention posed by the high price of American labor. If there is a discernible pattern in American innovation, it seems to have been the adaptation of processes originally used in Europe in ways that would allow for a greater economy of labor. Thus Oliver Evans, an extraordinarily fertile mind, devised an automatic mill in 1783 that processed grain into flour through a series of conveyors and gravity feeds, virtually without the need for human effort. And of course the famous invention of the cotton gin by

Eli Whitney in 1793—an overnight stroke of genius—was said by Whitney himself to make the necessary labor of cleaning cotton "fifty times less."

Interchangeable Parts

The great triumph of Yankee ingenuity, however, unquestionably lay in its early emphasis on a technique that would become more and more associated with "American" manufacturing techniques. This was the technique of mass production. But mass production is not a means of manufacture that can be adopted directly from handicraft. There is needed a crucial intervening step—the development of a technology of *interchangeable parts* in which the components of a finished article are so much alike that one can be substituted for another, at random, to make the final article.

The American style of this radically innovative system becomes more apparent when we learn that the technology itself was first developed in France and Britain. In 1785, as American minister to France, Jefferson was shown an interchangeable set of flintlock parts, but despite his efforts Congress refused to bring the inventor to this country. In England another interchangeable system, developed to manufacture pulley blocks, was also curiously neglected by Britishers, so that the idea never spread to other products.

A happy but not altogether fortuitous conjunction of circumstances led to the eventual application of interchangeable parts in America. At the close of the century Eli Whitney was already famous for his invention of the cotton gin, but he was also in considerable financial straits, having been unable to patent the gin. He determined to remedy his fortunes by undertaking a daring scheme. "I should like," he wrote to Oliver Wollcott, Comptroller of the Treasury, "to undertake to manufacture ten or fifteen thousand stand of arms."

Since Whitney had never manufactured so much as a single gun, and in view of the fact that the entire output of the federal arsenal at Springfield was only 245 muskets over two years, his proposal was indeed audacious. But Whitney had a plan. As he wrote to Wollcott:

> My general plan does not consist of one great complicated machine, wherever one small part being out of order or not answering to the purpose expected, the whole must stop and be considered useless. If the mode in which I propose to make one part of the musket should prove by experiment not to answer, it will in no way affect my mode of making any other part. *One of my primary objects is to form the tools so the tools*

themselves shall fashion the work and give to every part its just propor-
tion—which, once accomplished, will give expedition, uniformity, and
exactness to the whole.

. . . the tools which I contemplate are similar to an engraving on a
copper plate from which may be taken a great number of impressions, per-
ceptibly alike.[12]

The American System

We know little of the actual tools that Whitney designed to make
possible his system of interchangeable parts. We get some inkling of
the difficulty of the task, however, when we learn that in the Lowell
textile machine shops blacksmiths still cut each nut to fit its own bolt
and that mechanics considered a tolerance of $1/32$ inch to be the best
that could be hoped for. In England, where the firm of Watt and
Boulton turned out superb steam engines, it was considered a
triumph when a cylinder head was made accurate within the
thickness of an "old shilling."
Thus we are not surprised to learn that Whitney's contract was

Whitney's cotton gin

long delayed in being carried out. For twenty-eight months he labored to create his grinders and borers and lathes, and then in 1801 he brought ten (not ten thousand) muskets to show President Adams and Vice President Jefferson. Before their eyes he took the guns apart, separated the pieces into piles, and offered to assemble ten new muskets from parts selected at random. His audience was dumbfounded. Yet they did not begin to appreciate the extent of the revolution that was latent in those scattered bolts and stocks and barrels.*

The "American system," as it was soon called, was not instantaneously successful. It would not be so until a general technology of machine-tool production made the task of creating multiples a simple rather than a demanding one: as late as 1824 it was considered a feat when the Harpers Ferry arsenal produced muskets with interchangeable bayonets. In 1815 the new technique was applied to the manufacture of wooden clocks, and Eli and Seth Thomas began to assemble 500 wooden clocks at a single time. Thereafter Chauncey Jerome applied the idea to brass clocks; then in 1846 it was used in the making of sewing machines; in 1847, for farm machinery; in 1848, for watch parts; in 1853, for the famous Colt revolver.

However slow in spreading (the technique was used in only about twenty industries in 1860), the use of interchangeable parts was still almost exclusively an American process. When Colt set up a plant in London for the manufacture of small arms (perhaps the first multinational company!), he had to take his own equipment and personnel with him, for the American system was still largely unknown to English manufacturers. Indeed, James Nasmyth, who inspected the Colt factory, reported that it made him feel quite humble.

Other Breakthroughs

It was not, of course, just the "system" that provided the needed technological impetus to the nation. The first half of the nineteenth century also saw a flowering of American inventiveness applied to areas where American needs were different from those of the Continent. The American clipper ship was a breakthrough of no considerable dimensions, as were John Fitch's and Robert Fulton's steamers, and then the superb steamboats of the western rivers (built with so little draft that it was said they could sail in a heavy dew).

In agriculture, American efforts to cope with high ratios of acreage to labor led to early experiments with farm machinery. A man work-

* Another gun-maker, Simeon North, shared honors with Whitney for his vision of interchangeable parts but was never so successful in applying the idea.

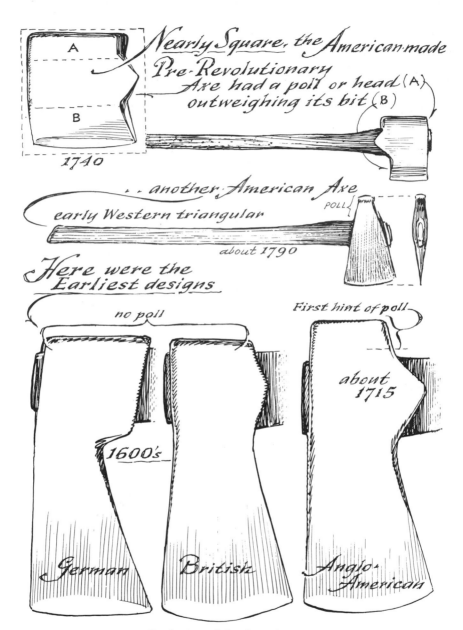

Nearly Square, the American-made
Pre-Revolutionary
    Axe had a poll or head (A)
      outweighing its bit (B)

A

B

1740

..another American Axe
early Western triangular

POLL

about 1790

Here were the
Earliest designs

no poll

First hint of poll

about
1715

1600's

German

British

Anglo-
American

Evolution of the American ax

ing with an old-fashioned cradle could harvest only two acres a day. By 1837 with the very imperfect Hussey reaper, he could bring in ten to fifteen, and the McCormick reapers made in 1849 were warranted to cut at least two acres an *hour.*

The Readying of the Economy

It is impossible to itemize all the technical improvements that now came with increasing rapidity—in water wheels, steam engines, blast furnaces, methods of canning, slaughtering, hat-making, building. Let us merely note that between 1840 and 1860 the number of patents increased by 1,000 percent.

Rather, what asks for emphasis is that the period of industrial preparation comes to fruition somewhere around the middle years of the nineteenth century. A transportation network had by then been solidly laid into place. A labor supply, willing to perform the monotonous tasks of machine tending, had been discovered. A technology capable of producing an industrial apparatus was well advanced. In a word, the prerequisites of an industrial society had been forged out of American and European sweat, skill, effort, and exploitation.

Yet, the age was still only one of preparation. The machine may have captured the American imagination, but it had not yet overrun American life. Still, the momentum of change was unmistakable. The pre–Civil War years saw only the beginning of the next phase of the economic transformation, but already the outlines of an impending change of vast dimensions were clear.

NOTES

[1] Carter Goodrich, *Government Promotion of American Canals and Railroads, 1800–1890* (1960), pp. 52–55.

[2] "The American System," *The Business History Review* (March 1955), p. 81.

[3] Quoted in Leo Marx, *The Machine in the Garden* (1964), p. 205.

[4] Quoted in Marvin Fisher, *Workshops in the Wilderness* (1967), p. 87.

[5] *McLane Report*, 1833, I, 1046.

[6] Quoted in Norman J. Ware, *The Industrial Worker* (1924), p. 202.

[7] *American Notes* (1842), p. 28.

[8] Ware, *The Industrial Worker*, p. 153.

[9] *Industry Comes of Age* (1961), p. 6.

[10] Quoted in Ware, *The Industrial Worker*, pp. 76–77.

[11] Quoted in John E. Sawyer, "The Social Basis of the American System of Manufacturing," *Journal of Economic History* (1954), vol. XIV, p. 377.

[12] Jeanette Mirsky and Allan Nevins, *The World of Eli Whitney* (1952), pp. 200–01.

The
Structural
Transformation

3

America on the Eve of the War

By every standard, the country was vastly richer in 1860 than it had been in 1800. Population had increased from 5 million to 31 million. In 1800 there was no city over 70,000; now there were already two cities with more than 500,000 people. In Washington's time 95 percent of the population lived in rural settings; in Lincoln's time the figure had fallen to 80 percent—one-fifth of the nation was already "urban." And whereas only 350,000 persons worked in factories or mills or hand trades in 1820 (the earliest date for which we have statistics), by the time of the Civil War there were 2 million men and women laboring in tasks that were neither agricultural nor "service" but industrial.

ECONOMIC GROWTH AND CHANGE

The Rate of Growth

Was this extraordinary change the direct product of that process we call "economic growth"? The question is not altogether easy to answer, for economic growth itself is not an easy concept to describe or measure. It would be one thing if economic growth consisted only in the augmentation of a *given* set of commodities—more and more corn, bricks, miles of turnpikes. But that is not the way in which growth occurs. Growth is an economic process of change as well as simple expansion. It is a process in which corn gives way to wheat, bricks to cement or steel, turnpikes to canals to rails—and then back to roads.

How can we measure growth under these conditions of change? The answer is that economic statisticians compute the dollar value of total output—*gross national product* (GNP) is the official designation.* For the early years of the nation, this is a difficult task, given the paucity of statistical information and the fact that much output in those years did not come onto the market for sale and therefore did not have an official price. From the estimated figures, economists then calculate the rate of increase of the total volume of output of the economy in dollars, making due allowance for changes in prices or (if they wish to discover how much output increased per person) for changes in population.

The calculation of actual growth rates is a technical matter into which we need not enter here. Suffice it to sum up the best estimates as showing a per capita growth rate of about 1.3 percent a year over the period from 1790 to 1860.[1] A rate of 1.3 percent may not seem very impressive, but it is more than sufficient to double per capita incomes over the period in question.

The Sources of Growth

For our purposes it is less important to calculate the rate of growth than to reflect on the sources of growth. We have watched the development of America from an untilled, untapped continent to a thriving society of farms and businesses. But we have not yet systematically inquired into the nature of the growth process itself. How can we now explain the process that has been at the center of our attention for so many pages?

* We will study this concept in greater detail in Chapter 11.

Mass consumption begins; bird's-eye view of the Wanamaker Grand Depot soon after its opening, 1877

The first source of the expansion in the value of total output must be self-evident. It is the sheer increase in the amounts of labor and capital that enter the production process. In 1860 our total labor force was about 11 million, over five times the 1800 labor force of 1.9 million. Over the same period the amount of capital—buildings, roads, livestock, machines—grew even more rapidly, although we do not have accurate estimates of the size of the capital stock comparable to those for the labor force.

Together, the increases in the man-hours of labor and "machine-hours" of capital explain much of the growth in GNP. But the increase in the quantity of inputs is not sufficient to explain the entire rise in the volume of outputs. Economists also emphasize the rise in *productivity* that augmented the contribution of both labor and capital. An average worker in 1860 was capable of turning out over 50 percent more than a worker in 1800.[2] This in turn was the consequence of two main improvements. First, the labor force was shifting out of agriculture into manufacturing, where its productivity per worker was higher. Second, labor was working with larger quantities and far better "qualities" of machines and tools of all kinds.

It is the second source that we should stress, for economic growth is much more attributable to improvements in the quality of inputs than to their increased quantities. Technology plays a central role here—the cotton gin, as we have seen, gave a tremendous impetus to the momentum of growth by multiplying the productivity of labor perhaps fifty-fold. So too the development of the "American system" of interchangeable parts greatly enhanced labor productivity.

From Quantity to Quality

In discussing the role of technology in growth, we reemphasize a point of great importance. It is that the economic transformation to which we give the name of "growth" is not just a change in volume of goods but in kinds of goods. The GNP of 1860 was not merely larger in the sense that it contained many more tons of wheat than the GNP of 1800; it also contained new products that made the output of the later date *different* from, as well as more valuable than, that of the earlier.

Nowhere was that difference more visible than in the first signs of a process that we will study in greater detail in the next period of the great transformation. This was the entrance of machines, en masse, into daily life. One immediately visible sign of the new times was the effect on the national imagination of the railroad. To quote from one social historian of the period, "Stories about railroad projects, railroad accidents, railroad speed [filled] the press; the fascinating subject [was] taken up in songs, political speeches, and magazine articles, both factual and fictional."[3] The cliché of the age, as one critic has observed, was "the annihilation of time and space," the telegraph here sharing honors with the railroad. It was, however, by no means an empty cliché. Chicago, once three weeks' distance from New York by canal, was now but three days removed. The railroad became a part of the life experience of millions of Americans, from the poorest immigrant families who traveled in boxcars across the nation to the social elites who traveled to spas and resorts in "saloon cars."

Less dramatic than the railroads but not less important was the introduction into daily life of objects that depended on machine production. There were the safety pin; large, cheap panes of window glass; the omnipresent cotton textiles; the new carpeting from the power looms of New England. In good but not lavish homes of the

1860s there were cast-iron stoves, spring mattresses, roller shades at the windows, flush toilets, wallpaper, gaslights, "patent" furniture, silver-plated tableware, a daguerreotype on the wall. Perhaps the most important change, in terms of the quality of life, was the invention of chloroform, the first effective anesthetic.

All these things were either unknown to or extremely expensive for Americans in the 1830s and 1840s, and unimagined by most Americans of 1800. Chester Wright has commented shrewdly on the importance of small articles in the wills of that earlier time: "The care with which a silver spoon, a silk dress, a bed, a chest of drawers, or a head of livestock is bequeathed shows a society where scarcity made little things important." But this concern for small articles of household wealth is lacking sixty years later.[4]

The Lower Classes

In terms of comfort and convenience, the material standard of the moderately well-off classes was appreciably above the level at the beginning of the nineteenth century, although in cities such as Pittsburgh another side of industrial abundance was already visible in a layer of soot and grime that lay over everything within miles of the iron foundries.

We should recognize, however, that the enjoyment of industrial abundance was mainly confined to the middle and upper reaches of the population and did not extend to the general run of the working class. Here the negative side of industrialization—the soot, the crowding—was all too evident, while the products of the new industry were beyond the reach of most. In the 1850s in Newburyport, Massachusetts, for example, the pay of a common laborer was insufficient to enable him to support his family without outside assistance,[5] and the situation was far worse in the larger cities into which the immigrants poured. In the crowded tenements of Boston and New York, conditions sometimes approached the depths of the English slums that Americans had once thought would never appear on their side of the Atlantic. Dr. Henry Clark, visiting Half-Moon Place in Boston, in 1849, discovered:

> One cellar . . . occupied nightly as a sleeping apartment for thirty nine persons. In another, the tide had risen so high that it was necessary to approach the bedside of a patient by means of a plank which was laid from one stool to another; while the dead body of an infant was actually sailing about the room in its coffin.[6]

The worsening slums make it clear that the meaning of economic growth was not a general improvement enjoyed equally by all. From a more general perspective we can also see that the transformation, though highly visible on the surface, had not yet penetrated into the whole structure of society. The persistence of log cabins and sod houses in the West testifies that the incursion of manufactures was a phenomenon mainly confined to the centers of population. Life expectancy at birth in 1855, if we judge by the statistics of Massachusetts hospitals, was still less than forty years, only four years more than in 1790. Municipal sanitation systems, fire-fighting forces, and public libraries were still rarities. The total number of school days in the lifetime education of an average citizen was less than 500.

The Effect on Life

Can we then sum up this irregular change with its differential impacts? We can venture three generalizations: The first is that *the transformation of the economy changed the character of domestic life, displacing many tasks formerly done at home into the market arena.* In the upper classes the home had never been an important locus of productive activity, except perhaps insofar as servants performed various tasks. But in the great majority of families milling, bolting, brewing, distilling, spinning, weaving, even simple metalwork were all done at home—even up to the Civil War every well-conducted farm had its salt tub, its smokehouse, its trying kettle, ash-leach, and candlemold.

Gradually the new "machinofacture" made these tasks unnecessary. Clothes were no longer made at home, nor were beer or soap or flour or tools. The tasks of lighting and heating the home were simplified by the invention of the safety match, the cast-iron stove, and the gaslight. The preparation of food had begun to change from a domestic chore to a factory task with the development of a canning industry. Later we shall see how all these changes affected the role of women in work.

A second general change was *the homogenization of material culture*—a leveling of material standards in many areas. The availability of cheap watches, railway travel, vulcanized mackintoshes, machine-sewn shoes narrowed the gap between the middle and the upper classes. There was still a vast difference between middle and upper, and a gulf between lower and upper; but the introduction of machine-made products set into motion a "democracy of things" that we can trace through the ensuing years down to our own time.

Third, there was an effect that was intangible, yet perhaps the most powerful of all. It was *the introduction of a new state of common expectation, a new state of mind about the material environment itself*. One can do no better than cite the words of the venerable historian of American manufacture, Victor Clark:

> Manufacturing is the phase of production that has modified most our national character and the constitution of society. The prolific output of machinery has made us prodigal in respect to things of which we were formerly thrifty, and has substituted a thirst for change in place of an earlier love for fixed order and familiar ways. The material environment, like the intellectual environment, of our forefathers was permanent. They lived in the same houses, used the same furniture, employed the same implements, wore the same clothes, and viewed the same scene from youth to old age. Their minds reflected the conservative habit of their surroundings. . . . In its fuller sense variety was the privilege of the few. That this condition has changed, whether for better or worse, is due mainly to the growth of manufactures, whose very end is to diversify our material surroundings.[7]

THE IMPACT OF THE WAR

The culminating and dominating event of our period was not, of course, the invention or introduction of machinery. At least on the surface it was not even an economic event. The terrible war toward which the country moved with a quickening pace and inevitability towered over the economic events of the times, and for all the economic motives and frictions so intimately entwined in the hostility of the North and South, no one then believed, and few today would hold, that the war was purely the result of an irreconcilable difference between a plantation economy and a factory economy. In the end the moral and political issue of slavery hung like a great noxious cloud between the sides, awaiting only a chance spark to flare into an immense conflagration.

Economic Conflict

But it is also true that economic interests, economic growth, economic transformations were inextricably involved in the development of the conflict. The problem was not so much the threat posed to the North by the presence of a slave economy in the South. At worst this resulted in the exasperating refusal of Southern con-

The machine process in rope-spinning

gressmen to vote for measures wanted by Northern businessmen, such as a protective tariff or a transcontinental railway. The economic threat was far more frightening when viewed from the Southern side. For not only was the North openly opposing the crucial institution of slavery on which the plantation system depended, but for all the contrary efforts of Southern congressmen it was evident that the industrial interests in the nation were clearly rising to dominance over the agricultural.

To put it bluntly, the North was rich and growing richer, and the South by comparison was poor and growing poorer. In 1860, not counting its slaves, the South possessed almost a quarter of the nation's population, but only a tenth of its capital. Worse was the seemingly unbreakable hold of agriculture, especially cotton, over the Southern economy. Central to this fatal involvement was the plantation aristocracy—the richest 10 percent of families who owned fifty slaves or more each. This plantation class regarded manufacturing and even mercantile pursuits with a near feudal contempt. Complaining endlessly of its dependence on Yankee middlemen, the Southern plantation aristocracy was unable to introduce Northern capitalist attitudes and customs into its treasured way of life.

Thus the two regions were from early times embarked on courses that were bound to bring them into conflict. In the South an economy had been built on a cheap, localized, passive labor force; in the North the economy had been adapted to an expensive, mobile, and active working force. In the South the ruling elites spurned the pursuit of money that was more and more the openly espoused social goal of the North. In the South, an absence of manufacturing made the region welcome the influx of cheap goods from Europe; in the North the presence of manufacturing caused the region to seek to exclude foreign wares. All these conflicts were integral to the growing tension, although they cannot be said finally to have precipitated that tension into outright war.

The Effects of the War

However fascinating, the problem of whether or not economic conflict was responsible for the Civil War is not that to which we must now address ourselves. For our theme of economic transformation suggests another question: what was the effect of the war on the subsequent course of economic events in America?

We begin with the question of economic growth itself. Did the war spur the rate of expansion? Until a relatively few years ago, most historians would have answered yes. The war was then generally regarded as the source of an immense impetus toward the industrial future. Then in a famous article in 1961 Thomas C. Cochran asked the opposite question: "Did the Civil War Retard Industrialization?"[8] Cochran pointed out that the war was not a time of booming production. On the contrary, cotton-textile production fell sharply, once Southern inventories were used up. Railroad trackage grew at a much reduced rate, because there was no iron to spare. Pig-iron output, a good barometer of overall activity, rose by only one percentage point between 1860 and 1865.

Cochran's point is a simple one. The economy in 1860 was essentially fully employed. Unlike the case in 1917 or in 1941 there was not a considerable body of unemployed labor or factory capacity that could be pressed into war service without reducing the production of other things. Therefore the material produced for the Union armies came at the expense of other goods, such as railroad tracks. The men who were recruited into the Union army came from the farm and the shop, not from school or from relief lines. Thus the impact of the war was to divert production rather than greatly to spur it on, although of course output soared in certain fields, such as arms and uniforms and farm machinery (to replace scarce labor). Furthermore, as Cochran wrote:

> [T]he Civil War was still unmechanized. It was fought with rifles, bayonets, and sabers by men on foot or horseback. Artillery was more used than in previous wars, but was still a relatively minor consumer of iron or steel. The railroad was brought into use, but the building of military lines offset only a small percentage of the overall drop from the prewar level of civilian railroad construction. Had all these things not been true, the Confederacy, with its small industrial development, could never have fought through four years of increasingly effective blockade.[9]

After the War

There has been a continuing debate among historians over the precise effect of the war on growth. No one doubts, however, that the end of the war witnessed a sharp change. Between 1860 and 1865 overall industrial production advanced only 7 percent. *Between 1865 and 1870 it rose by nearly 47 percent.* Per capita growth of GNP, long steady at 1.3 percent, now rose by about one-third.

It was as if the four years of the war, when the advance of manufacturing was slow, were a period during which the momentum of growth was actually being dammed up, waiting for release. For certainly progress was extraordinary once the war was over. Cotton-textile production doubled from 1865 to 1866, then climbed another 50 percent by 1869. Pig-iron output jumped from under a million tons in 1865 to two million tons in 1869, then to almost three million in 1873. New railroad trackage climbed from 819 miles in 1865 to 1,404 miles in 1866, 2,541 miles in 1867, over 4,000 miles in 1869, over 6,500 in 1871.

Did the Civil War cause this tremendous industrial spurt? The question is not easy to answer. The trend toward industrialism was already in motion, as we have seen, and part of the spurt was, therefore, nothing but the release of demands and plans that had been postponed by the war. Then, too, we must not forget that the war also brought enormous destruction in its wake. As Cochran pointed out, one major effect of the war was to set back Southern production so badly that even by 1880 the values of Southern farms and livestock were still one-fourth below those of 1860. And then, of course, there is the incalculable cost of the lost talents and energies of 620,000 Americans killed in the conflict.

Thus the war is not unambiguously the source of the postwar

boom. Yet we can also see that out of the war came specific stimuli, both for growth in general and for the future transformation of the country. Let us take a look at them.

Technology

First, the war provided encouragement to a few major industries. One instance was the clothing industry. The Northern army was wearing out 1.5 million uniforms and 3 million pairs of shoes a year. This required a substantial expansion in the woolen and leather processing industries. Moreover, to provide the mass production of clothing it was necessary to collect statistics on the average sizes of men's clothing. From this—and the forced reliance on sewing machines to handle the volume of output—came the men's ready-to-wear clothing industry, which grew from nothing in 1860 to 90 percent of all men's clothing thirty years later.

War becomes mechanized

Another high-powered technical advance was the invention of the universal milling machine. First developed in 1862 to drill holes in gun parts, it was soon generalized into a machine capable of cutting all sorts of metal shapes. Within ten years of its development, the Brown and Sharp Company was selling the machine to makers of hardware, tools, cutlery, locks, instruments, locomotives—in short to a whole spectrum of industrial companies.

Yet another specific impetus was given to the iron industry, impelled by the needs of war to improve its metal-handling abilities. At the outset of the conflict American mills had been unable to fill orders for 1½-inch steel plates because they had no way of trimming them. By the end of the war they were rolling and forging and cutting 5-inch plates.

Finance

A second direct effect of the war was its impact on finance. In our next chapter we will begin to study the emergence of business and business leaders as central agencies for economic change. Many of the fortunes that would power postwar expansion had their origins in the war itself.

Some of those fortunes were earned by dubious tactics or by outright fraud. A congressional committee investigating contracts for army provisions discovered that tents were made of such cheap stuff that soldiers testified they could better keep dry "out of them than under." Purveyors of knapsacks passed off as "linen" the shoddiest of cloth; suppliers of foodstuffs sold as "coffee" a mixture of roasted peas, licorice, and just enough coffee to give it a faint taste and aroma of the real thing. Blankets were often little better than rags. Freight rates charged to the government were higher than those charged to private commerce.

In other words, the war was the source of much "ill-gotten gains." But those same gains, in the period that followed, would be the source of investments that would account for much of the rush of growth and for the widening and deepening apparatus of industrial production.

Moreover, the rise of war-based fortunes accorded with the growing admiration of businessmen and business ways. Henry Adams, returning from Europe in 1868 after a ten-year stay, found himself in a world utterly strange to his prewar values. A new money-oriented, expansion-minded, hard-headed class had moved into prominence, elbowing aside the leaders of the prewar era to whom business was still a subsidiary and not a commanding social value. "One could divine pretty nearly where the force lay," commented Adams, "since the last years [have] given to the great mechanical energies—coal, iron, steam—a distinct superiority over the old . . . agriculture, handwork, and learning. . . ."[10]

Slavery

If we have hardly glanced at the "peculiar institution" of slavery, it is certainly not because the institution was unimportant. But in the economic transformation of the nation slavery plays a smaller role than in a history that seeks to trace our moral or social or political development.

What was the role of slavery in our economic history? We know that the institution was not essential for growth. The main success of the American economy was located in the North, where slavery played virtually no role at all. In the South, as we have seen, slavery was deemed essential for the operation of the plantation system, but whether that system was helpful or hurtful to the South (and to America) in general is not simple to say. The plantation system, with its gangs of slaves deployed in "brigades," certainly made possible the cheap production of cotton. Yet, without the invention of the cotton gin, it is likely that cotton would never have become King. It is even possible that cotton could have been profitably sold had the slaves been freed and paid as wageworkers. After all, in 1860 only one family in four owned any slaves, and only half the slave-owning families had more than five. Mainly slavery was essential to a plantation "way of life"—a way of life that, however congenial to its elites, was incompatible with economic growth.

The war brought an end to slavery. Did that mean the release of human energies for economic growth on a vast scale? That might have been the case had the slave population been schooled and trained and socially accepted as equals. As matters were, however, the emancipation of the slaves simply dumped upon a war-torn region a mass of wholly unprepared, unwanted, and unaccepted people. The freed slave was left to fend for himself or herself, and the only means available to most was to accept a kind of economic slavery as the tenant farmer or sharecropper for a white farmer. As late as 1900 three-quarters of all black farmers in the South were still in those categories, the victims of past injuries and contemporary oppressions. To this day we are suffering from the economic as well as the social wounds of slavery.

The Political Change

One last result of the war was a far-reaching change in the attitude of government toward manufacturing. The change was noticeable in many ways. As we have already mentioned, for a decade before the war Southern congressmen had blocked the approval of a transcontinental railway that would strengthen the hands of the nonslave states or territories; by 1862 that major step had been taken. Southern interests, as we know, were also bitterly opposed to a protective tariff, because that would raise the price of manufactures they could not make at home; by 1861 Congress had passed a strongly protectionist measure. The tariff was subsequently revised upward until average duties stood at 47 percent after the war compared with 18.8 percent at its beginning.

Not less important was the passage of a National Banking Act that greatly strengthened the banking system and eliminated the wildcat banks that had seriously undermined commercial progress. Yet another crucial act was the disposal of vast quantities of the public domain. The Homestead Act of 1862 opened the public lands to individual ownership and development; the principle was soon to be applied to the railways and other interests as well. In the eight years after the passage of the Homestead Act five times as much land was granted to the railroads as over the preceding twelve years—a total of 131 million acres, or 10 percent of the area of the states through which the lines passed, was handed over to the railroad-builders. Perhaps the lines could not have been built without this largesse, but largesse it assuredly was.

Nor does this recital exhaust the acts of the government favorable to business. Timber and mineral interests were able to profit in large measure from the Desert Land Act, the Timber Culture Act, the Timber and Stone Act, and others. Meanwhile, to ease the labor problems of both coasts, the Immigration Act of 1864 legalized the entry of cheap labor from Europe and China under contracts that have been called as harsh as those that brought indentured servants to America in the seventeenth and eighteenth centuries. And the capstone measure was the passage of the Fourteenth Amendment, which assured that "No State shall . . . deprive any person of life, liberty, or *property* without due process of law. . . ." A measure framed in the name of human rights was soon to become a bulwark in the defense of property rights.

This is not to imply that every act of the victorious North was unequivocally in favor of business, or that business interests themselves were always of one mind. What stands out, however, is the contrast between pre- and post-Civil War government. As Barrington Moore has pointed out, one must compare the program that we have just outlined with that of the South in 1860—"federal enforcement of slavery, no high protective tariffs, no subsidies or expensive tax-creating internal improvements, no national banking or currency system"—to realize the extent to which the victory of the North represented a victory for industrial capitalism.[11]

End of a Chapter

Like all "turning points" in history, the change from the prewar to the postwar economy was irregular, and it grows increasingly indistinct as we examine it closely. We have already pointed out that manufacturing had its roots deep in the past; we should emphasize as well that the age of agriculture did not come to a sudden stop with the war. Indeed, the period from 1860 to 1890 saw a doubling of cultivated land in the West, and to this very day farming continues to be one of the most productive economic sectors in the nation.

Nevertheless there is an unmistakable contrast between the nature of the economic transformation of the country before and after the war. We have watched the transformation of an undeveloped wilderness into a major economic power. Now we shall watch the transformation of a major economic power into an industrial civilization.

NOTES

[1] Paul David, "The Growth of Real Product in the United States before 1840," *Journal of Economic History* (June 1967), p. 195.

[2] David, "Growth of Real Product," p. 169.

[3] Leo Marx, *The Machine in the Garden* (1964), p. 191.

[4] Chester Wright, *Economic History of the United States* (1941), pp. 1022, 1025-32.

[5] See Stephan Thernstrom, *Poverty and Progress* (1964), p. 32.

[6] Norman J. Ware, *The Industrial Worker* (1924), p. 13.

[7] *History of Manufactures*, vol. I (1929), p. 578.

[8] *Mississippi Valley Historical Review* (September 1961). Reprinted in Ralph Andreano (ed.), *The Economic Impact of the American Civil War* (1967).

[9] *The Economic Impact of the American Civil War*, pp. 173-74.

[10] *Education of Henry Adams* (Modern Library edition, 1931), p. 238.

[11] Barrington Moore, *Social Origins of Dictatorship and Democracy* (1966), p. 151.

PART TWO

Industrialization Takes Command

The Age
of the Businessman

4

THE BUSINESS THRUST

We are about to examine a new "chapter" in our history of economic growth—a chapter that will change the character of life far more dramatically and decisively than anything we have witnessed thus far. In a dazzling period of sixty years following the Civil War, the face of the country will literally be made over. Enormous cities will arise out of prairie wildernesses; gigantic mechanical monsters will devour mountains in search of ore; astonishing inventions will enable individuals to talk to one another over wires; carriages will carry people about their business without horses.

In the background of these alterations a tremendous structure of steel will come to undergird the economy, and a torrent of power will come to drive it: the 16,000 tons of steel produced in 1865 will multiply to 56 million tons; the 16 million horsepower of energy used in the nation after the Civil War will become 1.6 billion horsepower by

1929. Perhaps we can sum up the change by saying that the omnipresence of machines will become more and more noticeable in the period from 1865 to 1929, when still another "chapter" of economic history will begin.

We call this era of intensified machine-building and machine use the *industrialization of America,* and our main task, in the chapters to come, is to examine the dynamics of industrialization as it actually took place. For the great cities, the gargantuan machines, the inventions and improvements did not come by some kind of miracle. They were built as part of a process that we have not yet had time to examine closely—the business process, or, as the economist would call it, the *market mechanism.*

The Market Mechanism

Business is a part of life that is familiar to nearly everyone. But the market mechanism is not, and we should spend a few moments making clear what we mean by it. There is no better way to begin than to ask: Who planned the industrialization of America? Who determined where the cities would grow and the iron mines be developed, who planned the changeover from horsedrawn to horseless carriages, or the knitting together of the nation by telephone wires?

The answer is that no one planned it. In contrast with the Soviet Union, where every steel mill, every technological change, every major new city was first determined by a group of planners and then built according to the blueprints of a central authority, no single individual or group of individuals designed the industrial transformation of America. Instead, the enormous process was largely left to the working-out of the market mechanism.

And what is this market mechanism? Basically it consists of two elements, each equally important. The first is the organization of the bulk of the nation's production as *profit-seeking enterprise,* free to carry on whatever activities are permitted by law. The drive for profit thus becomes the central driving force of the market system.

This search to make profits pushes business enterprises in two directions. It serves as a force for the *expansion* of business, because a large business almost always makes more money than a small one. And it also serves to put businessmen on the alert for *new opportunities* for profit-making. In this way the drive for profit propels business into the development of new products, as well as into the expansion of facilities to provide more of existing products.

Therefore we can see that the drive for profits serves as a generalized imperative for action. That imperative is lodged, however, not in the directives and blueprints of a central command agency, but in the acquisitive drives of thousands of business executives or capitalists.*

But the drive for profits is only one part of the market mechanism. If it were the only operating factor, the market would be better characterized as a profiteering system than a profit system. Each enterprise, out to maximize its income, would be able to charge all that the traffic would bear. Monopoly would be the natural result of such a system, with business enterprises charging extremely high prices, and reaping extremely high returns, on every article sold either to households or to other businesses.†

Thus a control system is a necessary part of the market mechanism. It is not a system of inspectors or rigidly enforced directives, such as we find in the Soviet Union or in any other centrally planned socialist system. *It is the institution of competition that provides control*—the institution of businesses vying one against another to obtain the favor of their customers. Competition thereby turns potential profiteering and monopoly into a struggle in which profits are constantly under pressure from enterprises eager to steal away the business of any firm that fails to trim costs or that prices its goods with a higher profit margin than is necessary for business survival.

Businesses

To learn more about the theory of the market mechanism we study economics, for a large part of that subject is concerned with elucidating the way in which the profit drive on the one hand, and the constraint of competition on the other, bring about the process of

---

* It is worthwhile learning a bit of terminology here. A capitalist is someone who owns capital and risks it in a business enterprise. An executive, or an entrepreneur (the word much used by economists), is a business decision-maker. One can be a capitalist without being an entrepreneur, as when a capitalist lends his money to or buys stock in an enterprise run by someone else. (We will learn more about stocks in Chapter 5.) One can also be an entrepreneur without being a capitalist—for example, a manager of a business who is paid a high salary or a bonus but who does not himself own a substantial portion of the enterprise.

† Just as a cautionary note, it should be added that monopolies cannot charge *any* price that they like if they wish to maximize their profits. If a monopoly railroad charged a million dollars per ticket, it would not sell many tickets. What a monopoly can do is to establish the price that gives it the highest profit obtainable. A competitive firm has to charge a price that "meets competition," and its profits are accordingly lower.

material replenishment and growth. But here we want to see the market mechanism in action. We want to follow the actual careers of nineteenth-century businessmen who were struggling to make money by expanding their business or by pioneering in new fields. We want as well to watch the competitive control system at work, for here lies one of the great sources of change in the period we are studying.

So let us begin by taking a survey of the business system as it existed in the first decade or two after the Civil War. There were about 500,000 business firms in America in 1870, not counting the nation's farms. Most of them were very small, employing one or two persons besides the owner-proprietor. A great many were small retail stores. But we are interested in a particular sector of the business world—the sector of manufacturing, for this is where the industrial growth of the nation will mainly take place.

From the census of 1870 we know something about that sector. Of the nation's total labor force of almost 13 million, nearly 2.5 million worked in manufacturing. The ten biggest industries were flour-milling, cotton goods, lumber, boots and shoes, men's clothing, iron, leather, woolen goods, liquor, and machinery—in that order. However, the biggest employer, lumber, gave work to only 160,000 employees—far fewer than we would find in one giant corporation today.*

Businessmen

Who ran these small businesses that were to play such an important role in our economic growth? They were a varied lot. A few were inventors, such as Thomas Alva Edison, who not only established the nation's first industrial research center—his so-called invention factory—at Menlo Park, New Jersey, in 1876, but who was actively engaged in creating companies to market his many inventions. Other businessmen had the prescience to put together other peoples' innovations to create new industries: Gustavas Swift, who left Massachusetts in the mid-1870s to become a butcher in Chicago and who combined the ice-cooled railway car with the ice-cooled warehouse to create the first national meat-packing company in 1885.

Still others were simply men with a talent for organization, finance, and management. James Buchanan Duke made his fortune by welding technology and merchandising. When the company in which he was a partner turned to cigarette manufacturing in 1881,

* Both A.T.&T. and General Motors employ over three-quarters of a million people.

Duke reduced the firm's operating costs by installing the new Bonsack cigarette-rolling machine, a one-ton contraption that fed paper and tobacco in continuous rolls, pasted and cut the tubes, and made 100,000 cigarettes in a single day. The resulting output threatened to glut the market. But by 1884, through the use of advertising and the creation of a crushproof sliding cardboard box, Duke had created a national demand for his product. In 1890 he combined the four major cigarette producers in the nation to form the American Tobacco Company.

But most of the nation's businessmen were not inventors, innovators, or merchandising pioneers. They were a much more conventional lot, no more remarkable (and no less) than the businessmen who run small factories or stores or wholesale establishments in the United States today. We tend to think of the entrepreneurs whose combined efforts brought so dramatic a change to the economic landscape as Horatio Alger success stories—men who rose from humble beginnings to achieve fame and fortune.* In fact, the business leadership largely came from substantial and conservative backgrounds.

A study by Francis W. Gregory and Irene D. Neu on the social origins of 303 business leaders in textiles, railroads, and steel during the 1870s finds that the overwhelming majority were born in the United States; that of those native-born executives only 3 percent had foreign-born fathers, the rest dating their American ancestry back to colonial times; that some 90 percent were raised in either a middle- or upper-class milieu; that roughly a third were college graduates; and that one-half did not go to work before age nineteen, and that less than one-quarter went to work before age sixteen. Summing up their investigation, Gregory and Neu conclude:

> Was the typical industrial leader of the 1870's, then, a 'new man,' an escapee from the slums of Europe or from the paternal farm? Did he arise from his own efforts from a boyhood of poverty? Was he as innocent of education and of formal training as has often been alleged? He seems to have been none of these things. American by birth, of a New England father, English in national origin, Congregational, Presbyterian, or Episcopalian in religion, urban in early environment, he was rather born and bred in an atmosphere in which business and a relatively high social

---

* No one reads Horatio Alger's business romances any more. If one did, he would soon discover a disconcerting fact. Alger's heroes did not get rich because they displayed sterling qualities of business acumen, loyalty, etc. Invariably success came to them because one day they had the chance to stop a runaway carriage in which sat a terrified golden-ringleted girl, who turned out to be—you'll never guess—the boss's daughter. After that things changed radically for plucky Dick, Tom, or Harry.

standing were intimately associated with his family life. Only at about eighteen did he take his first regular job, prepared to rise from it, moreover, not by a rigorous apprenticeship begun when he was virtually a child, but by an academic education well above the average.[1]

THE ROBBER BARONS

Thus the average business enterpriser does not seem like a very promising figure to be the agent for the industrial transformation of the nation. But what makes the businessman so dramatic a personage in the post–Civil War era is not the average entrepreneur. Rather, it is a handful of business leaders who arose in virtually every line of business to dominate and drive and dazzle their fellow businessmen. By virtue of their personalities, their ambitions, their talents or their tactics, these business leaders bestrode the economic landscape like Gullivers in the land of Lilliput, endowing the age with many of their personal characteristics. Because their characteristics included some of the predatory habits of feudal lords who exacted tolls and ransoms from those who strayed within their domains, these dramatic figures have been called the "robber barons," and the period of industrialization in which they played so powerful a role has been dubbed the Age of the Robber Barons. An examination of the career of one of them, Jay Gould, will give us some insight into the group as a whole.

Jay Gould

Jay Gould was the "Mephistopheles of Wall Street." He was perhaps the most money-minded man in a money-minded age. One historian writes: "No human instinct of justice or patriotism caused him to deceive himself, or to waver in any perceptible degree from the steadfast pursuit of strategic power and liquid assets."[2]

Gould's career begins in 1856, when he became a partner in a tanning factory in Pennsylvania. It was not long before he began investing a large percentage of the *company's* profits in his *personal* banking and real-estate ventures. After those embezzlements were discovered, Gould formed a new partnership—but he continued his embezzlements. This time one of his partners committed suicide; the other tried unsuccessfully to remove Gould from the tannery. It was not until 1861 that Gould was ousted, but by that time he had already extracted most of the firm's assets.

Jay Gould

It was during this period that Gould first turned his attention to the railroad industry. In 1867, Daniel Drew put Gould and Jim Fisk on the board of directors of the Erie Railway. It was quite a trio. Fisk was a man of rapacious appetites and extraordinary unscrupulousness, of whom it was said that he regarded business "as a kind of joke." [3] Drew was famous for having introduced the idea of "watered stock"—driving thirsty cattle to the market and then bloating them with water just before they were weighed in for sale.*

---

* Drew was also known for the bandanna trick. Feigning confusion and dismay on the floor of the stock exchange, he would mop his forehead with a red bandanna, causing a slip of paper to fall from his pocket. Another speculator would retrieve the note on which were written Drew's instructions to his brokers to buy or sell stocks. Thinking that Drew's plans were now discovered, his adversary would place his stock orders to take advantage of Drew's plans. But of course the whole thing was a ruse that enabled Drew himself to outwit his opponents because he knew what *their* operations would be.

Beginning in 1868 the triumvirate of Drew, Gould, and Fisk engaged Cornelius Vanderbilt in a struggle for control of the Erie. The threesome began by issuing some $8 million in "watered" stock—corporate securities as bloated as water-filled cattle—despite a judicial restraining order. Thereafter they dispensed $1 million in bribes to obtain passage of a New York law to authorize the stock issue. These manipulations were too much even for Drew and Vanderbilt. Drew recalled the $8 million stock issue, and he and Vanderbilt turned the Erie over to Gould and Fisk, who thereupon issued $23 million in watered stock.

Even in an age of unbridled acquisitiveness, Gould's tactics earned him an unenviable reputation. Yet we should recognize that his chicanery and unscrupulousness represented an exaggeration of, but not a departure from, the behavior of many of his fellow business titans. Bribery, for example, was not uncommon—even Thomas Edison promised certain New Jersey representatives a thousand dollars apiece if legislation favorable to his interests was passed. Stock-watering and disregard for the law were widespread. After obtaining control of the New York Central Railway, Cornelius Vanderbilt arbitrarily increased its capitalization by $23 million. When told that this was illegal, he supposedly replied: "Law! What do I care about the Law? Hain't I got the power?" [4]

Fraud and deception were thus all too common practices of the day—the federal government, for example, was billed at three times actual cost by the first transcontinental railway construction company, whose expenses Congress had agreed to underwrite; and afterward, when the depredations of the company were in danger of being dragged into the open, the company's books were brazenly burned.

The Celebration of Wealth

We will have a chance to look more deeply into the business behavior of the age and its relation to economic growth, for the era of industrial expansion could hardly have flourished if Gould's or Fisk's tactics were ubiquitous. Nonetheless, the styles and aims of the robber barons have an important bearing on the tenor of the times. For they typify a country that had become enamored of wealth. Business became the great avenue of success, and anything that delayed one's entrance into the world of business, including education, was frowned on. It was often remarked with approval that Cornelius Vanderbilt, who left $90 million at his death, had read but one book in his

A horseback dinner

life, and that one at an advanced age. (It was *Pilgrim's Progress;* we can doubt that he learned very much from it.)

Not only was the accumulation of wealth regarded as the most fitting and admirable of all careers, but its ostentatious expenditure was generally admired. Social commentators of the period delighted in describing parties where cigarettes made of dollar bills were smoked for the pleasure of inhaling wealth; where extravaganzas of decoration were employed, including the conversion of one New York hotel into a fake coal mine; where newly made millionaires vied with each other for social distinction, one giving a party where monkeys were seated between the guests, another a dinner party on horseback, yet another a party where each lady found a gold necklace tucked in her napkin as a favor.

Moreover, the love of money and success permeated all ranks of society, not just the top. Historian Henry Steele Commager comments, "The self made man, not the heir, was the hero. . . ."[5] Small wonder, then, that panegyrics and encomiums celebrated the "captains of industry," and that a general philosophy of "rugged individualism" reached down through all the ranks of American society. Even among the working classes, Charles Beard remarks, "all save the most wretched had aspirations. [T]here was a baton in every toolkit."[6]

Social Darwinism

The worship of success thus provided an important source of the drive for profit that set into motion the industrialization process. We should note as well that the quest for wealth was supported by an important intellectual current of the day—a current we call Social Darwinism because it translated the biological theories of Charles Darwin into a social theory that blessed the business struggle as an indispensable means to "progress."

Darwin's theory of evolution did not make pronouncements about "progress." It was essentially a generalization about the struggle for survival in which some species survived and some perished. But in the hands of the English sociologist Herbert Spencer, Darwin's theory became interpreted as a process that chose the "better," as well as the tougher or stronger, among competing individuals or species. Thus the competitive struggle of business was viewed as a contest in which the survivors were the "fittest"—not merely as businessmen, but as champions of civilization itself.

Little wonder that such a theory won the approval of big businessmen—Andrew Carnegie, for example, was a disciple of Spencer's and wrote to him as " Master." Social Darwinism became a means of excusing as well as explaining the competitive process from which some emerged with power and some were ground into poverty. As one millionaire member of the United States Senate said of himself: "I do not know much about books; I have not read very much; but I have traveled a good deal and observed men and things and I have made up my mind after all my experiences that the members of the Senate are the survivors of the fittest."[7]

Thus Social Darwinism joined with the general adulation of wealth to create an atmosphere in which aggressive business expansion was given the unstinting and uncritical approval of virtually all sections of society. Even the churches were strong supporters of the business ethic, equating worldly success and spiritual superiority in a manner that would have made Cotton Mather blush. An estimated 13 million people heard Reverend Russell Conwell deliver his "Acres of Diamonds" sermon: riches were to be had almost for the asking by a little hard work, he claimed, and riches were "holy" because money could be used for good purposes. Conwell certainly had *his* acre of diamonds: his publications earned him over $8 million.* We shall see

---

* Most of Conwell's wealth was channeled into social and educational causes, including the founding of Temple University.

in later chapters how these prevailing attitudes played an important role in determining the character of the industrialization process.

FROM BARON TO BUREAUCRAT

We have looked into the career of Jay Gould to get some feeling for the roistering atmosphere of the post–Civil War period. Yet it must be apparent that industrialization would never have found its realization under a business elite composed only of Goulds and Fisks. Therefore we must acquaint ourselves with another type of business tycoon, typified by a man very different from Gould in his view of the aims of the business enterprise; Gould is a caricature of the worst of the robber baron age; Andrew Carnegie represents the best of it.

Andrew Carnegie

Born in Dunfermline, Scotland—a center of the Scottish weaving industry—in 1835, Carnegie was the son of a hand-loom weaver who had been thrown out of work by the coming of the Industrial Revolution. When Carnegie was thirteen the family emigrated to Allegheny, Pennsylvania. There he worked as a bobbin boy in the textile mills at $1.20 a week; then as a machine wiper deep in a factory cellar at $3 a week—to the end of his days the merest whiff of machine oil could make him deathly ill.

In America Carnegie found the thing that was so noticeably absent in Scotland—opportunity. When the telegraph came to nearby Pittsburgh in 1849, he got a job as a messenger boy. Like the hero in a Horatio Alger story, he came to the office early and left it late in order to watch the operators at work; then at night he studied Morse code until he became a skilled telegrapher himself. In fact he was soon one of the very few operators in the country who could take messages direct from the buzzes of the machine rather than from its printed dots and dashes: people used to drop into the telegraph office to watch him take a message "hot from the wire."

Also as in every Horatio Alger story, luck played an important role. One citizen who saw Carnegie at work was Thomas Scott, then the local superintendent of the Pennsylvania Railroad, later to become a great railway baron in his own right. In 1853 Scott took Carnegie on as his assistant, and after the young man had gained his trust offered him a chance to buy a $500 interest, ten shares, in a company called

Andrew Carnegie

Adams Express. Carnegie did not have $50, much less $500, but Scott lent the funds to this young man of "great expectations." Adams Express prospered mightily and soon paid its first dividend. It was a turning point for Carnegie. As he later wrote: "I shall remember that check as long as I live. It gave me the first penny of revenue from capital—something I had not worked for with the sweat of my brow. 'Eureka!' I cried. Here's the goose that lays the golden eggs."[8]

In 1859 Scott promoted Carnegie to superintendent of the western division of the Pennsylvania Railroad at a salary of $1,500 a year. And when Scott became Assistant Secretary of War in 1861, he appointed Carnegie superintendent of military transportation and director of the Union's telegraph communications.

Meanwhile, another goose came his way. Riding the railroad in 1860, Carnegie was approached by a stranger carrying a green bag. The stranger introduced himself as T. T. Woodruff and inquired if Carnegie was connected with the railway. Woodruff then opened his bag and showed Carnegie a small model. It was, in miniature, the first sleeping car. Carnegie arranged for Woodruff to meet Scott, and soon a company was formed in which Carnegie was given a one-eighth interest for his services. Within two years the Woodruff Palace Car Company was paying Carnegie dividends of over $5,000 a year.

Investments now became the center of Carnegie's interest and the means to his initial fortune. The Palace Car Company was followed by an interest in the Keystone Bridge Company, the first successful manufacturer of iron railroad bridges, which were needed to sustain the weight of ever heavier locomotives. Next came a share in the Pittsburgh Locomotive Works; thereafter a share in a local iron foundry that would become the nucleus of Carnegie's steel empire.

By 1868 Carnegie was already rich. Yet, unlike the great majority of his fellow budding captains of industry, he was troubled by his wealth. In a suite in the opulent St. Nicholas Hotel in New York he wrote a memorandum to himself:

> Thirty-three and an income of 50,000$ per annum . . . Beyond this never earn—make no effort to increase fortune, but spend the surplus each year for benevelent [sic] purposes. Cast business forever aside except for others. . . .
>
> Man must have an idol—The amassing of wealth is one of the worst species of idolitry [sic]. . . . To continue much longer overwhelmed by business cares and with most of my thoughts wholly upon the way to make more money must degrade me beyond hope of permanent recovery.
>
> I will resign business at Thirty-five. . . .[9]

Odd thoughts for a robber baron! And of course Carnegie did not "resign business." On the contrary, his real business career was soon to begin; everything previous had been a harbinger of what was to come. On a trip to England to sell railroad bonds, he had a chance to see the astonishing new way of making steel invented by Henry Bessemer (we will find out more about that method in our next chapter). Carnegie was awe-struck—perhaps something about the spectacular volcanic eruption of the flames appealed to his fiery temperament. At any rate, he jumped on the first available steamer home, convinced that the day of cheap steel had come. Assembling his partners, he announced his intention of building the biggest steel plant in the United

States, equipped with the Bessemer process. It is interesting that the year of his return was 1873, and that the United States was in the throes of the most severe business depression it had ever experienced. But Carnegie was convinced that the future was bright. By 1875 the plant was in production and he was on his way to becoming the most renowned industrial businessman in the world.

The Rise of the Business Manager

Carnegie's career is a corrective to that of Jay Gould in that it gives us a sense of the men and motivations that lay behind the market mechanism. But before we are finished with our study of businessmen, we must pay heed to one extremely significant development of the sixty-year period in which we are interested. This is the gradual emergence of a new "style" of businessman—no longer a robber baron, or even a captain of industry, but a corporate manager, indeed a business bureaucrat.

Sociologist Reinhard Bendix describes him this way:

> Entrepreneurs start firms of their own at some point in their careers; bureaucrats do not. At the climax of their careers entrepreneurs are substantial owners of a firm, while bureaucrats are typically salaried executives. Entrepreneurs sometimes spend parts of their careers as salaried employees, bureaucrats do so invariably and for a major portion of their careers.[10]

Bureaucrats are peculiarly creatures of organizations rather than founders of them, and it was inevitable that a business bureaucracy should develop as the size of industry grew. A Lowell cotton mill or a Pittsburgh rolling mill was an operation that could still be housed in a single large shed or in a small complex of buildings, where the owner or his mill foremen could take in the entire works in an hour's tour of inspection. But once a certain size of endeavor was reached, the possibility for direct supervision disappeared and an effective *organization* became essential. By the 1850s Henry Varnum Poor, editor of the *Railway Journal* (and later the founder of the first manuals of statistical information for investors), was tracing the misfortunes of the railroads to the fact that the owners of the roads could not manage them, and that the managers did not own them. What was lacking, in other words, was a managerial element—a group of executives subordinate to the ultimate decisional authority of the owners in matters of grand strategy, but possessing the authority to run complex enterprises according to their own expertise.

Thus, as we might expect, we find the first efforts to create systems of administration in the largest industry of the times, the railroads. The pioneer of industrial organization was Daniel A. McCallum, a talented engineer and inventor who was asked in 1854 to become general superintendent of the Erie Railroad. It is ironical that the railroad of the greatest robber baron pirate, Jay Gould, was to be also the source of a profound managerial reorientation, but the credit certainly does not belong to Gould's concern for service as such. Rather the directors of the road, worried about rising costs and declining efficiency, engaged McCallum to establish a "system" to assure better accountability of both managers and men.

The First Table of Organization

McCallum responded to the challenge eagerly. As he pointed out in his report a year later:

> A Superintendent, if a road is fifty miles in length, can give its business his personal attention and may be constantly on the line engaged in the direction of its details; each person is personally known to him, and all questions in relation to its business are at once presented and acted upon; and any system, however imperfect, may under such circumstances prove comparatively successful.
>
> In the government of a road five hundred miles in length, a very different state exists. Any system that might be applicable to the business and extent of a short road would be found entirely inadequate to the wants of a long one; and I am fully convinced that in the want of a system perfect in its details, properly adjusted and vigilantly enforced, lies the true secret of [the road's] failure; and that this disparity of cost per mile in operating long and short roads, is not produced by any difference in length but is in proportion to the perfection of the system adopted.[11]

To achieve his desired system, McCallum drew up what is probably the first table of organization for an American company—a tree with the roots representing the president and the board of directors, and five branches showing respectively the main operating divisions—engine repairs, cars, bridges, telegraph, printing—plus the service division. On the branches, leaves represented the various local agents, train crews, foremen, and so on. Furthermore, within the smaller units of the system, such as the machine shops, the same hierarchical system prevailed, with duties prescribed for each grade, and the grade of each individual indicated on the uniform he wore.

Orders were to go from roots to leaves, but as economic historian Alfred Chandler points out, "McCallum realized that the most essential communication in his organization was from subordinate to superior rather than vice versa.''[12] Thus a continuous flow of upward-rising reports constantly informed the managers as to the day-by-day, and sometimes hour-by-hour, location of rolling stock, or the occurrence of tie-ups or accidents, and provided them with a detailed, regular scrutiny of the costs of operating the system, not alone as a unit, but in each of its numerous constituent parts.

Henry Varnum Poor considered McCallum's work so remarkable that he had the organizational tree lithographed and offered it for sale at $1 a copy; the tree was reported on in Parliament and was even popularized in the *Atlantic Monthly*. Thus its influence on the development of internal business organization was widespread.

Organization Enters Business

Other large enterprises soon followed suit by "rationalizing" their own internal structures of command. In *The Inside History of the Carnegie Steel Company*, James Howard Bridge describes the metamorphosis there. Of the early days of the company, he writes:

> While the workings of every furnace and every machine were carefully watched and tabulated, the operations of the greatest machine of all, its brain, were spasmodic, unmethodical, and for the most part unnoted. The Board of Managers met by chance, there being no fixed time for meetings. Consultations and deliberations were conducted in a haphazard way, and often no minutes of them were taken. If an important change was to be made, perhaps a meeting would be called; or it might happen that the managers most interested in it would have an informal meeting at the works, when the matter would be decided. The old minute-books of the various companies often show a gap of several months without an entry.
>
> With the accession of Mr. [Henry Clay] Frick to the headship of the concern, this was promptly changed. A rule was made that the Board of Managers should meet every Tuesday at lunch, and that a full report of their subsequent deliberations should be kept. Similarly, every Saturday at noon, the different superintendents and their assistants, some foremen, purchasing and sales agents and their principal assistants, to the number of thirty or more, met about a larger table, and after lunching together, talked over all matters of common interest.[13]

We find the same organizational scaffolding arising elsewhere. In Standard Oil, for example, an elaborate system of committees superintended the various aspects of the trust's affairs. Each day at lunch at 26 Broadway their work was coordinated and supervised by the management committee that provided the central guidance for the whole concern. Similarly in the very large merchandising and manufacturing operations of Swift or Armour, of Duke, of Preston (who created a merchandising operation for refrigerated bananas similar to that of Swift's for meat), in the promotion of McCormick's reaper and Singer's sewing machine, the functional requirements for growth and success were first and foremost the creation of effective and smoothly running organizations.

Bureaucrats versus Barons

What relationship did these committee men have to the robber barons, whose presence still dominated the years during which the committees were proliferating? At first they tended to assume subsidiary roles in which their rise to power depended on the patronage of the central figure. Thus Carnegie steadily promoted men like Charles Schwab and W. E. Corey, and J. P. Morgan assisted the rise of Charles Mellen to become "Railroad Lord of New England." Mellen candidly admitted that he wore the Morgan collar, saying after Morgan's death, "I did what I was told."[14] Others, such as H. H. Rogers of Standard Oil, served their terms as organization men and then left to become independent capitalists on their own. Still others rose to high rank and salary, while never quite emerging as leaders in their own right.

But the change induced by the need to administer the larger scope of enterprise did not end with the production of internal bureaucracies. Soon we find that the bureaucracy itself was producing the leading business figures—the route to power had changed from the assumption of capitalist risk to the exercise of organizational expertise. A study of over 1,000 biographies of prominent businessmen shows that only 5 percent of the business leaders born before 1800 rose to success by way of the bureaucratic route; 16 percent of those born between 1801 and 1830; 21 percent of those born in the 1831–1860 period; 29 percent of the group born from 1861–1890, and 48 percent of those born between 1891 and 1920.[15] A study by William Miller of 185 business leaders in the decade 1901–1910 confirms this finding (see table, p. 84).[16]

Thus by the end of the period we are interested in, *nearly half of the great industrial leaders were products of the organizational structure of industrial enterprise.* The managerial-minded men desired by Henry Varnum Poor had moved from a subsidiary to a primary function, no longer merely assisting the personal aggrandizement of the great

American Business Leaders by Type of Career		
Type of Career	*Number*	*Percent*
Professional (lawyers)	23	12
Independent Entrepreneur	25	14
Family	51	27
Bureaucratic	86	47

barons but now taking into their own hands the direction of the great corporations within which they had climbed to the very top.

Their advent brought with it a change in the character of business leadership. The piratical tactics, the zest for competitive combat, the personal generalship so characteristic of the robber barons were not the style of men who had patiently worked their way up the organizational ladder. The new captains of industry were not practiced in the arts of risk but in the arts of negotiation—80 percent of the bureaucratic business leaders studied by Miller had never in their entire careers headed a company or assumed any significant risk of financial responsibility for their business enterprises. Significantly, they were also less successful financially. Of the 303 leading entrepreneurs studied by Gregory and Neu, only 54 were considered millionaires. Hence, despite the lingering presence of a few baronial types, the dominant businessmen of the twentieth century would be men who built organizations, not monuments. Theodore Vail, who guided American Telephone and Telegraph; Walter Teagle, who reorganized Standard Oil; Gerard Swope, who made (but did not start) General Electric; Alfred Sloan, who rebuilt General Motors—all were representatives of an entrepreneurial type very different from the dominant figures of the previous generation.

This is by no means to say that they were less successful as businessmen. Indeed, the very point of the shift in the locus of power was that it reflected a changing attribute of the business system itself. Bureaucratization did not mean the slowing down of industrial growth, but rather its adaptation to an environment in which the buccaneer's mode of operation was no longer the mode best suited to the survival of the system.

What is striking is that the profoundly significant rise of business bureaucracy was rooted in the very period when the robber baron seemed to occupy the center of the stage. Thus, at a time when every American knew the names of the greatest enterprisers of the time, the age was already foreshadowed when no one would know any names except those of the great enterprises themselves.

NOTES

[1] Francis W. Gregory and Irene D. Neu, "The American Industrial Elite in the 1870's: Their Social Origins," in William Miller (ed.), *Men in Business* (1962), pp. 193–211.

[2] Matthew Josephson, *The Robber Barons* (1934), pp. 192–93.

[3] Quoted in Edward C. Kirkland, *Dream and Thought in the Business Community* (1956), p. 40.

[4] Quoted in John Tipple, "The Robber Baron in the Gilded Age," in H. Wayne Morgan (ed.), *The Gilded Age* (1963), p. 36.

[5] *The American Mind* (1950), p. 13.

[6] Charles and Mary Beard, *The Rise of American Civilization* (1933), vol. II, p. 395.

[7] Quoted in Matthew Josephson, *The Politicos* (1938), p. 445.

[8] *Autobiography* (1920), p. 80.

[9] Quoted in Joseph Frazier Wall, *Andrew Carnegie* (1970), pp. 224–25.

[10] *Work and Authority* (1956), p. 229.

[11] Quoted in Alfred Chandler, "Henry Varnum Poor," in Miller (ed.), *Men in Business*, p. 260.

[12] *Men in Business*, p. 262.

[13] 1903, pp. 275–76.

[14] Quoted in William Miller, "The American Business Elite in Business Bureaucracies," in *Men in Business*, p. 290.

[15] Reinhard Bendix, *Work and Authority*, p. 229.

[16] "The American Business Elite," in *Men in Business*, p. 290.

THE RISE OF STEEL

We have become familiar with the men who guided the process of industrialization—barons, captains of industry, and, later, bureaucrats. But we have not yet explored the process itself. We are interested, of course, in the gradual introduction of machines and capital goods throughout American life. But we need to examine the technology of industrialization as closely as we examined the reality of the market mechanism if we are to gain a clear sense of what was happening in the eventful years of our study.

Technical Problems

A good place to begin is with steel, for the age of industrialization can almost be summed up as the age of steel. The reason is that machinery requires steel. You can make machines of wood, as in medieval times, but wood has limited strength. You can make them out of iron, as in the early Industrial Revolution, but iron snaps and bends. Hence from earliest times men have sought to improve iron by heating it, combining it with other materials, or cooking it at high temperatures to make what we call steel—a metal of tremendous strength, resiliency, and versatility.

But the cost of converting iron into steel was tremendous. Steel swords were treasures in medieval Europe, rarities to be handed down from father to son. Moreover, not only was the product extremely expensive, but it could not be made in large quantities. At the time of the American Revolution steel was made in crucibles not much larger than a vase. At the great Crystal Palace Exposition of 1851 a 2½-ton ingot of steel (made by combining the outputs of many crucibles) was a sensation.

The steel bottleneck was broken by an extraordinarily versatile English inventor, Henry Bessemer. Bessemer was an inspired tinkerer who had already made his fortune by inventing a way of using brass to make "gold" paint. Thereafter he became interested in increasing the range and accuracy of artillery by designing a projectile that would spin. The projectile, however, required a rifled gun barrel that would far exceed the strength of wrought iron. Since steel barrels were much too expensive, Bessemer set to work to make his projectile practical by inventing cheap steel.

Bessemer devised a solution of amazing simplicity—once it was discovered.* Instead of refining pig iron into steel by heating its surface, he blew air right through the molten metal. The heat generated by the oxidizing iron kept the iron liquid, and the enormous temperatures rapidly burned out the carbon that made untreated iron brittle. Through the Bessemer process three to five tons of iron could be converted into steel in ten or twenty minutes, compared with the laborious process of heating and stirring and reheating, which used to take a day or more. Meanwhile, as the air shot through the container, a veritable volcano of sparks and fire erupted. Then when the miniature hell subsided, pure steel could be poured out.

That was the process that captured Carnegie's imagination. But it was only the beginning of the new steel technology. When Carnegie built the Thomson works, its converters held five tons of molten iron. Within twenty-five years they held twenty tons—converters as large as small houses were cradled by immense gantry cranes that raised

---

* Curiously, the process was independently discovered by William Kelly, an American ironmaster. Kelly made the great mistake of keeping it secret.

The Bessemer process

and lowered and tilted them as easily as sand toys. Equally important, machines also performed the operations before and after the
conversion into steel. Mechanization began at the mines, where the
ore was scraped up by shovels capable of loading a freight car in a
few swings. The cars themselves rolled directly into the mills, where
a giant dumper picked them bodily off the tracks and cascaded their
products into vast bins. Electric cars then hauled the ore to the tops
of furnaces ten stories high. Emerging from the converters in a
Niagara of molten metal, the white-hot steel was sent through a succession of rollers that squeezed the glowing metal thinner and
thinner and faster and faster until finished rails shot from the last
pair of rollers at speeds of forty to sixty miles an hour.

The Birth of an Industry

The Bessemer process did more than revolutionize the making of
steel. As costs fell, steel became the basic building material of a host
of other industries. In 1873, steel was selling at over $100 a ton.
Although railroad executives badly wanted to replace their iron rails
with steel—the iron rails were splintering under the weight of the big
new engines—they could not afford to do so at that price. But the
Bessemer process reduced the cost of steel dramatically. When Carnegie's new plant (thoughtfully named the Edgar Thomson works in
honor of a top official of the Pennsylvania Railroad) began production in 1875, it cut the cost of rails to $50 per ton. Two years later the
cost had fallen to $40. By 1885 it was reduced to $20; by the late
1890s, to $12. Selling his rails at $18 a ton, Carnegie made a very
large profit and still offered the railroads an unprecedented bargain.

The new low-cost steel did more than open a vast market for rails.
Carnegie soon saw the versatile possibilities of steel and converted
another mill from steel to structural shapes. Again he was right. By
the mid 1870s steel began to edge iron out as the material used for
railroad bridges: in 1879, for instance, the builders of New York's
famous Brooklyn Bridge decided to construct the entire middle section of steel. Within a few more years another market opened. The
Masonic Temple in Chicago, which was to rise a dizzying twenty
stories into the sky, gave rise to an order for 4,000 tons of girder, all to
be made of steel.

After steel beams came steel nails, steel wire, steel tubes. Total
steel output, which amounted to barely 157,000 tons the year before
the Thomson works opened, grew to 26 million tons by 1910. Carnegie's plants did not produce all of this steel; Carnegie had formi-

dable competitors, and in our next chapter we will be looking into the problem that this competition caused. But the Carnegie complex of mills, valued at $700,000 when the Thomson works were opened, doubled in value in five years, doubled again in three more years, and rose to an official valuation of $300 million by the turn of the century.

Technology and Growth

How did the business grow? In large part, as we have seen, it grew because the master key of technology opened vast new market demands for a commodity that had previously been too expensive for extensive use. First the 100,000 miles of railroad trackage, as of 1881, was converted to steel; then the 100,000 miles of new trackage laid down in the next decade was built of steel; thereafter the entire national network had to be relaid in a heavier grade of steel rail as locomotives continued to grow in weight. In 1907 the Tennessee Coal, Iron and Railway Company placed an order for 150,000 tons of rail, which was only 3 or 4 percent of the nation's steel output.

The demand for structural steel provided another vast new market. When the Thomson plant opened there was very little demand for steel beams, but within twenty-five years over 2.5 million tons of steel went into girders and plates for bridges and buildings. Steel nails alone took 300,000 tons of output by 1889; steel wire soon approached 1 million tons a year as telephone poles festooned railroad tracks and as barbed wire enclosed hundreds of thousands of farms.

In this process of expansion, the Bessemer method paved the way. Without it we would not have had the steel rails, wires, nails, girders, plates, bolts, needles, screws, and springs that gave us the skyscraper and the steamship, the scalpel and the jackhammer, the train and the sewing machine, the tin can (actually made of steel) and the tin lizzie. Yet it must be clear that steel alone could not have changed the face of America. Industrialization also required power—the electric dynamo, the internal combustion engine, gasoline. It required communication—the telegraph and the telephone, the typewriter and the high-speed press. It required enormous supplies of materials to be wrested from the earth and used as inputs into the production process—sulfur, tin, lead, zinc. It required complex processes that were invisible to the eyes of consumers but indispensable to the production of the goods they bought—methods of making chemicals, for example, without which rubber tires or photographic film or dyed cloth could not be made.

Industrialization was the sum total of all these technological advances, most of them first invented by some gifted individual like Bessemer and then launched into economic importance under the business generalship of a man like Carnegie. Without the generalship the technology would have lain dormant or would have been diffused only very slowly into the bloodstream of the nation. Carnegie threw into it the force of his dynamic, driving personality.* He pitted one manager against another, paying big bonuses for higher output, shaming laggards with telegrams: "Puppy dog Number Two has beaten puppy dog Number One on fuel."[1] Carnegie recognized no substitute for success; and success meant expansion, expansion—and then more expansion.

THE ECONOMICS OF SIZE

The new technology and the aggressive tactics of the age provided a powerful mixture for economic growth. But they were also a dangerous mixture for economic stability. For the technology and the tactics combined to alter the organizational structure of industry quite as profoundly as it altered its physical configuration.

The table below indicates that change:

Iron and Steel Firms: 1870 and 1900		
	1870	*1900*
No. of firms	808	669
No. of employees	78,000	272,000
Output (tons)	3,200,000	29,500,000
Capital Invested	$121,000,000	$590,000,000

The Increase in Size

The effect of technology is not immediately apparent in these figures, but it quickly becomes apparent when we relate the number of firms to the figures for employees or output or capital. Then it be-

---

* Carnegie was actually not the first person to use the Bessemer process in the United States. He was, however, the first person to take full advantage of its economic potential.

comes clear that the thirty-year span is marked by a *dramatic increase in the size of the average enterprise.*

In 1870 the average iron and steel firm employed fewer than 100 men; in 1900, over 400. During the same period, average output per firm jumped from under 4,000 tons per year to nearly 45,000 tons, and the capital invested in an average company rose from $150,000 to almost $1 million. Moreover, these figures understate the "look" of what was going on, because the statistics include numerous small but unimportant firms. We get a clearer picture of the change when we learn that it cost about $156,000 to build a new rolling mill in Pittsburgh at the time of the Civil War whereas a new rolling mill in 1890 cost $20 million.

It was not only in iron and steel that the size of the typical industrial establishment grew. A glass furnace in the 1860s was deemed an

Pittsburgh steel mills (around 1880–1890)

adequate size if it had the capacity of 6 tons. By 1900, an efficient glass furnace had to produce 1,000 tons. Between 1865 and 1885, the typical railroad grew in length from 100 to 1,000 miles. The cost of an oil refinery in the 1850s, when a "refinery" was little more than a shed with distilling equipment, came to less than $500. By 1865, when Rockefeller bought his first refinery, he paid $72,500*—a sizable fortune for those days—and by 1900 a refinery cost over $1 million.

Thus in nearly every industry we witness a vast increase in size. Already in 1888 a middle-sized railway with headquarters in Boston employed three times as many people and enjoyed six times as much revenue as the state that had created it. In manufacturing, an "enterprise" came to mean not a single modest building but a multiacre complex of structures; machinery grew in size from assemblies that fitted comfortably into a room to constructions that required immense sheds; the work force swelled from troops or companies to regiments and divisions that thronged the streets as they entered or left the factory gate. From one industry to the next, this increase in size varied according to the technology of the product or process, but when we look at the country as a whole, and especially at its industrial core, we cannot mistake the phenomenon of business growth.

The Pattern of Growth

Moreover, the growth of business followed certain common patterns. Much as we have seen in steel, businesses in many fields diversified their products, multiplied their sites, expanded their size of plant. In this way the one-man, one-plant enterprise grew into the bureaucratic organization that we have already studied. And the pattern of growth did not merely involve diversification or geographical extension. Companies grew vertically as well as horizontally, buying up sources of supply or reaching forward to the final sale of their products. The arch-example of successful vertical integration was the oil industry. Standard Oil began in 1870 as a refining company. Shortly thereafter it expanded "backward" into the actual drilling for oil, and it was also extended "forward" as a direct seller of products such as kerosene to the consumer.

Not every enterprise pushed its vertical integration that far. But in many industries we see an effort to grow in "depth" as well as in "extent." Carnegie's great steel plants, for example, were only the

---

* By the end of the year that one refinery grossed over $1.2 million!

disgorging end of a still larger organization that extended far behind the making of steel to a variety of industrial undertakings that fed into the final steel complex. Behind the Thomson and Homestead and Keystone plants were the famous Lucy and Carrie furnaces for making pig iron; and behind them was the enormous Henry Clay Frick Coke Company with its 40,000 acres of coal land, its 2,688 railway cars, and its 13,252 coking ovens; and behind this in turn were 244 miles of railways (organized into three main companies) to ship materials to and from the coking ovens; and then at a still more distant remove were a shipping company and a dock company with a fleet of Great Lakes ore-carrying steamers; and then, at the very point of origin of the steel-making process, was the Oliver Mining Company with its great mines in Michigan and Wisconsin.

What was the point of this vertical organization? Partly it was an effort on the part of business managers to assure a steady flow of necessary raw materials, or to head off the possibility of being "held up" by some strategically placed railroad or mine company. In part it was also a natural avenue of expansion for companies that were seeking profitable areas for investment but that feared to extend themselves further in their own markets. And in part the vertical organization of business expressed the "logic" of a technology that was increasingly knitting the production activities of industrial society into one vast, interconnected process.

Expansion Overseas

We have seen how expansion led the successful business from typical one-plant, one-product beginnings to both horizontal and vertical growth. But we must not overlook one very interesting aspect of that growth. This was the expansion of business overseas.

Such expansion typically began with exports. As a firm grew larger, its market expanded from locality to region, from region to the nation. But why stop at the frontiers of a nation? Would not Canadians and Mexicans, English and Germans also consume the goods a firm could produce if it could manage to sell them cheaply enough to cover transportation costs and meet competition abroad? That was clearly the trend by the late 1800s. Between 1870 and 1900, total United States exports tripled from $450 million to $1.5 billion, and, even more significant, the percentage of those exports that consisted of manufactures (rather than agricultural or raw materials) jumped from 15 percent to 32 percent.

Thereafter only one avenue of expansion remained to be explored.

This was actual production overseas—that is, the establishment of branches abroad, not to sell goods but to produce them. Thus by 1897 American companies had invested some $635 million abroad—in oil wells, railway ventures, mines, plantations, and—most interesting of all—in manufacturing. By that date $94 million was already invested in foreign factories, such as the giant Singer Sewing Machine factory at Kilbowie, Scotland, as large as the company's largest domestic plant. Because Singer was selling half its output overseas, foreign production, rather than exports, made economic sense. It came to make the same sort of sense to a wide variety of industries, some of which expanded overseas "horizontally" (like Singer), some of which expanded "vertically" (like Standard Oil, seeking oil wells).

Thus from an early date business exerted an expansive thrust that brought the American economy into involvement with economies throughout the world. Moreover this internationalist, "imperialist" impulse was strongly encouraged and supported by American government policy. In 1900 the United States dispatched 2,500 American soldiers to join an international European "rescue" expedition aimed at suppressing the Boxer Rebellion—a Chinese uprising against foreign economic influence in Chinese affairs. Within a few years American foreign policy would openly be called "Dollar Diplomacy." President William Howard Taft was not reluctant to admit—indeed, to advertise—the close association of American military might and the promotion of American commercial interests. In his annual message of December 3, 1912, Taft spoke of the new diplomacy as "an effort frankly directed to the increase of American trade upon the axiomatic principle that the Government of the United States shall extend all proper support to every legitimate and beneficial American enterprise abroad."

In this book we shall not trace the complex story of the expansion of American economic influence abroad. Only toward the end of our narrative will we return to the theme of overseas expansion when we examine the modern multinational corporation. But at least we can see that the roots of the giant multinational can be discovered almost one hundred years ago—and that the pressures for international growth were only the final expression of an expansive process of capitalist enterprise whose domestic stages we are now familiar with.

The Struggle for Market Shares

Now we must return to our central theme—the economic transformation of the country. For we have hitherto only attended the causes of the change in size that marked the post–Civil War years. We have yet to investigate the consequences of that change.

The most important immediate effect was a devastating new form of competition. Competition, we recall, was the disciplinary process of the market system. But this disciplinary effect held true only in a milieu of small firms, none of which could take over the entire market. With the coming of the new technology the nature of this disciplining process altered completely. A firm with great economies of scale—the economist's term for the advantages in cost resulting from large-scale production—often had the ability to take away the entire business of a competitor. Competition thus awarded to the more efficient firm the power not merely to "discipline" the prices of a laggard or overly avaricious firm, but literally to wipe out such a firm.

Fixed Costs

Moreover, technology changed competition in another way. Typically, the expensive new machines and equipment added to the "fixed costs" of business—a steel mill that put in Bessemer converters, for example, had to pay interest on the money it borrowed to pay for them and had to bear the cost of the depreciation of the new investment. These large fixed costs also served as a powerful stimulus for aggressive business behavior.

Suppose, for example, that a steel plant put in a Bessemer process and thereby incurred new interest and depreciation costs of $1 million per year. Those costs had to be paid whether the plant was running or not. Therefore there was a tremendous temptation, whenever business was dull, to cut prices in order to bring in *some* revenues, even if they were not enough to make a profit. Carnegie put the matter in a nutshell when he said that it cost less to keep the machines running, even when there was no market in sight, than to shut down the factories.

Cutthroat Competition

Thus the growing investment in new technology exerted a powerful inducement to price-cutting as a means of stealing a march on competitors. Price-cutting was all right—until the going got rough and the bigger firms, with more wealth, began to cut prices *below* costs, accepting a loss in order to keep revenues coming in. As Carnegie wrote in 1902, "Political economy says that . . . goods will not be produced at less than cost. This was true when Adam Smith wrote, but it is not quite true today." [2]

Not just in steel, but in virtually all industries with heavy fixed costs—railroads, oil, coal, copper—"cutthroat" price wars repeatedly broke out as producers desperately struggled to find markets for their products when business was slack. "A starving man will usually get bread if it is to be had," said James J. Hill, President of the Great Northern Railway, "and a starving railway will not maintain rates." [3]

As we would expect, this cutthroat competition soon forced smaller firms, with less wealth, against the wall. We can see this tendency if we examine the statistics of the iron and steel industry once again (see p. 92). Notice that there were *fewer* firms in operation in 1900 than in 1870, even though the industry's output had increased enormously. Obviously some firms had grown at the expense of others.

It was not just in iron and steel that dog-eat-dog competition winnowed the ranks of the firms. In 1900, for example, the number of textile mills in the country was one-third fewer than in the 1880s, although textile production was up threefold. In similar fashion, the number of manufacturers of agricultural implements had fallen by 60 percent despite a rapid increase in the use of farm machinery.

We can sum up the change in a sentence: *Competition became a process in which firms struggled for shares of the market.* The result was a desperate contest whose consequences would have profound effects on the workings of the entire economy. We shall trace those consequences in our next chapter. But first, while we are still focused on the role of technology in the economic transformation, we must stop to consider another change, without which the thrust of economic growth would have been expressed in very different fashion. This is the *social technology of organization,* and specifically the development of the organizational form we call the corporation.

THE TECHNOLOGY OF ORGANIZATION

Corporations and Proprietorships

The corporation can be traced very far back into history. The early colonial settlers had corporations for the performance of certain activities, such as charity work and other activities that were associated with the public welfare. These corporations were entities organized by the state or colony—that is, organizations that received a corporate "charter" from the local government permitting them to carry on their business.

But certainly the corporation was very much the exception rather than the rule until well into the nineteenth century. Corporations required the approval of legislatures and therefore entailed a degree of government intervention into economic life that appeared both unnecessary and burdensome to enterprisers in the eighteenth and early nineteenth centuries. The typical enterprise was a proprietorship or a partnership—forms of organization in which the principals of a business "owned" it very much as they owned their private assets, such as their house or other personal effects.

There were obvious conveniences to such a simple mode of establishing a business, but there were also difficulties and problems. For if a proprietorship or a partnership failed, its creditors could sue the owners personally, forcing them to pay any debts of the business from their personal assets. Proprietorships thus exposed their owners to considerable financial risk in case of business failure. Moreover, they were ill-suited to businesses that were expected to last beyond the life of the proprietor, because the enterprise had to be legally reorganized every time its owner or partners died.

Corporate Advantages

The corporation avoided those difficulties. Because it was an entity created by the state, it existed in its own right as a "person" created by law. As such a legal person, the corporation could do anything that a private person could—own, buy, or sell property, carry on business affairs, sue or be sued. But it had these extraordinary features:

The "person" of the corporation did not die when any official or shareowner of the corporation died. It went on forever—or at least until the state that issued its charter revoked it.

The corporate person was responsible only for "its" own obligations. If a corporation went bankrupt, it met as much of its debts as it could from its own assets, but neither its officials nor its shareowners could ordinarily be asked to pay any remaining debts from their personal wealth.

Corporate Ownership

Clearly the corporation had substantial advantages over proprietorships and partnerships. But who owned it? How did it run?

A corporation today as in the past is owned by individuals who buy "shares" in it. Suppose that a corporation is granted a charter to carry on a business, say in retail trade. The charter also specifies how many shares of stock this business enterprise is allowed to issue. For

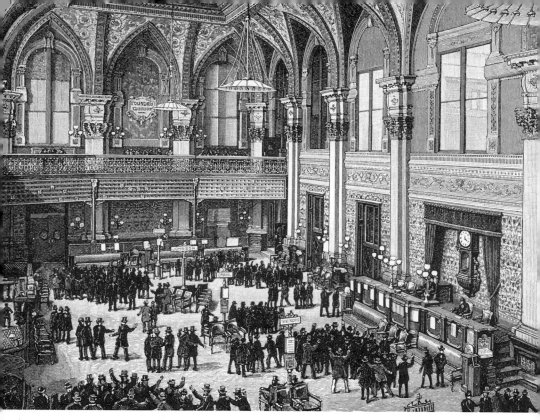

The New York Stock Exchange

example, a corporation may be formed with the right to issue 1 million shares. If these shares are sold to individuals at a price of $10 each, the original shareholders (also called stockholders) will have put $10 million into the corporation. In return they will receive stock certificates indicating how many shares each person has bought.

These stock certificates are somewhat like a partnership agreement, although there are very important differences. If someone buys 1,000 shares in our imaginary corporation, he or she will own .1 percent of the corporation. He will have the right to receive .1 percent of all income that it pays out as "dividends" on its stock. He will also be entitled to cast 1,000 votes at the meetings of shareholders that all corporations must hold. In this way a shareholder is very much like a junior partner who was given a one-tenth of one percent interest in a business.

But here are the critical differences:

As we have already said, a stockholder is not personally liable for any debts that the corporation cannot pay from the money it has taken in from its stockholders or from its earnings. If the company goes bankrupt, the shareholder will lose his investment of $10,000 (1,000 shares at $10), but no one can sue him for any further money. *His liability is thereby limited to the amount he has invested.*

Unlike a partner, who usually finds it very difficult to sell his shares, a stockholder may sell his shares to anyone he likes, at any price he can get. If our imaginary corporation prospers, he may be able to get $20 for each share. He is perfectly free to sell as many shares as he wishes at that price. Moreover, marketplaces for stocks and bonds have developed along with the corporation to facilitate sales of stock. The most important of these markets, the New York Stock Exchange, was organized in 1817. By 1900 over 100 million shares a year were being traded on its floor. *Thus with the corporation came the advantage of a much greater "liquidity" of personal wealth.*

Shares of stock entitle the stockholder to the dividends that the directors of the corporation may decide to pay out for each share. But as a stockholder he is not entitled to any fixed amount of profit. If the corporation prospers, the directors may vote to pay a large dividend. But they are under no obligation to do so—they may wish to use the earnings of the corporation for other purposes, such as the purchase of new equipment or land. If the corporation suffers losses, ordinarily the directors will vote to pay no dividend, or only a small one, to be paid from past earnings. *Thus as an owner of ordinary "common" stock, the stockholder must take the risk of having his dividends rise or fall.* *

---

* Corporations are allowed to issue bonds, as well as common stock. A bond is different from a share of stock in two important ways. First, a bond has a *stated value* printed on its face, whereas a share of stock does not. A $1,000 bond is a certificate of debt issued by the corporation. It makes the bondholder not a sharer in the profits of the company but a creditor of the corporation—someone to whom the corporation is in debt for $1,000.

Second, a bond also states on its face the *amount of income* it will pay to its bondholders. A $1,000 bond may declare that it will pay $80 a year as interest. Unlike dividends, this interest payment will not rise if the corporation makes money, nor will it fall if it does not. Thus there is no element of profit-sharing in bonds, as there is in stocks. However, there is a compensation for this. The risk of owning a bond is much less than that of owning a stock. A bond is a legal obligation of the corporation, which *must* pay interest, and which must buy back the bond itself when a fixed term of years has expired and the bond becomes "due." (If it fails to do so, the bondholder can sue the corporation.) A stock has no such obligations attached to it, and a share of stock never comes "due." No stockholder can sue a corporation if it fails to pay a dividend. Last, bondholders' claims come ahead of stockholders' if a corporation goes out of business or becomes bankrupt.

Ownership and Control

One last matter is also of significance in discussing the organization of the corporation. The new mode of structuring enterprise brought a development of great moment for the captains of industry and their successors, the business managers and the bureaucrats. It enabled a small group of men to direct the affairs of an enterprise *even if they did not personally own it.*

As we have seen, stockholders are the actual owners of a corporation. But it is obviously impossible for large numbers of stockholders to meet regularly and run a company. A.T.&.T., for example, today has well over 1 million stockholders. Where could they meet? How could they possibly decide what the company should do? Even in the 1870s, how could the shareowners of a large railway company have gathered to run their enterprise?

Therefore all corporations are run by boards of directors elected by the stockholders. At regular intervals, all stockholders are asked to elect or reelect members of the board, each stockholder casting as many votes as the number of shares he or she owns. In turn the board of directors appoints the main officials of the corporation—for example, its president and vice-presidents. In turn the main officials hire the rest of the employees.

As a result, a corporation is something like a private government. It has an electorate—its shareholders. It has an elected governing body —its board of directors. It has an executive—its officials. Needless to say, there are very important differences between a government and a corporation, but it is not too misleading to think of corporations as a means of governing the complicated affairs of a business enterprise.

Moreover, as the number of shareowners grows, power tends to drift into the hands of the board of directors and the officials whom it appoints. Consequently, it becomes extremely difficult to round up enough votes to elect a slate of directors different from the directors in office. Who, after all, has the money and the time to write to a thousand—much less a hundred thousand—shareowners, recommending a special candidate? Thus boards of directors tend to become self-perpetuating, each year mailing to the company's stockholders a mail ballot (called a proxy) on which are printed the names of their own candidates—usually themselves. Except in unusual circumstances, the shareowners obediently vote the slate that the directors have designated. It is easier for a shareholder who "wants out" to sell his company shares than to get a new management in place of the old. (This is not to say that directors are indifferent to stockholders' opinions, for they are not. All directors are concerned about their company's image, especially if they plan to offer more stocks and bonds for sale at a future date.)

Thus power comes to settle in the hands of a board of directors whose members may own only a tiny fraction of the total outstanding stock of the company. We do not have statistics for the early years of corporate activity, but in 1929 the board of directors of the United States Steel Corporation held in all only 1.4 percent of the company's stock. In contrast, in 1900 Andrew Carnegie had personally owned over half of Carnegie Steel, Ltd. Needless to say, the passing of effective control from the hands of a few wealthy capitalists into the hands of a small group of self-chosen directors further enhanced the change from the captain of industry to the industrial manager.

The Corporation and Economic Growth

The development of the modern corporation did not take place overnight. In Pittsburgh in 1860 there were 17 foundries, 21 rolling mills, 76 glass "factories," and 47 other manufacturing establishments to be seen, but not a single one of them was incorporated. As late as 1878 in Massachusetts there were only 520 businesses organized as corporations out of 11,000 manufacturing enterprises, but those 520 corporations already produced one-third of all the state's manufacturing output. As we will see in our next chapter, the legal powers and flexibility of the corporation changed considerably as various state legislatures altered the requirements for corporate charters. But we can already understand how this enormously important development in social technology assisted in the growth of the economy.

To the robber barons and the captains of industry the corporation offered immediate advantages. The corporation limited their personal financial risk and increased their liquidity—that is, their ability to raise cash by selling their stock. Therefore their ability to move into and out of businesses was vastly increased. The possibility of steering the policy of a large enterprise without necessarily owning a majority of its shares was still another gain for them.

More important in terms of economic growth was the possibility for successful businesses to tap a source of capital that would have been impossible to reach without the limited liability and high liquidity of stocks and bonds. In the early days of enterprise, businessmen had to look to their own resources, or to those of capitalists at home or abroad, to raise the money needed for their operations. Once the market for stocks and bonds was organized, a whole new layer of capital became available among small merchants or moderately well-to-do citizens who were eager to share in the rising fortunes of the great railways and major companies, or who simply wanted a chance to "play the market" in the hope of getting rich quick. As we have noted in the case of the Pennsylvania Railroad, many of the early railroads were financed by sales of stock to small stockholders.

The corporation was therefore an extraordinarily useful adjunct to the machine technology. As a means of attracting capital, it far surpassed the proprietorship or the partnership. As a way of organizing a vast enterprise, it lent itself naturally to the emergence of managerial bureaucracy, at which we looked in the preceding chapter. Today, of course, the corporation is the dominant economic institution of our age. What we should remember is that, like the industrial processes it coordinates, the corporation was also a technological innovation, and one that was no less important for our economic growth than the vast equipment it came to control.

NOTES

[1] Quoted in J. H. Bridge, *The Inside History of the Carnegie Steel Company* (1903), p. 113.

[2] *The Empire of Business* (1902), p. 154.

[3] Quoted in Thomas Cochran and William Miller, *The Age of Enterprise* (1942), p. 141.

From Trust to Antitrust

6

So far we have examined particular elements of the industrialization process—the evolution of the businessman who was its main human agency, and the development of the technologies that were its most powerful material agencies. Now we must put these elements together, watching what happened as the aggressive drive of the business search for profit combined with the new industrial techniques and the new forms of social organization.

THE SPIRIT OF THE AGE

A good way to begin is to put ourselves into the business frame of mind of the late nineteenth century. We tend to think of those years as a time of easy money-making, when everyone prospered and businesses grew effortlessly from small firms into large enterprises.

But that is not at all how things looked to the businessmen of the time. The "Gilded Age" (as Mark Twain dubbed the '70s and '80s) was a period of extreme business uncertainty. Periods of prosperity were interrupted by long and frequent stretches of business depression. Indeed, of the twenty-five years between 1873 and 1897, fourteen were viewed by contemporaries as times of recession or depression.

Panic and Pain

The businessmen of that time were not mistaken: those *were* difficult years. In retrospect the depression of 1873 has been adjudged the most severe in American history, save only for the Great Depression of the 1930s. In the terrible debacle that began in 1873 the general price level dropped by a quarter; the rate of business failures doubled; more than half the nation's steel furnaces and rolling mills were idle; the New York Stock Exchange was even shut down for ten days. "Business since 1873," said the *Commercial and Financial Chronicle* at the beginning of 1879—*six years* after the onset of the recession— "has been like a retreating army on the march."[1] Indeed, reflecting on his years in the oil business John D. Rockefeller later wrote:

> [I wondered] how we came through them. You know how often I had not an unbroken night's sleep, worrying about how it was all coming out. All the fortune I have made has not served to compensate for the anxiety of the period. Work by day and worry by night, week in and week out, month after month.[2]

Hence business enterprisers did not enter on their search for profit and expansion confident that all would end well. As a "planning agency" the market was a harsh pacesetter, urging business into hell-for-leather expansion when the outlook seemed bright, exacting terrible penalties when the outlook changed. The expansion of output and the accumulation of wealth took place, not in an atmosphere of security, but in one of "panic and pain," as historian Edward Kirkland has described it.

The Business Cycle

In a word, economic growth did not proceed along a smooth upward path but took the form of booms and busts. Economists call this irregular wavelike motion the *business cycle:* and they attribute it to the very phenomenon we have seen—a rush of business expansion in one period, normally lasting four to five years, followed by a period of doldrums typically lasting another three, four, or five years.*

These business cycles were not a totally new experience in economic life, for we can trace waves of faster and slower growth back to the years before the Civil War. But the industrialization process brought much sharper swings in prosperity and recession. "In the three decades after the Civil War," write Thomas Cochran and William Miller, "as confident entrepreneurs raced to take advantage of every ephemeral rise of prices, of every advance in tariff schedules, of every new market opened by the railroads and puffed up by immigration, they recklessly expanded and mechanized their plants, each seeking the greatest share of the new melon. The more successful they were in capturing such shares and the more efficient they were in promptly satisfying the new market, however, the greater was the number of buildings and machinery left idle when the new market approached the saturation point and the rate of expansion declined."[3]

But the business cycle was more than just the cause for "panic and pain." It was also a prime factor in that concentration of business in fewer hands that we noted in our last chapter. During the years of panic and depression, many smaller, weak firms went under, and bigger, rich firms survived; so that when the cycle was over and the forward movement resumed, the new (and usually larger) volume of production was lodged in a smaller number of firms than before. And then, quite independent of the cycle, the bigger and more aggressive firms pursued expansive strategies of the kind we have seen, forcing competitors to the wall and further accelerating the "concentration" of industry.

Competition and Combination

Thus the struggle for markets brought fear in its wake. "Competition is industrial war," wrote a large manufacturer of envelopes in 1901. ". . . [U]nrestricted competition, carried to its logical conclusion, means death to some of the combatants and injury for all.

---

* Actually, there is more than one cycle in the pattern of growth. Statisticians identify at least three different cycles: a short one, of one to three years' duration, commonly associated with swings in inventories; a very long cycle of about twenty years, probably the result of swings in housing construction and household formation; and the "regular" seven-to-ten-year cycle we mention above.

Even the victor does not soon recover from the wounds received in combat."[4]

The Pittsburgh *Commercial,* a newspaper concerned with the oil industry, bemoaned "a ruinous competition between refineries, by which all parties have lost money."[5] Even the Social Darwinists, who extolled the virtues of the competitive struggle, felt the strain was too much: "The struggle for existence and survival of the fittest is a pretty theory," said George W. Perkins of the Chicago, Burlington and Quincy Railroad, "but it is also a law of nature that even the fittest must live as they go along."

An obvious response to the anxiety and threat of cutthroat competition was for the firms in a given industry to get together and to agree not to undercut one another—to "live and let live." From pre-1865 days—indeed, back to colonial times—this had been a constant aim of businesses in many fields, who formed "pools"—informal agreements on prices—to avoid their suicidal race for markets.

In 1876 the Cleveland *Gazette* described how a pooling arrangement worked on a local steamboat route:

> The object of the pool line (so called because each boat is required to put up a certain amount of its receipts—about 45 percent—each trip into the hands of the treasurer, when it becomes the property of the line) . . . is to maintain a regular rate on freights at Cincinnati and all points on the river, to, and including, Cairo.
> . . . In case of opposition, the pool boat on "berth" will take freight at figures so low that the opposition will lose money, and the regular boat's rate is made up to the established rate out of the pool's fund. . . . After 60 days a division of the pool money is made, retaining 20 percent of the whole amount to maintain organization. The assessment of the pool is very heavy . . . so that it does not take long to get enough money on hand to make all boats "stick," for, if they do not live up to their agreement, they forfeit all the money they have paid into the pool.

By the 1880s there was a cordage pool, a whiskey pool, a coal pool, a salt pool, and endless rail and other pools. For the growing scale of individual firms provided a strong new impulse to avoid the mutual bloodletting of cutthroat competition. As fixed costs grew, the incentive to take in business at any price was often irresistible.

Yet, none of the pools worked. As soon as business worsened, the need to assure revenues led one firm after another to reduce its prices. At a meeting of railway managers called to agree on a schedule of freight rates, the president of one railroad slipped out during a brief recess to wire the new rates to his company so that it could be the first to undercut them. "I suppose they will cheat," sighed one railroad executive, "but we can stand a great deal of cheating better than competition."[6]

Trusts and Mergers

The basic reasons that pools could not prevent all-out competition was that they were illegal. A long tradition in English and American law forbade *contracts* in "restraint of trade." Therefore no company could sue another for breaking its "gentleman's agreement."

The failure of the pools did not, however, bring to an end the search for a means of enforcing price discipline. It merely turned that search in a new direction—a direction happily provided by the growing predominance of the new corporate means of organizing business. For the corporation was soon discovered to offer a highly effective way of avoiding the internecine economic wars that upset the business community.

The architect of the new method was Samuel C. T. Dodd, the chief counsel of John D. Rockefeller's Standard Oil Company. Dodd saw that the corporation, with its control vested in a small number of directors, provided a legal means of achieving what could not be done under the common law. His "invention" was the trust—a legal arrangement under which stockholders in a corporation gave their stock to a central board of directors "in trust." The board members were authorized to vote the stock as they wished, while the dividends on the stocks continued to be paid to the shareholders, who had surrendered their stock for trust certificates.

In 1882 Dodd established a trust for Standard Oil that permitted its board of directors to control the overall policies of forty corporations from Standard's headquarters in New York City. Soon the trust idea spread to other industries: there was a sugar trust, a cottonseed oil trust, and a dozen more. By the late 1880s, trusts were a well-nigh ubiquitous feature of industry, much talked about in the press. One commentator said that an average citizen was born to the profit of the milk trust and died to the profit of the coffin trust.

The voting trust was, however, only a stepping stone to a still more effective means of avoiding competition. This was the corporate merger, a very simple device by which one corporation bought up the stock of another, thereby winning control of its price and other policies. Why was such an obvious means not used before? The principal reason was that corporations were not at first allowed by their charters to own stock in other companies. Then in 1889 New Jersey amended its incorporation laws to make mergers possible, and businessmen quickly took advantage of the new law.

Morgan and U.S. Steel

One such businessman was John Pierpont Morgan, the dominant (and domineering) figure of finance at the turn of the century. Morgan lorded over the financial world with a passion for order and a fierce hatred for the financial havoc that competition brought. He also had a shrewd eye for the profits that could be made by merging warring corporations into one giant firm and then selling the stock of the new giant for more than the combined values of the corporations that comprised it. "I like a little competition," he was quoted as saying, "but I like combination better."[7] Between 1892 and 1902 Morgan was instrumental in merging competitive firms to create such new giant corporations as General Electric, American Telephone and Telegraph, and International Harvester. But the capstone of his career was the formation of the United States Steel Corporation, the first billion-dollar company in American history.

One evening in 1900 Morgan was invited to a dinner of leading industrialists, where Charles Schwab, the dynamic young operating president of Carnegie Steel, sketched out his vision of a unified steel industry. We have already mentioned that Carnegie had competitors. Other capitalists had also formed Bessemer-based operations that fought Carnegie in every aspect of his operations. There was the American Can Company, American Steel and Wire, Federal Steel, National Steel, National Tube, American Bridge—a whole regiment of steel-producers. Schwab painted the picture of an industry rid of this competitive duplication of factories and mills, guided by a single great corporation charged with the orderly development of American industrial power. Needless to say, such a vast steel corporation would also be immensely profitable.

Morgan's imagination was kindled. He took Schwab aside and plied him with questions about his absent master. On what terms would Carnegie sell his interests? What companies would be inside the new supercorporation; what ones could safely be left outside? In turn Schwab conferred with Carnegie, and the veteran steel-maker, tired of business, agreed on a price for selling out to Morgan: $492 million, of which $250 million would go to Carnegie, the rest to his

J. P. Morgan

partners. Morgan looked at the scrap of paper on which the number was scrawled and brusquely said: "I accept."

Morgan then set about acquiring the other firms he needed for his supercorporation. One of them was American Steel and Wire, controlled by John Gates, a swashbuckling robber baron whose latest scandal had been to risk a million dollars on the turn of a single card. (He lost.) Gates was reluctant to sell. At last Morgan stormed into his office, pounded on the table, and, fixing Gates and his associates with his fierce eyes, said, "Gentlemen, I am going to leave this building in ten minutes. If by that time you have not accepted our offer, the matter will be closed. We will build our own wire plant." Gates capitulated.

The firm assembled by Morgan consisted of Carnegie Steel and its eight largest competitors. It had a capacity of two-thirds of the nation's steel castings and ingots. It embraced every aspect of steelmaking from ore beds to finishing plants. It had 156 major factories.

It was the largest industrial company the world had ever seen, and the wealthiest. For Morgan sold the shares of the new United States Steel Corporation for $1.4 billion. Of this enormous sum, perhaps $700 million was "water." The shares were bought at their inflated price only because Morgan's prestige convinced investors that their value was real.

THE MERGER MOVEMENT

What Morgan brought to pass in steel was also rapidly coming about—often at Morgan's doing—in many other industries. For beginning in 1898, the merger device was producing a tremendous wave of amalgamation.

Year	Number of Firms Bought	Capitalization of Firms Bought (in $ millions)
1895	43	40.8
1896	26	24.7
1897	69	119.7
1898	303	650.6
1899	1208	2262.7
1900	340	442.2
1901	423	2052.0
1902	379	910.8
1903	142	297.6
1904	79	110.5

The effect of the merger wave was to change the structure of American industry almost overnight. In 1865 most industries were competitive, with no single company dominating any field. By 1904 one or two giant firms—usually put together by merger—controlled at least half the output in 78 different industries. In the locomotive field nineteen firms had shared the market in 1860. Two merger-created firms ruled the roost in 1900. In the biscuit and cracker market—formerly a scatter of tiny companies—one giant merged firm, the National Biscuit Company, controlled 90 percent of the industry's market. In oil, the Standard Oil Company, under the shrewd and aggressive leadership of John D. Rockefeller, grew from insignificant beginnings in the 1860s to a supercorporation that owned well over 80 percent of the nation's refining capacity by the turn of the century.

Another way of looking at the transformation is to note the change in sheer size. In 1865 it is doubtful if there was a single firm in the United States worth $10 million. In 1896, except for the railroads, there were not a dozen $10-million companies. In 1904, after the merger wave, there were 300 such firms which together owned $20 billion—over 40 percent of all the industrial wealth of the nation. As two of America's leading economists wrote in 1912, "If the carboniferous age had returned and the earth had repeopled itself with dinosaurs, the change in animal life would scarcely have seemed greater than that which has been made in the business world by these monster corporations."[8]

The Results of Combination

Did the trusts achieve their end? Yes and no. Investigating the course of steel prices from 1880 to 1901, one scholar has discovered that the monthly average price per ton for standard Bessemer rails ranged from $16.50 to $85. For the next fifteen years, following the merger that produced the United States Steel Corporation, they sold for $28 a ton without deviation, save for occasional rush orders. During this period steel prices still fluctuated considerably, and once or twice the price of pig iron rose *above* the price at which rails sold. But rails, which were the main focus of cutthroat competition, held firm. The perils of competition had been effectively eliminated.

In oil, farm machinery, lead, biscuits—in short, in most heavily concentrated industries—one large corporation now emerged by tacit consent as the price-maker, the remaining firms following closely or exactly in its tracks.

We should note, however, that price leadership did not necessarily ensure price stability, despite the extraordinary results in steel rails. Indeed, according to a study prepared by the National Industrial Conference Board in 1929, the trusts as a whole did not diminish the scope of price swings over the business cycle. But we must remember that the purpose of the consolidation movement was not to counteract the business cycle (which was then regarded as beyond the intervention of man), nor was it even to raise prices "unduly." Above all, *the aim of consolidation was to remove the threat of the unrestricted price*

Cartoonist Nast views the trust problem

competition that proved so dangerous for a world of large-scale enterprise.

Viewed in this light, the combination movement was a considerable success, for it did mute price competition. Yet, surprisingly, the merger movement never succeeded in wholly stamping out competition by other means. In fact, one of the most interesting "post-mortem" findings about the trusts is that the shares of the market commanded by the great corporate giants steadily declined, as smaller and more aggressive firms stole business away from the large conservative monoliths, or as new firms were formed to enter the industry. In the table below we see the steady erosion of the market share of the biggest firms over time:

Share of Market of Leading Mergers		
	At Time of Merger	*Later Date*
U. S. Steel (1901)	62 %	40% (1920)
Standard Oil (1882)	90+	64 (1911)
Int'l Harvester (1902)	85	64 (1918)
Anaconda Copper (1895)	39	12 (1920)
Am. Can Co. (1901)	90	50 (1913)

Thus the trusts were a mixed success. They did mitigate the severity of the price competition that had demoralized business for so long. They did not, however, secure monopoly positions, or even commanding shares of the markets, for the biggest firms. And perhaps most important of all, by their very efforts to achieve economic success, the trusts brought upon themselves the political animus of the nation. Let us next follow that development.

THE ANTITRUST MOVEMENT

Popular Opposition to the Trusts

Grass-roots opposition to the trust movement was a sentiment of long standing. What historian Arthur Dudden has called a "simmering ferment of anti-monopolistic ideas" was discernible through most of the late nineteenth century: "The corners and pools of the eighteen sixties and seventies," he wrote, "the oil trust of the seventies together with its imitators of the eighties, and the multitudinous mergers and consolidations throughout, were assailed by their detractors not only as particular evils but as overall manifestations of foreboding portent."[9]

These antitrust feelings were at first of little importance. Then, as the railway pools began to squeeze the small businessman and the farmer, voices began to rise in protest. A resolution passed in 1873 by the Illinois State Farmers Association read:

> Resolved, that the railways of the world, except in those countries where they have been held under the strict regulation and supervision of the government, have proved themselves arbitrary, extortionate, and as opposed to free institutions and free commerce between states as were the feudal barons of the middle ages.[10]

Labor organizations, such as the Knights of Labor and the American Federation of Labor, also feared the rise of mighty concentrations of business power: "The great corporations, the trusts, with their capital, their machinery, special privileges and other advantages, are overwhelming the individual, reducing him to the condition of a mere tool, to be used in their great undertakings for their individual profit, and of no more consequence than a dumb piece of machinery," wrote John Hayes of the Knights.

And by no means least influential, a group of journalists began to call attention to the practices of the robber barons. In *Wealth Against Commonwealth*, published in 1894, Henry Demarest Lloyd excoriated big business in general and the Standard Oil Company in particular. Lloyd's book, detailing the transgressions of the great oil company, was the first of a series of "muckraking" exposés that would do much to mobilize outrage against the tactics of business aggrandizement and the general indifference, not to say contempt, evidenced by business for the public.

As a consequence of all these protests, public sentiment began to change. Significantly, whereas the Anti-Monopoly Party polled but 173,000 votes in the election of 1884, four years later even the Republican Party declared itself against "all combinations of capital organized in trusts," and Democratic President Grover Cleveland asserted that the people were being "trampled to death" beneath the iron heels of the trusts. Clearly a new political theme was being sounded; as Henry Demarest Lloyd wrote, "If the tendency to combination is irresistible, the control of it is imperative." By 1890 twenty-one states had attempted to curb monopoly with antitrust statutes of varying kinds.

The Regulation of Enterprise

The question was: What to do? By the early 1890s one remedy had been tried and found wanting. Many states had gone to court to sue the trusts on the grounds that they were "restraining" trade—Louisiana sued the cottonseed trust, Nebraska the whiskey trust, New York the sugar trust, Ohio the almighty oil trust. Yet, although the states generally won their court cases, the trusts were not so easily vanquished. As we have seen, they abandoned the "trusteeship" idea, only to achieve the same dominating effect through mergers and other corporate devices, or simply by moving their headquarters from a state in which they were being attacked to another, more obliging one.

It was the failure to achieve control over the trust at the state level that brought pressure on Congress to intervene at the federal level. The first target was the railroads, now accused by merchants all over the country of charging exorbitant rates. One newspaper in Sacramento, California, for example, published a schedule of freight rates between that city and a number of points in Nevada, showing that far lower rates had been charged by wagon-teams before the railroad was built! In addition, there was growing outrage at such practices as charging more for some short hauls than for long hauls, or for the nefarious granting of secret rebates or kickbacks to favored shippers.

The Interstate Commerce Commission

In a mood of indignation Congress passed the Interstate Commerce Act of 1887, establishing the first federal *regulatory agency*, the Interstate Commerce Commission. As its title makes clear, the commission was limited to the regulation of railroad rates in interstate commerce, for the Constitution had specifically provided Congress with the authority only to regulate commerce between the states. The act declared that railroad rates must be "reasonable and just," that railroads had to publish their rate schedules, and that most of their shadier practices, such as granting rebates, were unlawful.

The ICC had immense obstacles to overcome. To begin with, the law itself was obscure: What was a "reasonable and just" freight charge?

In its *First Annual Report,* the Committee stated:

> Of the duties devolved upon the Commission by the act to regulate
> commerce, none is more perplexing than that of passing upon complaints
> made of rates as being unreasonable. The question of the reasonableness
> of rate involves so many considerations and is affected by so many
> circumstances and conditions which may at first blush seem foreign,
> that it is quite impossible to deal with on purely mathematical principles,
> or on any principles whatever, without a consciousness that no conclu-
> sion which may be reached can by demonstration be shown to be
> absolutely correct.[11]

Yet another difficulty the commission had to contend with was the
flood of requests for action that it received. Over a thousand cases
were presented to its tiny staff in its first few months of existence.
And not least, the ICC had no way of enforcing its decisions except to
sue in the federal courts.

Taking advantage of the confusion, the railroads paid little attention to the commission, often continuing to charge their high rates
even after the commission had directed them not to. Four or five
years later, when the erring railroad was finally brought to court, the
roads generally gained from judicial interpretations of the law that
gave the benefit of every doubt to the railroads and that regarded the
new federal authority with grave suspicions. Of sixteen cases brought
to the Supreme Court between 1887 and 1905, fifteen were decided in
favor of the railroads. One railroad executive announced that "there
is not a road in the country that can be accused of living up to the
rules of the Interstate Commerce Law."[12]

In time the situation changed. The powers of the ICC were gradually expanded and its staff enlarged. By the beginning of the twentieth century the commission was effectively regulating the rates on
virtually all rail transportation, and no railroad dared flout its
rulings. Ironically, by the midpoint of the twentieth century, the ICC
had become the *protector* of the railroads, establishing freight schedules for trucking that prevented this new, aggressive form of freight-
handling from undermining the dwindling profits of "their" industry. This conversion of an agency charged with the suppression of
abuses into an agency concerned with the protection of its client industry has since been many times repeated, as the ICC model was extended into other fields—banking, food inspection, communications,
drugs, airlines.

Opposition to the trusts

The Sherman Act

Regulation, however initially ineffective, was not the only sign of a gradual swing of public sentiment against the big corporations. Equally important was the growing movement that we call "antitrust"—a movement designed to break up the big companies and to restore competition rather than to restrain it.

Like the simmering discontent against the trusts because of their abuse of power, there had long existed an undercurrent of mingled fear and dislike directed against them sheerly because they represented a threat to the ideal of democratic equality. A strain of "populist," anti-wealth, anti-big-business ideas had always tinctured American thought, even in the years of all-out celebration of wealth. Gradually that strain received popular support as the trusts waxed fat and the books of the muckrakers began to make a deep popular impression. By 1890 the political feeling had swelled to such an extent that a bill directed against the trusts—the Sherman Anti-Trust Act—passed Congress without a murmur of dissent.

The Sherman Act declared that "every contract, combination in form of trust or otherwise, or conspiracy in restraint of trade among the several States . . . is hereby declared to be illegal," and "that every person who shall monopolize or attempt to monopolize or combine or conspire with any other person to monopolize any part of trade or commerce among the several States . . . shall be deemed guilty of a misdemeanor." This surely seemed a radical departure for a nation that had always extolled its business leaders and admired their exploits. How did such a bill pass through a highly conservative Congress whose Senate was called—with good reason—"The Millionaires Club"?

Looking backward we can see a number of explanations. The mood of the country was strongly "antitrust," and the bill satisfied the need of Congress to go to the electorate and declare that it had passed a bill to punish the trusts. Then, too, the bill did not really break new ground in its economic philosophy but merely moved the long-standing disapproval of monopoly from the exclusive concern of the states to the mixed concern of the states and the federal government. Another reason was the genuine desire of Congress to "do something" about the trusts, although no one was able to say exactly what should be done: the bill in its general condemnation of monopoly seemed as good an answer as any. And then there was the knowledge that the actual impact of the law would depend on the interpretation of the judiciary, which in turn could be depended on for a conservative reading of the law.

Business Ignores Antitrust

Certainly Congress was correct in not expecting the law to make a great change. Most business leaders simply ignored it. Testifying before the Stanley Committee investigating the United States Steel Corporation, Carnegie was nonchalant about the Sherman Act: "Do you really expect men engaged in an active struggle to make a living at manufacturing to be posted about laws and their decisions, and what is applied here, there, and everywhere?" Pressed further, as to whether his lawyers might not have advised him about the law, he answered: "Nobody ever mentioned the Sherman Act to me, that I remember."[13] Carnegie's indifference must have been widespread, for, as we have seen, the merger movement gained its greatest impetus in the decade *following* the passage of the Sherman Act. Thus if the act was supposed to halt the growth of trusts, it clearly failed.

The failure was traceable in large part to the extremely conservative interpretation that the Supreme Court put on the law, as expected. In the first important case in 1895, involving the American Sugar Company's control over 98 percent of the nation's refining capacity, the judges decreed that the company's mergers concerned *manufacture* and therefore did not fall within the scope of interstate *commerce.* In the face of such decisions, we can understand why a humorist of the times wrote, "What looks like a stone wall to a layman is a triumphal arch to the corporation lawyer."

Following the Court's conservative interpretation, the Sherman Act lay dormant, having virtually no effect in breaking up the trusts or slowing down the process of business amalgamation. Then, in 1902, the act was rejuvenated. In that year President Theodore Roosevelt ordered his Attorney General to prosecute the Northern Securities Company under the Sherman Anti-Trust Act. The Northern Securities Company was a corporation formed by J. P. Morgan to control the Northern Pacific, the Great Northern, and the Chicago, Burlington and Quincy railroads, giving it a monopoly of western transportation. The Court dissolved the Northern Securities Company in 1904, earning for Roosevelt the sobriquet "trust-buster." Roosevelt also initiated a suit against the Standard Oil Company, which was adjudicated under Taft in 1911. Although the Court dissolved the Standard Oil Trust, the Standard Oil Company of New

Jersey promptly used the device of the holding company (a corporation that owned stock in other corporations) to reestablish direct control over some seventy companies that had been severed from it by the antitrust decision.

The Effect of Antitrust

Thus, just as in the case of regulation, it is difficult to claim that the immediate aims of the antitrust movement were achieved. Even today, after the Sherman law has been strengthened by other legislation, many economists doubt whether the dynamics of industrial concentration have been much affected by efforts to curb the tendency toward monopoly. Yet, as is also the case with regulation, perhaps it is possible to see the problem from a perspective that does not focus directly on the success or failure of the legislation.

For in retrospect what seems most significant about the Sherman Act or the ICC and its subsequent regulatory agencies is the expression of a new concern on the part of the national government. We have seen how the expansion of business size was intimately related to the whole process of industrialization. During the early years of that process, the change in the texture and scale of business life was a matter of indifference to the national government. Indeed, the government watched with admiration as the captains of industry built a mighty industrial economy; and both state and federal legislatures were generous with help to hasten that process along.

Slowly, however, another view began to manifest itself—a view quite different from the uncritical approval of business expansion and private enrichment so characteristic of attitudes at the beginning of the period of industrialization. In 1890, ex-President Rutherford B. Hayes, certainly no radical, wrote in his diary about the "wrong and evils of the money-piling tendency of our country." Theodore Roosevelt, though deeply concerned about the "socialistic" tendencies of reformers like Henry Demarest Lloyd, nevertheless shared their disdain for what he called the "malefactors of great wealth": "I am unable to make myself take the attitude of respect toward the very wealthy men which such an enormous number of people evidently feel," he wrote. As we have seen, it was under Roosevelt's presidency that the first efforts were made to enforce antitrust legislation against the "bad" trusts (Roosevelt also believed that some trusts were "good").

Woodrow Wilson went even further in his crusade against the trusts. "If monopoly persists," he wrote, "monopoly will always sit at the helm of government. I do not expect monopoly to restrain itself. If there are men in this country big enough to own the government of the United States, they are going to own it."[14] And under Wilson the Federal Trade Commission and the Clayton Anti-Trust Act (both passed in 1914) greatly strengthened the hand of government vis-à-vis the corporation.

A Final View

How can we sum up this complicated chapter of economic history? It would be wrong to view the tendency to giant size or to monopoly as an indication of evil intentions on the part of business. The captains of industry, seeking to aggrandize their firms by price competition or by merger, were only following the profit incentive that is the legitimate objective of market behavior. Although their tactics were outlandish by present-day standards, their motives were beyond reproach. Rather, we must see the emergence of giant corporations as the natural, even the logical, outcome of this motivation coupled with the new technologies of mass production and corporate organization that we have previously examined.

The businessman was not to blame for this turn of events: he was only the agent of economic forces and developments beyond his control. But the businessman was never the only, though he may have been the dominant, figure in the social system. As the reach and power of business organizations increased, other elements within the body politic began to search for effective countermeasures to be applied against the emerging business monoliths. There was only one agency capable of applying those countermeasures—the government. Thus, from many quarters pressure mounted to use the government as a deliberate force to contain or guide or even inhibit business growth.

As we have seen, the application of government power was halting, was at best only partially effective, and was even used, in the regulatory system, to bolster the fortunes of portions of the business world.*

---

* A school of "revisionist" historians, challenging the conventional interpretations of political and economic history, contends that much of the regulatory or antitrust sentiment came from big business itself, eager to establish rules of behavior that would eliminate the smaller concerns nibbling at their markets. Gabriel Kolko has presented the most effective case for this view in *The Triumph of Conservatism* (1963) and *Railroads and Regulation* (1965). His general contention that "big business led the struggle for the federal regulation of the economy" is still under debate. But there is no doubt that some business leaders did cooperate with the government in seeking a means to achieve through legislation what business could not do by itself—namely, to lessen the pressure exercised against major firms by the price- and standards-cutting behavior of smaller companies.

This outcome is hardly surprising. The regulation or curtailment of business does not easily accord with the basic beliefs in "free" and "private" enterprise that underlie the capitalist market system. Moreover, efforts to interfere with the natural expansive tendencies of business threaten to dampen the expansive forces of the economy itself. A society that depends on the workings of a business system cannot easily interfere with the dynamics of that system.

Yet it would be wrong to conclude this chapter on a note that stresses the unsolved aspects of controlling big business, although that problem is still very much with us. Rather, we should come away with two conclusions:

The first is that the process of economic growth, though lodged mainly within business enterprises, has gradually required the intervention of government—in part to protect the market mechanism from destroying itself, in part to assert the claims of the larger society over the blind workings of that mechanism.

The second is that economic growth, which we have hitherto considered mainly as a force for economic expansion, is also a force for profound structural change. With this change come problems for which no immediate or easy social solution may be at hand. More and more, as we proceed with our theme, this disturbing aspect of economic growth will come to our attention.

NOTES

[1] Quoted in Norman S. B. Gras and Henrietta Larson, *Casebook in American Business History* (1939), p. 718.

[2] Quoted in Edward C. Kirkland, *Dream and Thought in the Business Community* (1956), p. 9.

[3] *The Age of Enterprise* (1942), p. 139.

[4] Quoted in Gabriel Kolko, *The Triumph of Conservatism* (1963), p. 13.

[5] Quoted in Allan Nevins, *A Study in Power* (1953) I, p. 96.

[6] Quoted in Thomas Cochran, *Railroad Leaders* (1953), p. 163.

[7] Quoted in John Tipple, "The Robber Baron in the Gilded Age," in H. Wayne Morgan (ed.), *The Gilded Age* (1963), p. 26.

[8] J. B. and J. M. Clark, *The Control of Trusts*, pp. 14–15.

[9] Arthur Dudden, "Men Against Monopoly," *Journal of the History of Ideas* (October 1957), pp. 587–88.

[10] Quoted in Jonathan Periam, *The Groundswell* (1874), p. 286.

[11] Interstate Commerce Commission, *First Annual Report* (1887), p. 36.

[12] Quoted in John A. Garraty, *The New Commonwealth* (1968), pp. 119–20.

[13] Quoted in E. C. Kirkland, *Industry Comes of Age* (1961), p. 323.

[14] Quoted in Richard Hofstadter, *The Age of Reform* (1955), p. 231.

Workers
and
Work

7

The end of our last chapter provides a good beginning for this one. Until now, we have examined economic growth as if it were a process that mainly affected business. This is because business enterprise, as we have seen, was the agency through which the process of growth was expressed and by which the forces of growth were mobilized. Economic growth in a capitalist market system is set into motion by business expansion, and it makes sense, therefore, to focus initially on the men, the techniques, and the problems associated with that business effort.

Yet, as our first pages indicated, we mean more by "economic growth" than just the expansion of output that was its most striking result from a business point of view. Growth was also a process that changed American society at every level, bringing new ways of life, new stresses and strains, new difficulties as well as new advantages and improvements. In our next chapter we will look again into some of the social aspects of the process of industrial transformation. But first we must examine an attribute of the changing society that is closely associated with the development of business, though submerged beneath it. This is the effect that economic expansion—specifically, industrialization—exerted on the working men and women whose energies were harnessed within the business system.

THE CONDITIONS OF WORK

Homestead

Let us start by taking a tour of a great new steel mill that Andrew Carnegie built on the banks of the Monongahela River in 1879. When the site was chosen, Homestead, Pennsylvania, was a hamlet of 600 people. By 1892 the population had swelled to 11,000. Almost every able-bodied man and youth worked in the sixty-acre assemblage of sheds—there were 3,800 employees, including the mayor of the town who worked as an assistant roller earning $65 a month. This was a good wage, considerably above the $40 per month average earnings of manufacturing workers. And prices were far lower than they are today: one could keep body and soul together on those wages, especially if more than one member of the family worked or if the family had a small vegetable garden or kept a cow.

We do not know what Homestead looked like before the mill was built; in all likelihood it was another sleepy Pennsylvania town, with a few stores, and a generally rural air. By 1892 that rural aspect had vanished. The Monongahela was so polluted with wastes from the mill that it was said no self-respecting microbe would live there (perhaps just as well, since many a typhoid microbe lived in the Ohio River near Pittsburgh). Cinders and dust covered the area—even the trees were gray with soot, except after a heavy rain. Hamlin Garland, a novelist, found the vista depressing:

> The streets of the town were horrible; the buildings poor; the sidewalks were swaying, sunken and full of holes. . . . Everywhere the yellow mud of the street lay kneaded into a sticky mass, through which groups of pale lean men slouched in faded garments, grimy with soot and grease of the mills.[1]

Life was certainly hard in Homestead, and in dozens of industrial towns like it. The men worked every day of the year except Christmas and July 4th, twelve hours each day except for a swing shift every other week when they worked twenty-four hours straight.

There was no lunch period, no shower rooms, only primitive sanitary facilities. When the day was over the men sloshed off the dirt in the same troughs in which they washed their tools and trudged home for an exhausted sleep—perhaps stopping for a drink at one of the many saloons on Eighth Avenue.

Inside the mills a fearful scene greeted Garland's eye. In the furnace room he saw "pits gaping like the mouth of hell and ovens emitting a terrible degree of heat, with grimy men filling and lining them. One man jumps down, works desperately for a few minutes, and is then pulled up, exhausted. Another immediately takes his

Work in a steel mill

place. . . ."[2] Garland spoke to the men about the heat. They told him he was lucky he was there in the winter.

A modern historian of the Carnegie mill describes some of the less arduous jobs as follows:

> Pressure work in the rolling, blooming, and plate mills (as contrasted to hot jobs) was cooler but equally nerve-racking, due to the incessant vibration of the machinery and the maddening screech of cold saws ripping through steel. In time the men became hard of hearing. The din within the huge sheds forced them to yell to each other all day long. They and their clothes were covered with miniscule, shiny grains of steel. They complained about respiratory ailments and drank liquor after work, as one man said, to 'take the dust out of my throat.'[3]

Work was dangerous as well as hard. We do not have precise statistics of industrial safety for those years, but we know that in a single year 195 men were killed in Pittsburgh's iron and steel mills: twenty-two from hot metal explosions, five from asphyxiation, ten from rolling accidents, twenty-four falling from heights or into the pits. Men worked only inches away from white-hot metal; terrible burns were frequent. In the hot departments the steel floors hissed when water was poured on them. In 1893 Homestead alone had sixty-five accidents, seven of them fatal, two necessitating amputations. Not a cent of recompense was paid for most injuries or even for death—not because Carnegie was a meanspirited employer—on the contrary, "Andy" was admired and even loved by his men—but because the idea of workmen's compensation was unknown anywhere in the country at that time.

It is a chilling picture. Of course we must be careful not to assume that work everywhere in America was as arduous, dangerous, and exhausting as work in the steel mills. Only a small fraction of the total labor force was exposed to the full rigors of the industrial work process. Total employment in all the iron and steel mills of the nation amounted to less than 1 percent of the jobs in the country. Yet, for reasons that will become clear as we go along, the experience of the industrial force was as decisive for our future as was the experience of trustification, which affected far fewer than 1 percent of all the business firms in America.

Immigrant Labor

But we are not quite finished with our tour. As we go about the plant we notice another thing: how "foreign-looking" so many of the workers are. We are right—about a third of all workers in 1870 in manufacturing industries were foreign-born, perhaps more than a third in "dirty" industries such as steel. By 1907, over four-fifths of the laborers in the Carnegie plants of Allegheny County were eastern Europeans.

We have already seen how significant was the contribution of immigrant labor before the Civil War. Now, with the full-scale advent of industrialization, the role of immigration in providing a labor force became even more indispensable for the expanding business system. Driven by hunger and lured by visions of a promised land, beginning in the third quarter of the century, immigrants arrived in enormous numbers: 138,000 in 1878, 789,000 in 1882; in all, over 6 million between 1877 and 1890; 14 million from 1860 to 1900! The immigrants brought extraordinary vitality and sometimes business acumen. But the greater part of them were pressed into the service of the industrial sector where they helped sustain the momentum of expansion, first by providing sheer labor power, second by holding down wages and thereby enabling businessmen to reap larger profits which were plowed back into still more expansion.

Mainly between the ages of 15 and 40, poor and unskilled, the immigrants were drawn like iron filings to a magnet toward the growing industrial centers of work. There they took on jobs at pay that native-born American working men and women would not accept. "Immigrants work for almost nothing and seem to be able to live on wind—something which I cannot do," said one American worker. Another objected that immigration brought wages "below the bread line."[4] A reporter, Margaret Byington, inquiring into weekly wages at Homestead in 1907, found that native white Americans averaged $22; English-speaking Europeans (mainly Irish and Scots), $16; "Slavs" (Slovaks, Croats, Magyars, Russians, Italians), a miserable $12.

It was not just in steel that the immigrant played a major role in providing the muscle power and the docility that enabled crushing work to be performed at cheap rates. Upton Sinclair, describing the Chicago stockyards in his famous novel *The Jungle*, published in 1906, wrote about "Hunkies" and "Polacks" who performed their work in a sea of blood and a miasma of fetid stench. In the West 9,000 pigtailed Chinese toiled on the plains and in the mountains, building the Central Pacific transcontinental line. In the cities of the East, sweatshop industries, such as clothing, were "manned"—we need quotation marks because so many workers were women—by immigrant Jews, largely from Poland and Russia.

Labor's Attitude Changes

Immigrants fitted into the picture in yet another way. Because they were often from peasant backgrounds, unused to the ways of city life, and because they had much less independence than native workers—if they lost a job there was often no family to turn to—immigrants were much less likely to join the labor unions of the time. Not only did employers find it easier to dissuade them not to unionize, but American workingmen were reluctant to admit "foreigners" into their union lodges.

It may come as a surprise that there were any unions at all. Yet, just as business had begun to consolidate to escape the rigors of competition, so working people had begun to unite to protect themselves against their powerlessness in the giant firm. Prior to the advent of full-scale industrialism, unions were few and weak. Many workers even regarded unions as un-American, believing they stifled individual initiative and prevented one from becoming a capitalist. Others were more interested in panaceas, such as the Greenback movement.

But the gradual change in the environment of work and the breaking down of the older personal relations between the "boss" and his men began to make these sentiments outmoded. Because of the entrepreneur's desire to increase efficiency and reduce waste, the factory worker's routine became more and more regimented. Workers complained that in a factory a man lost his identity as a man and took a number like a prisoner in a penitentiary. Instead of being responsible to a boss who knew his needs and with whom he was in daily contact, the workingman was now accountable to an impersonal foreman who usually did the hiring and the firing. ". . . I never do my talking to the hands," said a New England mill owner, "I do all my talking to the overseers."[5] This new state of affairs was summarized in 1883 by a brass worker:

> Well, I remember that fourteen years ago the workmen and the foremen and the boss were all as one happy family; it was just as easy and as free to speak to the boss as anyone else, but now the boss is superior, and the men all go to the foremen; but we would not think of looking the foremen in the face now any more than we would the boss.[6]

Unionization

Unionization was thus labor's response to the problems of technology and large-scale organization, just as "trustification" was the response of business. Actually, unions of workingmen were very old—we can trace them back to colonial times. But they were mainly unions of craftsmen—skilled workers who joined together to form local mutual-benefit associations and to bargain with employers over wages and working conditions.

The idea of a nationwide labor union was slower in coming. In 1866 the so-called National Labor Union was formed in Baltimore. It was an amorphous body, composed of sovereign constituent units and embracing at its height somewhere between 200,000 and 400,000 members. Its financial strength, however, lagged far behind its numerical strength. In 1870, the union's best fiscal year, its expenses were nearly double its receipts. The primary objective of the National Labor Union was to abolish the wage system and to inaugurate worker-owned cooperatives. "By cooperation," said William Sylvis, the union's first president, "we will become a nation of employers—the employers of our own labor. The wealth of the land will pass into the hands of those who produce it."[7] The National Labor Union was short-lived—little wonder, with such ambitious plans and such weak finances.

The Knights of Labor and the AFL

Of longer duration were the Knights of Labor, founded in Philadelphia in 1869. Originally a secret organization with an elaborate ritual, the Knights tried to organize—with the exception of liquor dealers, gamblers, bankers, and lawyers—into one "great brotherhood." Under the leadership of Uriah Stephens, a garment-cutter who had once studied for the ministry, the Knights were an idealistic organization, more interested in the "rights of man" than in the dollar-and-cents concerns of the wage-earner.

By 1879 the Knights claimed some 9,000 members. In that same year the Knights were taken over by Terence V. Powderly, a Pennsylvania machinist and one-time mayor of Scranton, Pennsylvania. While Powderly was in office the Knights abandoned secrecy and opened their ranks to women, blacks, immigrants, and unskilled workers—a radical step in a period when most craft unions would admit none of them. In addition, the Knights came out in favor of the eight-hour workday. Curiously, Powderly matched his radical view of membership requirements with an extremely conservative view of his union's role. He refused to sanction strikes, engage in collective bargaining, or recognize any discernible differences between labor and management. Because the rank and file took union matters into its own hands, there *were* a number of successful strikes, and membership in the Knights jumped to about 700,000 by the mid-1880s. But its subsequent fall was as meteoric as its rise. An unsuccessful strike against Jay Gould's railroad was followed by accusations—wholly untrue, it was later discovered—implicating the Knights in a bombing incident in Haymarket Square, Chicago, in 1886. In the national hysteria that followed, the union dissolved.

In that very year, however, another union emerged—a union that was to succeed where the Knights had failed. Organized by Samuel Gompers, a cigarmaker by trade, the American Federation of Labor (the AFL) brought together a number of craft unions into an effective national body. Much more practical-minded than the Knights, the union threw its energies into "bread and butter" issues—wages, hours, collective bargaining—rather than into vague plans for social change. Samuel Gompers was once asked what was the philosophy of the AFL. He answered succinctly: "More."

THE WORKER'S STANDARD OF LIVING

Did the union actually win "more" for its members? In a few pages we shall trace its efforts to do so at Homestead. But we can readily see that as a force for raising wages on a national scale unions could not have been very important.* Trade unions were still in their embryonic stage, and much too small to be of any real significance. In 1870 membership in trade unions was approximately 300,000, and, although the labor force more than doubled by 1890, trade unions could boast of only 370,000 members at that time.

Then how did the workingman or workingwoman fare during the period of high industrialization? Our first impression is very favorable. If we take average industrial wages in 1880 and compare them with wages in 1850, making due allowance for the general decline in prices over the period, we find that "real" wages rose by about 40 percent.

Hidden Hardships

But this statistical fact conceals a great deal of variation among working groups and hides much economic hardship that accom-

---

* In his important work *Wages and Earnings in the United States: 1860–1900* (1960), Clarence D. Long states (p. 4) that "it is highly questionable whether, up to at least 1880, most firms in manufacturing were either touched directly by unions, or obliged in setting wage rates to take the threat of unionization very strongly into account." To the extent that wages rose, then, it was the consequence of the growth of the economy, not of union pressure.

panied the economic gain. For one thing, the upward trend in purchasing power ignores the "panic and pain" with which workingmen and women also had to deal during the depression phases of the business cycle. The business collapse of 1873, for instance, took a terrible toll. "Probably never in the history of this country has there been a time," reported the Pennsylvania Bureau of Labor Statistics at the end of 1873, "when so many of the working classes, skilled and unskilled, have been moving from place to place seeking employment. . . ."[8] In its annual report of 1874 the American Iron and Steel Institute said that as of November 1874 "at least a million" workers across the nation were unemployed. During the winter of 1877–78 total unemployment reached a peak of 3 million.

Meanwhile, workingmen who were lucky enough to maintain their jobs were forced to accept wage cuts and longer hours of work during periods of depression. Between 1873 and 1879 the McCormick Harvester Company in Chicago cut salaries on five separate occasions; in 1875 the Whitin Machine Works in Massachusetts instituted the first pay cut in its history. Unskilled laborers who were averaging about $1.81 a day in 1873 were getting $1.29 in 1879. Artisans in the New York City building trades who were making from $2.50 to $3.00 for an eight-hour day in 1872 were receiving $1.50 to $2.00 for a *ten-hour day* in 1875.

We could repeat these statistics of unemployment and wage cuts for the depressions of 1882–85 and 1893–97. But the point is clear. The rough waves of the business cycle affected labor just as painfully as they affected business. The overall climb in labor's earnings masked a great deal of hardship and uncertainty. When a man enjoys an increase in pay for, say, nine years, but is unemployed for the tenth, it is hard to say that his standard of living has risen.

Moreover, even at their best, the wages paid industrial workers were barely enough to sustain a family. The Homestead laborers, as we have said, earned a modest living wage. Elsewhere in the nation, wages were often not up to subsistence for the family. In Massachusetts, for example, studies show that living costs for a worker's family exceeded the earnings of the head of the family by almost a third. The difference had to be earned by other household members, taking part-time work. In the coal mines, Robert Layton of the Knights of Labor said that "absolute necessity compels the father in many instances to take the child into the mine with him to assist in winning bread for the family."[9] In the South, particularly, children were sent to work at tender ages under the duress of need: in the nation as a whole in 1880 approximately 6 percent of the children between the

Women enter the labor force

ages of ten and fifteen were employed in some kind of industrial work.

Women at Work

An increasing fraction of the country's women were also working for wages. In 1870 only about 15 percent of all women aged sixteen or over were at work, and a much smaller percentage of white women. By 1929 over a quarter of the nation's women were working.

Of course women were at work in the 1830s and 1840s. But in those days it was held that there were only seven occupations open to women—teaching, needlework, working as domestics, keeping boarders, setting type, and working in bookbinding and cotton factories. By the census of 1890, of the 369 listed occupations, at least some women were engaged in all but 9. Mainly, as we might expect, women entered fields with which they had some familiarity. The factories they entered were extensions of the work they did at home: clothes-making, textile and millinery work, and food-processing.

Industrialization thus provided new avenues of opportunity for women, for many of the jobs they entered were directly created by the new technology of industry. By the First World War there were already some 2 million women working in offices, many serving as "typewriters." It was no longer unusual for women to think in terms of entering business. The heroine of Sinclair Lewis' novel *Main Street,* published in 1920, has no hesitation about discussing her business aspirations upon graduating from college.

The entrance of women into the labor market had an effect on others than the new workers themselves. As women proved that they were capable of doing many kinds of work, they began to displace men. Salesmen gave way to salesladies. Male telephone operators disappeared before telephone girls. With few exceptions, women earned much less than men for the same work. Therefore their entrance into the labor force served to hold down the pay of their male counterparts. Women gained in their economic emancipation, but men lost. The day of economic equality was—and still is—in the future. Indeed it was not until 1920 that women gained political equality with the passage of the Nineteenth Amendment.

The Overall Change

Our glance at the changing market for labor makes it clear that it is not easy to generalize about the well-being of the working family. Perhaps it is not even wise to do so. As the nation moved off the farm and into the city, as family size gradually diminished, as new patterns of consumption created new demands for income, as the hours worked per week slowly fell, the meaning of a given dollar income changed. We are probably correct in envisaging a considerable general improvement in the economic situation of most working-class families during our sixty-year period, but we are wise to remember that that impression ignores the periods of severe hardship and the plight of backwater areas or trades. Not least, it overlooks the growing strains and strife of industrial work.

The Strike at Homestead

We will get a glimpse of that strife if we return to the Carnegie mill at Homestead, Pennsylvania, where the AFL had a strong local union of 800 men. Those men were part of the Amalgamated Association of Iron and Steel Workers. With 24,000 dues-paying members and 300 sublodges, located mainly in western Pennsylvania, this was one of the largest unions within the AFL.* We focus on 1892 because that was the year of the terrible Homestead struggle. Meeting with the management in a year of adverse business conditions, the Amalgamated was faced with a demand for a *reduction* of wages of about 18 percent. Negotiations were in vain; in desperation the union struck. In retaliation, Henry Clay Frick, Carnegie's partner (with full support from Carnegie, who was enjoying life in his castle in Scotland), closed the plant and announced that he would hire a new labor force. Frick secretly hired the Pinkerton Detective Agency, an organization whose activities included labor espionage and strike-breaking, to send an armed force of 300 men to seize the Homestead plant from the striking workmen who were picketing it.

What happened thereafter was a miniature war. The Pinkertons approached the works by barge along the Monongahela under cover of night, but the landing went astray. To their dismay, the Pinkertons found themselves surrounded, rounded up, and marched as a body of captives toward the main gate. All might have ended without further incident, but along the march someone's anger snapped and the crowd of workmen fell upon the Pinkertons, savagely beating them. When the melee was over, seven Pinkertons and nine workmen were dead.

The victory of the workmen proved short-lived, however. The governor of the state sent in the national guard; arrests followed; and within a few months the strike was hopelessly lost. Henry Clay Frick had the vindictive pleasure of watching his men file back into the plants on his terms. Of 3,800 strikers, only 1,300 went back on the payrolls—none of them Amalgamated men. The few gains the Amalgamated had won were washed away. The twelve-hour day was imposed on almost all workers. Grievance committees were abolished. Extra pay for Sunday ceased. Labor espionage became an established practice. Wages were reduced not by 18 percent but by approximately 50 percent.

Labor versus Capital

Homestead interests us because it tells us something about the attitudes against which workers had to struggle, as well as about the physical conditions they faced. Frick's hostility toward unions was by no means unusual in that period. Historian John A. Garraty has assembled a collection of views typical of the times:

---

* By 1892 the AFL had a quarter of a million members.

John H. Devereux, railroad general manager: I would proceed to discharge every man . . . who continued to foment, and cause a disturbance . . . It would be a sad thing for some of the old white-haired Engineers to be thrown out of work, but I told the Committee I should strike with an unsparing hand.

N. F. Thompson, secretary, Southern Industrial Convention: Labor organizations are today the greatest menace to this Government that exists . . . [A] law should be passed that would make it justifiable homicide for any killing that occurred in defense of any lawful occupation.

A Massachusetts textile manufacturer: As far as [collective bargaining] is concerned, we will not agree to that. Our money built these mills, and we propose to secure whatever benefits may be derived from the business.[10]

Not all manufacturers were so adamantly opposed to unions. Despite his support of Frick's policy at Homestead, Carnegie had written with sympathy about the plight of the workers and had gone so far as to endorse the eight-hour day—as a long-term goal. But even Carnegie could not bring himself to see that the new conditions of industrial labor made his words often seem unrealistic: "The lot of the skilled workman," he had written, "is far better than that of the heir to an hereditary title, who is likely to lead an unhappy, wicked life."[11] We read the words and smile. But then, Carnegie's sentiment aside, what about the *unskilled* workman? What about the immigrant jumping into the pits? What about the vast numbers of Homestead employees who were losing their skills because of industrialization itself? There was a side to the industrial expansion of America that Carnegie did not clearly see. Let us take a look at it.

THE WORSENING OF WORK

If we survey the era of industrialization with regard to its impact on labor, it is not the change in the living standards of workers that impresses us. It is the change in the nature of work itself. For one element that Carnegie either did not see or did not understand was the significance of a process to which he himself was surely a major contributor. This was the increasing division of labor, far and away the most significant effect that industrial growth exerted on the life of the worker.

The Industrial Division of Labor

We are all familiar with the idea of the division of labor. But now we must distinguish between a division that allows workers to specialize in a single craft and one that breaks down that craft into specialized tasks that are performed by several people. In the 1770s, Adam Smith, the first great economist, noticed that this second kind of division of labor was taking place in England and wrote about it in a passage that has been famous ever since:

> To take an example . . . from a very trifling manufacture . . . , the trade of the pin-maker. [A] workman not educated to this business . . . , nor acquainted with the use of the machinery employed in it . . . could scarce, perhaps, with his utmost energy make one pin a day, and could certainly not make twenty. But in the way in which the business is now carried on . . . one man draws out a wire, another straights it, a third cuts it, a fourth points it, a fifth grinds it at the top for receiving the head, to make a head requires two or three distinct operations; to put it on is a peculiar business; to whiten the pins is another; it is even a trade by itself to put them into paper. [T]he important business of making a pin is, in this manner, divided into about eighteen distinct operations. . . .[12]

Why should labor be divided into these "distinct" operations, instead of having each person make pins from start to finish? Smith provided an answer: "I have seen a small manufactory of this kind where only ten men were employed. . . . When they exerted themselves [they could] make among them about twelve pounds of pins in a day. There are in a pound upwards of four thousand pins of a middling size. These ten persons, therefore, could make among them upwards of forty-eight thousand pins in a day. . . . But if they had all wrought separately and independently . . . , they certainly could not have each of them made twenty, perhaps not one pin in a day."

The fragmentation of labor, in other words, enormously increases the productive power of human energy—a crucial fact for the phenomenon of growth itself. We will come back to it shortly. But here we want to note two other aspects of the industrial division of labor. First, as Adam Smith makes clear, it requires machinery if it is to be effective (and there would be no point in seeking a division of labor if it were not). Thus the ability to set up a small "manufactory" of ten men, grinding out pins, requires that machinery exist to enable each workman to accomplish his specialized job much more rapidly than he could do it unassisted.

Second, the industrial division of labor requires organization. The flow of work must be studied; the object, the task itself, must be scrutinized as if they were strange and unfamiliar. The product called a "pin" has to be examined very carefully. What does it consist of? How many different activities need one person undertake to make a pin? Can these activities be established as independent tasks, accelerated with machinery, and linked with the activities of other persons working on other aspects of that peculiar object, a pin?

Homestead was a pin factory on a giant scale. For what the Bessemer converter and the rolling mill, the giant presses and the railroad cars filled with ore, represented was a realization of the principle of the division of labor to a far greater extent than was attainable in Adam Smith's day. Here not ten men, but 3,800 men, were coordinated into a single workteam. Not all of them did different tasks, of course; but the plant as a whole divided the complex task of making steel into the much simpler tasks of loading furnaces, cleaning out ovens, guiding machinery, picking up and moving ingots, shoveling fuel. If you had stopped a workman at Homestead and asked him what he did, he would have had to answer that he ran a hoist, or handled billets, or stacked bars, or scrubbed floors. None of them could have answered "I make steel," because no one person did make steel.

The division of labor, as Adam Smith's pin factory reveals, is much older than the era of rapid industrialization. Frederick Olmstead, the architect who designed New York's Central Park, visited Cincinnati in 1850 and described how rows of men transformed a carcass, traveling before them on an overhead conveyor, from hog to pork in a matter of minutes: "No iron cogs could work with a more regular motion," he wrote of their steady chop, chop, chop.[13]

What industrialization did was to give an enormous impetus to the process by which labor could be subdivided and given the strength, speed, and steadiness of machines to augment its human exercise. But industrialization also brought a renewed effort to organize the flow of work in a new manner. Not only machines but method were the secret of the Carnegie plants, and of successful industrial operations everywhere.

Taylorism

One of the most far-reaching changes in the organization of work was the product of a strange man named Frederick Winslow Taylor. The scion of a well-to-do Philadelphia family, Taylor gave up the study of law at Harvard and decided to work his way up from the bottom in a steel plant. Beginning as an apprentice in 1874, he used his intelligence, diligence, and sheer drive to rise to the position of "gang boss" of the lathe department in the Midvale Steel Works.

By temperament Taylor had been a curious personality since boyhood, given to splitting the world into its smallest parts. He counted his steps when he walked to learn the most efficient stride, calculated the angles of his shots at croquet, and chafed at anything that displayed less than the efficiency of a finely planned machine. The most irritating thing to Taylor was the extreme "inefficiency" with which most men worked. As gang boss he told his men that he intended to get much more work out of them—and he did, by alternately bullying and persuading them to work quicker, more accurately, harder.

But Taylor was not content merely to be a driver of men. He began to see that much more work could be performed if men would break their accustomed habits and perform their tasks in a "scientifically" planned way. Early in his career, he studied a seemingly simple task—the loading of 92-pound "pigs" of iron into freight cars. Picking up his 92-pound pig, walking up an inclined plank to the top of a freight car, and dropping his load into the car, an average worker loaded some 12½ tons of iron a day. Taylor watched each motion, each step; and then he taught his first subject exactly what to do. As he explained it later to a Congressional committee in 1912:

> Schmidt started to work, and all day long, and at regular intervals, he was told by the men who stood over him with a watch, 'Now pick up a pig and walk. Now sit down and rest. Now walk—now rest.' etc. He worked when he was told to work and he rested when he was told to rest, and at half past five in the afternoon has . . . 47½ tons loaded on the car.[14]

Taylor's method was to search for the tool or the technique that would be exactly suited to a given purpose. "When we went to the Bethlehem Steel Works," he told the committee, "and observed the shovelers . . . , we found that each of the good shovelers . . . owned his own shovel. There was a larger tonnage of ore shoveled in that works than of any other material, and rice coal came next in tonnage. We would see a first class shoveler go from shoveling rice coal with a load of 3½ pounds to the shovel, to handling ore from the Massaba Range, with 38 pounds to the shovel. Now, is 3½ pounds the proper shovel load or is 38 pounds the proper shovel load? They cannot both be right. Under scientific management the answer to this question is not anyone's opinion: it is a question for accurate, careful, scientific investigation."

Taylorism became the rage in the first decade of the twentieth century; a new profession was born—the study of time-and-motion, whose experts watched workers, stop watch in hand, and then taught them to move differently, to retime their motions, to discard old ways and learn new ones. For each job a precise description was now possible: reach, move, grasp, hold, release, and so forth, with each motion timed, and with a standard output therefore calculable. Equally significant, Taylorism deliberately separated the performance of labor from the planning of work. The management engineer was now entrusted with more and more of the thought that went into the making of steel or cloth or whatever; the working man or woman was more and more asked to carry out instructions and not to disturb the engineer's plan by varying the prescribed routine.[15]

The Assembly Line

Machines and method came together most dramatically not in steel but in automobiles, in the famous "assembly line" technique developed by Henry Ford during the first decade of this century. Allan Nevins, the biographer of Ford and his company, has described the process as it existed in 1914:

> Four great principles [were] applied throughout: the use of the latest machinery of original design; the placing of men and machines in operation sequence; the employment of work slides and moving assembly lines; and the installation of overhead carriers to bring up materials. The period for assembling a motor, which only the previous fall had been about 600 minutes of one man's time, had been lowered to 226 minutes. The period for assembling a chassis had been reduced from 12 hours 28 minutes . . . to 1 hour and 33 minutes. . . .
> . . . [Y]ou see men whose function is to join parts together and insert a bolt; others who put nuts on bolts; others who tighten the bolts and insert cotter pins; one who uses a hand lever . . . press to impose the inside ball-bearing cone upon the stub-axle; another who applies a more complicated machine to bring steering arms and stub axles into combination.[16]

Without machines and method, the mass-produced, cheap car would have been impossible, just as without machines and method the production of cheap steel would never have been achieved. But here we want to summarize the effects of Taylorism on the worker who was exposed to it.

Two consequences stand out. First, *the pace of work was deliberately*

The assembly line

speeded up. In 1890, Samuel Gompers was quizzed by a special Commission on Capital and Labor:

> Q. Would you say that the new machinery, bringing in more rapid processes of production, has lightened the toil of the operatives?

> A. No. . . . As a matter of fact, the velocity with which machinery is now run calls forth the expenditure of nearly all the physical and mental force which the wage-earner can give to industry. . . .

I can say . . . that in every mechanical trade, when European workmen come over to this country and stand beside their American fellow workingmen, it simply dazes them—the velocity of motion, the deftness, the quickness, the constant strain.[17]

Second, *the character of work was changed.* In place of the variety of tasks demanded of a farmer, a fisherman, a potter, a carpenter, or even an old-fashioned "mechanic," work was now more and more patterned after the impersonal repetition of machinery itself. Many years later, an operative in an automobile factory was to tell a visiting researcher:

> I work on a small conveyer which goes around in a circle. We call it a "merry-go-round." I make up zigzag springs for front seats. Every couple of feet on the conveyer there is a form for the pieces that make up the seat springs. As that form goes by me, I clip several pieces together, using a clip gun. I then put the pieces back on the form, and it goes around to where other men clip more pieces together. By the time the form has gone around the whole line, the pieces are ready to be set in a frame, where they are made into a complete spring seat. That's further down the main seat cushion line. The only operation I do is work the clip gun. It takes just a couple of seconds to shoot six or eight clips into the spring, and I do it as I walk a few steps. Then I start right over again.[18]

PRODUCTIVITY

Taylorism raises a question of great importance. For in the dehumanization of factory work, we sense the seeds of an immense latent conflict. The struggle between those who "owned" the jobs and those who performed them—between capital and labor—had long provided a major theme for history, a theme that Karl Marx had elevated to the main process of historical change when he wrote in the *Communist Manifesto* that "the history of all hitherto existing society is the history of class struggles."

The Missing Class Struggle

In Europe there was indeed a brooding revolutionary spirit. Though it was mainly muted, it broke into violent expression in 1848, again in Paris in 1870, in Russia in 1917, and in Germany after the First World War. In America, however, a revolutionary temper had never been an integral part of the labor movement. As we have seen,

Samuel Gompers

labor unions—especially the successful ones—were concerned with defending and trying to better the lot of the worker under the existing scheme of things rather than striking out against the whole framework of capitalist society. Perhaps this pragmatic, nonrevolutionary turn of mind reflected the pervasive air of American democracy, so markedly different from the European feeling of inherent class differences. Perhaps it was the consequence of the extraordinary openness of the vast American continent with its beckoning, if often delusive, opportunities for the "common" man. Perhaps it was simply the result of the economic improvement that proceeded so much more rapidly in America than abroad.

Whatever the reasons, the idea of a self-conscious, revolutionary working class never made much headway in nineteenth-century America. But with the advent of Taylorism, the stage seemed set for a decisive change in sentiments. The progressive reduction of the working person within the factory to a mere robot, a pair of hands whose very movements were no longer determined by their possessor, seemed likely to sharpen the sense of class solidarity among working people and to rouse a feeling of class antagonism against the system that had so diminished their status.

Yet it did not. Why not? The history of the American labor movement is complex, and the reasons for its divergence from the more revolutionary European example are many. But one central part of the answer interests us, because it is intimately connected with the very process of industrialization that degraded the labor process.

This antirevolutionary effect of industrialization lay in the immense impulse that industrialization gave to *labor productivity*. Behind this surge in productivity were many factors with which we are now familiar. There had been an enormous accumulation of capital in the form of machines, buildings, railroads, and highways. There had been dazzling advances in technology. Although we have not heretofore called attention to it, human effort was itself becoming more adept and skillful as the consequence of education. In 1870 only 57 percent of the population between the ages of five and seventeen was in school; by 1929 the percentage had grown to 80. And not least there had also been the "militarization" of labor—its reduction to the robotized, armylike functions that Taylorism so avidly promoted. Together, all these causes accounted for the stunning increase in productivity that tripled the tonnage of steel produced per man in the thirty years between 1870 and 1900 and that would triple it again in the years between 1900 and 1929.

To be sure, the total output of the nation did not grow at anything like the explosive rates of its most advanced industrial salients, but overall output increased mightily in the period from 1865 to 1929. In round numbers a person living in 1929 produced about four times as much as his father or grandfather living in 1865.

The Effects of Productivity

This increase in productivity meant, of course, that the amount of goods and services available per capita in the nation was steadily growing. And in turn this meant that the standard of living of most working people—with all the exceptions and irregularities that we have pointed out—was gradually increasing. Thus one reason why the harsh process of labor discipline did not give rise to a revolutionary labor movement was that it was tempered by a feeling of slowly improving conditions.

But this was not the only, and perhaps not the most important, reason. For despite the growth in income, had the industrialization process subjected ever more people to the rigors of factory life the course of American (and, indeed, European) labor history might have taken a different course. But that is not the way industrialization worked. We would think, for example, that the rise of industrial technology meant that vastly larger numbers of men and women worked in factories and manufacturing establishments in 1929 than in 1865. In fact, the actual numbers did increase sharply, from 2.3 million to 10.9 million. But if we look at the *percentage* of the labor force in manufacturing we find an unexpected result. In 1865 about 18 percent of all workers were employed in "manufacturing and hand trades," to use the classification of official government statistics. In 1929 this percentage had indeed grown—but only to 22.5 percent, hardly a dramatic change.

This gives us a new insight into the economic transformation of the country. The rise of a highly mechanized industrial sector, marked by tremendous productive powers, did not mean that a rapidly growing portion of the American working force was subjected to the harsh discipline of the assembly line. On the contrary, it made it possible for more and more labor to be switched from onerous tasks whose output was enormously leveraged by industrialization into other, less physically demanding tasks.

The Reallocation of Labor

This release of labor did not mainly occur within the industrial sector where, after the 1890s, the proportion of the work force remained approximately constant. The main impact of the industrialization process was in another area—agriculture. In 1870 one worker out of every two was employed in agriculture. If there had not been a steady growth of the use of machines on the farm—such as the reaper, the combine, the tractor—Americans would have had to use half of the work force in 1929 just to feed the nation. That would have made it impossible to man the factories, the offices, the stores, the public services that they enjoyed in 1929. It also meant that the United States would have remained a nation of farm workers.

In fact, however, industrialization made labor much more productive in agriculture. From 1870 to 1929 the value of farm tools and equipment increased from $271 million to over $3 billion. Better machinery lowered the number of man-hours required to tend an acre of wheat from twenty to less than twelve. Thus, even though the actual output of all crops tripled from 1865 to 1929, the proportion of the labor force on the farm dropped from one worker out of every two to one worker out of every five. Instead of only half the labor energies of the nation being available for nonagricultural work, four-fifths were available. Today, we use only 5 percent of our labor for agricultural work.

The Rise of the Service Sector

Still more significant, from our point of view, the industrialization process allowed large numbers of the working force to be employed in the growing array of white-collar "service" jobs. In 1865 only 12 percent of the work force was employed in education, professional and personal services, trade, and government. In 1929, these white-collar tasks absorbed almost double that proportion of the labor force. By the middle of the twentieth century, about two-thirds of the working population had moved into service occupations.

Many of these service tasks were as routine as those on the assembly line, but they were typically located in offices and stores and not in factories or farms, they were performed by men and women in street clothes and not in overalls, and they carried with them the feeling that one belonged to a middle-class not a working-class way of life.

Thus economic growth defused the revolutionary potential inherent in factory life by using the productivity of the machine to support the rise of nonfactory occupations. Technology made America a "middle class" nation. This process was not, of course, the outcome of anyone's decision. Like much of the economic history we have traced, it followed from the blind workings of the market mechanism. But the changing shape, as well as the changing content, of the labor requirements of industrial America helps us understand something more of the dynamics of the economic transformation itself—a process that brings change, often difficult to measure in terms of better and worse, along with mere expansion. The radical alteration of the labor process, both within the factory and in the society at large, is perhaps the most dramatic instance of this, but it is not the only one. In our next chapter we will see similar effects of growth and industrialization, for better and worse, in other areas of our national life.

Afterword

Today we are beginning to find that work brings dissatisfactions to the office worker as well as to the factory worker. A report of the Department of Health, Education and Welfare stated in 1973:

> What is striking is the extent to which the dissatisfaction of the assembly line and blue-collar worker is mirrored in white collar and even managerial positions. The office today, where work is segmented and authoritarian, is often a factory. . . . Secretaries, clerks, and bureaucrats were once grateful for having been spared the dehumanization of the factory. . . . But today the clerk, and not the operative on the assembly line, is

the typical American worker, and such positions offer little by way of prestige. Signs of discontent among white collar workers include turnover rates as high as 30% annually, and a 46% increase in white collar union membership between 1958 and 1969.[19]

Is it possible that the neglect of work will finally surface as an active element in American political and social life? We do not know. All that can be said is that the problem whose roots we have examined in this chapter remains very much with us as one of the unsolved aspects of our economic transformation.

NOTES

[1] "Homestead and Its Perilous Trades," *McClure's Magazine*, vol. 3 (June 1894), pp. 3, 5.

[2] Quoted in R. G. McCloskey, *American Conservatism in the Age of Enterprise* (1951), p. 145.

[3] Leon Wolff, *Lockout* (1965), p. 37.

[4] Quoted in John A. Garraty, *The New Commonwealth* (1968), p. 142.

[5] United States Senate, Committee on Education and Labor, *Report on the Relations Between Labor and Capital* (1885), III, 38.

[6] U.S. Senate, *Report on the Relations Between Labor and Capital*, I, 473.

[7] Quoted in Samuel P. Hays, *The Response to Industrialism* (1957), p. 33.

[8] *Second Annual Report*, 1873–74, p. 433.

[9] U.S. Senate, Committee on Education and Labor, *Report on the Relations Between Labor and Capital*, I, 19.

[10] *The New Commonwealth*, pp. 144–45.

[11] Quoted in McCloskey, *American Conservatism in the Age of Enterprise*, p. 145.

[12] *The Wealth of Nations* (Modern Library ed., 1937), pp. 4–5.

[13] Quoted in S. Giedion, *Mechanization Takes Command* (1948), pp. 217–18.

[14] Frederick Winslow Taylor, *Scientific Management* (1947), p. 106.

[15] See Harry Braverman, *Labor and Monopoly Capital* (1974), pp. 85ff.

[16] Allan Nevins and F. E. Hill, *Ford* (1954), vol. I, pp. 504–05.

[17] *Report on the United States Industrial Commission on Capital and Labor* (1901), vol. VIII, pp. 606ff.

[18] Quoted in Charles R. Walker and Robert H. Guest, *The Man on the Assembly Line* (1956), p. 46.

[19] Special Task Force to the Secretary of Health, Education and Welfare, *Work in America* (1973), pp. xvi–xvii.

Industrialization Rubs Off on Life

8

So far we have observed the impact of industrialization on the structure of business enterprise, on government, and on work. Yet if we could somehow manage to look simultaneously at the whole range of everyday life in 1865 and 1929, it would probably not be those economic aspects of industrialization that would first engage our attention. Rather, we would be struck by a series of other changes, also connected with the process of industrial growth, that would account for the wholly different "look" of the country at those two times.

URBANIZATION

The first of these changes would surely be the sharp contrast in the habitat of Americans. "The United States," writes Richard Hofstadter, "was born in the country and has moved to the city."[1] In 1865 no city had yet reached a million inhabitants; in 1929 there were five such cities. Even more striking, in 1865 only fourteen cities had populations over 100,000. By 1929, there were ninety-three such cities. Half the population was now classified as "urban"—that is, living in towns of 8,000 or more. Equally telling, between 1860 and 1920, for every urban dweller who moved to a farm, twenty farmers moved to a city.

From Farm to City

Who were these migrants? Small-town laborers in search of better jobs; farmers who were unable to secure a good piece of land or to make their farms pay; rural dwellers who were tired of the narrow scope and isolation of rustic life; young Dick Whittingtons who believed that the streets of the cities were paved with gold.

Above all, however, it was the pressure of the economic transformation that served as the catalyst for urbanization. People came to cities to find work. The farm lands were booming in terms of output but not as places of employment. As we have seen, the new industrial machinery of agriculture steadily lessened the need for labor to bring in the crops. As the reapers and combines and tractors arrived in the fields, they displaced the farm hands who had previously done the reaping and binding and hoeing and plowing. It took twenty man-hours to bring in an acre of wheat in 1880; less than ten by 1930. As a result, the proportion of the total work force needed on the farm dropped from over half in the 1860s to less than a quarter in the 1920s.

Simultaneously, the expansion of industrial output steadily created new opportunities for employment in the urban areas. New York's sweatshops produced the blouses and skirts and shirts worn by Americans who never came within a thousand miles of the metropolis. Pittsburgh produced steel for the entire continent. Chicago slaughtered and packed the country's bacon and beef. And the cities were, par excellence, the locus of the burgeoning service tasks of trade, finance, government.

Urbanization changed not alone the distribution of our population but the quality of its life. America became a nation of city dwellers, enjoying the excitement of city life, suffering the evils of urban sprawl. For just as no one planned the overall economic expansion of the nation, so no one planned the expansion of the cities. As with industrialization, it was the lure of profit and the counterforce of

Slum life

competition that mainly directed the process of urbanization, with results that mixed gains and losses in often unexpected ways. Let us examine some of them.

The Tenement

One of the losses was the deterioration of the city, symbolized by the rise of the tenement. Because of steady population growth, urban real estate steadily rose in price. In Washington, D.C., for example, land that went for eight cents a square foot in 1882 was selling for forty-eight cents in 1887. In their quest for profits landlords subdivided and partitioned apartments, converted private residences into rooming houses, and built new tenement apartments to accommodate as many people as possible in the smallest amount of space.

In 1869 New York City had 14,872 tenements housing a population of 468,492; in 1890 there were 37,316 tenements with 1,250,000 dwellers; in 1900, 42,700 tenements contained 1,585,000 people. In some New York tenements as many as twelve families lived on one floor, in rooms that often had no direct ventilation. In 1867 the New York State legislature passed "An Act for the Regulation of Tenement & Lodging Houses in the Cities of New York & Brooklyn," whose requirements tell us much about prevailing conditions. The law demanded that stairs have banisters, that roofs be kept in repair, that proper ventilation be provided, and that cellars could not be used as dwellings unless the ceiling was one foot above street level. In addition, the act stipulated that there must be one toilet for every twenty-one inhabitants, although it permitted the toilet to be located in the back yard.

In 1879, Henry C. Meyer, editor of the trade journal *Plumber and Sanitary Engineer*, sought to alleviate the tenement problem by announcing a prize for the design of an apartment building on a 25 × 100-foot lot that would best combine safety and convenience for the tenant and maximum profits for the investor. Of the 204 plans submitted, James E. Ware's design for the so-called dumbbell tenement was awarded first prize. This was a five- or six-story building, with front and rear rooms connected by a hall. Each floor had space for four families living in fourteen rooms—seven on either side, going back in a straight line—with two toilets (opposite the stairs) on each floor. Ventilation was provided by a narrow, enclosed, twenty-eight-inch indentation on the side of the building (see illustration).

Yet even these reforms were inadequate. The air shafts formed by the indented flanks of the adjacent dumbbells failed to provide ade-

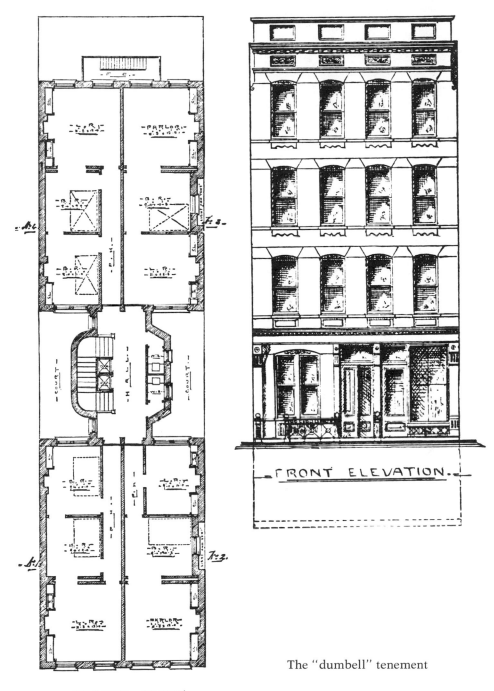

FRONT ELEVATION.

The "dumbell" tenement

SECOND STORY.

quate ventilation. Moreover, they served as ducts to convey flames from one story to the next, and as garbage chutes that created a fetid odor. Seeing the way people lived in these tenements, Southern visitors to New York once suggested that antebellum slaves on plantations had lived more comfortably.

The Ghetto

Among those who gravitated to the cities in search of jobs and housing were many Negroes. With their arrival we witness the appearance of ghettos and the special problems that come in their wake.

Of all the nation's ghettos, probably the best known is Harlem, a thousand acres of concentrated misery that begins north of an ill-defined frontier across Manhattan Island and disappears in the dreary stretches of the Bronx. Few people realize that this was once one of the choicest neighborhoods in New York. Indeed, if we look at Harlem's housing we see that many of the decrepit brownstones and run-down apartment houses are the remains of what were once elegant town houses and expensive apartment dwellings built during the late 1800s.

What happened to Harlem? A building boom, fueled by extravagant and unrealistic expectations, played itself out in 1904. Vacancies began to appear, first scattered, then wholesale. As the neighborhood began to deteriorate, whites moved out and blacks were able to locate good housing at low prices. By 1914 some 50,000 blacks were in Harlem, many of them enjoying very good, low-priced housing. But this very good fortune served as a magnet to attract other, less well housed, black families. Soon Harlem was overcrowded: by 1929 its population had doubled, mainly by in-migration from out of state. Three-quarters of New York's blacks were now crowded into those 1,000 acres.

As population rose, so did rents, for landlords were quick to charge what the traffic would bear. Rents doubled between 1921 and 1927, and many black families—most of whom earned low wages—were forced to subdivide their apartments or to take in boarders. The ghetto syndrome began to appear: high rents, high density, low amenities. "The state would not allow cows to live in some of these apartments used by colored people," said the chairman of the city's Housing Reform Committee in 1927.[2] Overcrowding and unsanitary conditions soon took their toll. Between 1923 and 1927 the death rate in Harlem was 42 percent higher than anywhere else in New York.

Urbanization and Industrialization

The point, however, is not to lament the appearance of the ghetto, but to relate it to the larger development of industrial growth. The connection is not difficult to make. The rise of industrial employment and the decline of rural employment together served as a powerful stimulus to uproot blacks from their rural habitat. Bad as the city was, it was better than the rural slum; and as the nation's economy grew, it pulled the black population cityward. Between 1865 and 1929, millions of blacks left the South, most of them for city life in New York or elsewhere. During the 1920s alone, 600,000 blacks moved north, many of them to Harlem.

In the cities, the blacks provided an underlayer of cheap labor that served the economic needs of the growing industrial metropolis. Black males became the city's day laborers, its casual dockhands, its dishwashers, hallmen, bellboys. The black female workers became its servants, laundresses, cleaning women. The presence of this low-paid, easily abused black labor force provided a lubricant for the growing economy. The last to be hired and the first to be fired, the black worker served as a buffer for the white worker, absorbing much more than his or her share of unemployment when times were bad, yet not competing strongly enough to prevent the rise of white wages when times were good.

But there is a last lesson to be learned from the rise of the great city, with its ghettos and slums. The big city also testified to the growing interdependence of life in an industrial society. In the 1860s many city dwellers still had their tiny truck gardens; in Homestead, a worker could still have one foot in the factory and one on the farm. By the 1920s the link between rural and urban life had been largely severed. The city dweller was now almost entirely dependent on the network of rails and roads that brought his food from a country-side hundreds of miles distant. The citizens of New York and Chicago ate wheat grown in Kansas and meat raised in Texas and lived in houses built of Vermont stone and Pittsburgh iron and steel. Without the intricate web of transportation that bound together a thousand trades and localities, the city could not have existed for a week.

Industrialization is inextricably bound up with this kind of interdependence. Yet the effects of urbanization extended far beyond even this deep-reaching change, touching life in innumerable ways: technical, cultural, political. Urban agglomerations that had grown up without plan or foresight had to find means of disposing of garbage and sewage on a mass scale. The city had to provide transportation from one area to another. It offered a new market for mass entertainment. It brought into being a class of office workers who sought to imitate their "betters" in stylish dress. It jostled races and cultures together: it was the city, not the country, that was the "melting pot." It was also the scene of loneliness and isolation for the newcomer: suicide rates rose from 3.18 per 100,000 in 1860 to 11.9 in 1922.

None of these problems was new, of course. Cities have always had their special attributes. But the extent and ubiquity of these urban traits were new. In 1860 cities were few in the United States and their excitement and despair were the exception in a land where rural placidity was the rule. By the first quarter of the twentieth century the city, with its strains and its vitality, had become the norm. It was a long while before the political structures and the prevailing beliefs and self-images of the nation caught up with the realities of its urbanized life: to some degree they have still not embraced the importance of the city. This lag is itself one reason why the city has remained a "problem." We continue to see our urban ills as intrusions upon, rather than as embodiments of, our economic evolution.

MACHINERY AND DAILY LIFE

A second change brought about by industrialization affected both city and country. It was the enormous acceleration of a trend whose beginnings we saw before the Civil War—the introduction of machinery into everyday life. This change was so pervasive, so all-embracing, that it is impossible to itemize its particulars. Let us simply consider some of the differences that it brought.

Mobility

The first difference we notice is in mobility. In the 1860s the basic means of local transportation was the horse. But the horse was ill-suited to an urbanized nation: Where could a million New Yorkers or Chicagoans stable their steeds? Urban life became constricted, limited to journeys on foot or to occasional ventures on trains or steamboats.

But the constriction was not long-lasting. The first breakthrough was the development of the horse-pulled streetcar—the first urban mass transit. By 1895 the electrically powered trolley was running over 10,000 miles of track in the cities; indeed, by changing from one streetcar line to another you could even journey from New York to Boston.

Even more pervasive was the influence of the bicycle. It is hard to realize today how vast a change the bicycle ushered in. Small enough to be parked in a hallway, inexpensive enough to be bought by a working-class family, simple to maintain, the bicycle reopened the country to the city dweller. First introduced into the country in 1878, in less than two decades bicycle-manufacture had become a major industry. By 1900 the industry was turning out over a million vehicles, and an estimated 4 million persons could be seen riding a strange assortment of high-wheelers, low-wheelers, bicycles built for two, bicycles with sidecars. The mass use of the bicycle also brought pressure on Congress to improve the road system of the country: the League of American Wheelmen was a kind of precursor of the American Automobile Association in the campaign for good public roads. As the census report for 1900 states, "It is safe to say that few articles ever used by man have created so great a revolution in social conditions as the bicycle."

Then, of course, there was the automobile. The first gas-powered auto appeared in the nation in 1892; in 1896 its inventors, the Duryea brothers, actually sold 13 cars. That was the year in which a thirty-two-year-old mechanic named Henry Ford sold his first "quadricycle." In 1909, with the advent of the Model T, he sold 10,660 cars. By 1929 there were 23 million cars on the road—one for every five Americans.

The rise of the automobile industry affected economic growth in a number of ways. It was the prime center for the application of the mass-production techniques whose impact on labor we witnessed in our previous chapter. It was a stupendous source of employment—indeed, soon the largest employer in the country. It was the biggest customer for steel, rubber, sheet steel, lead, leather. It became the origin of one-sixth of all the patents issued in the country. With 2,471 plants in 1923, the automobile industry was the largest in the nation.

But we are interested in the automobile as a concrete manifestation of growth that changed daily life. To the average American family it became the most prized (and most expensive) of all its possessions, save only its home. It was the means for cheap and easy travel that made Americans, always a restless people, into a nation of motorized vagabonds. It changed the location of industry and of workers' housing, for it was no longer necessary to live within walking distance of work or near a trolley route. It altered urban configurations: the move to the suburbs was made on rubber tires and would have been impossible without them. (Later, during the Great Depression, Will Rogers would claim that America went to the poor-

The traffic jam appears

house in its automobiles.) It changed social habits. Vacationing became a national passion. Sex mores were radically affected by the
car. The city was stretched beyond its capacity by the vehicles that
jammed its streets. The nation's police force had to be expanded to
cope with a new major source of accidents, of theft, of exasperation.
Not least, the car provided the greatest joy ride in the nation's
history.

Power in the Home

Next to mobility, the most visible change in daily life is the increased use of energy. In 1860 the total amount of energy delivered by
all "prime movers," such as steam engines, water wheels, windmills,
and farm animals, totaled 13 million horsepower. By 1930 the
amount of energy used by the nation was 1.6 *billion* horsepower. Of
this total, 1.4 billion was provided by that extraordinary power
source, the automobile. But the power delivered by stationary motors
of all kinds was also some twenty times as much as in 1860.

A great deal of this increased power was used by the factories of the nation, now mechanized to a degree unimaginable in 1860. But we are interested in the direct use of power by the average family as it ran the machines that were more and more part of the normal household's equipment. Here we have but to trace the growth of the use of electricity following Edison's installation of the first power-generating plant in New York in 1882. By 1907 only 8 percent of all homes had access to electricity, mainly because the problem of sending current over cables for long distances had not yet been solved. But by 1929, 85 percent of all nonfarm residences had wall receptacles that enabled them to "plug in" to this new source of energy. The residential use of electricity grew from next to nothing in the 1890s to 9 billion kilowatt hours in 1929.

Electricity brought power into the home. Perhaps the least revolutionary of its effects was the electric light, for candles or gas burners had provided reasonably good illumination before Edison perfected the carbon-filament lamp in 1887. The real change was the possibility of using machines in domestic life in a manner impossible before this extraordinary source of invisible, easily conducted energy became available. The washing machine and the refrigerator, the vacuum cleaner and the electric iron were the creations of electric power. Their effect on household life was dramatic. The availability of mechanical servants made it possible for the housewife to venture into the labor market and still to maintain her traditional role of "homemaker." Thus the advent of the working woman was intimately connected with the mechanization of household work.

Electricity also vastly increased the ability of households to communicate with one another. In 1887 there were 170,000 subscribers to the new telephone service; in 1917 nearly 12 million phones were in use. "What startles and frightens backward Europeans," said a visiting English author, "is the efficiency and fearful universality of the telephone."

The phone, and then the radio, served to open the ordinary household to events far beyond its previous ken. Together with the movies, those devices were probably more important than the schools as a force for social education and for the spread of sophistication. The jazzy, freewheeling spirit of the twenties would have been unthinkable without the electrical technology of communication. How few people had ever actually heard or seen Abraham Lincoln or Mark Twain! How few had not seen or heard Calvin Coolidge or Al Jolson!

The dream of affluence

THE TRIUMPH OF INDUSTRIALIZATION

These snapshots by no means fully reveal the changes that the industrial era brought to the United States. They overlook, for example, advances in medicine associated with the increased interest in and application of science. Life expectancy between 1865 and 1929 rose from just under forty years to just over sixty, mainly through the conquest of childhood diseases. The death rate from typhoid fell by 95 percent; from measles, by 75 percent.

Second, our overview has by-passed an important change in the tempo of life that also arose from the increased productivity of the age. This was the gradual decline in working hours from over sixty per week in 1865 to about forty-four in 1929. In 1923, after protesting for years that it could not be done, the U. S. Steel Works at Gary, Indiana, went from two grueling twelve-hour stints to three eight-hour shifts. In 1926 Henry Ford, who had already astonished the business world by instituting a $5 work day in 1914, announced that henceforth his plants would work on a five-day week. The International Harvester Company started another trend by granting its workers a two-week vacation with pay.

Still another change was a greatly lengthened attendance at school. In 1929 30 percent of the seventeen-year-old population was in high school. This may not seem like a very high figure—today about 80 percent of this age group is in school—but in 1865 the percentage of seventeen-year-olds in school was 2.

Not less significant, although less apparent on the surface, was the change in America's position in the world. Alone among the participants in the First World War, the United States emerged stronger than when it entered. Formerly a debtor to Europe—it entered the war with $3.5 billion in debts—it now became the great lender to Europe, with credits of $12.5 billion. By 1929 almost half of the world's industrial production was located in the United States. Meanwhile, the international thrust of business continued apace: exports rose by a third between 1913 and 1929, and United States investment abroad in factories and mines and plantations rose from the $635 million we saw in 1897 to $7.5 billion.

In 1919, looking ahead to the postwar era, Woodrow Wilson had said: "The financial leadership will be ours. The industrial primacy will be ours. The commercial advantage will be ours."[3] He was right.

The National Feeling

All these new ways, and others that we have not included, constituted the reality of a vast economic transformation. Not all of it by any means was benign, as we have seen from our view of the ghetto, and its outcome would be anything but happy, as the impending—and wholly unsuspected—Depression would prove. Yet there can be no doubt that a general consciousness of prosperity was widely felt and much celebrated.

"No Congress of the United States ever assembled," said President Calvin Coolidge in 1928 surveying the state of the Union, "has met with a more pleasing prospect." Coolidge was a very conservative man who believed that "The man who builds a factory builds a temple." His contemporary, Lincoln Steffens, was not. Once a famous muckraking reporter for *McClure's* magazine, he had reported with enthusiasm on the early days of the Soviet Union: "I have been over into the future, and it works." Now Steffens was himself saying, "Big business in America is producing what the socialists held up as their goal: food, shelter, and clothing for all."[4]

Certainly Coolidge's successor, Herbert Hoover, regarded the prospect as bright:

> We in America [he said to a Stanford University Audience in 1928] today are nearer to the final triumph over poverty than ever before in the history of any land. The poorhouse is vanishing from among us. We have not yet reached the goal, but, given a chance to go forward with the policies of the last eight years, we shall soon with the help of God be in sight of the day when poverty will be banished from this nation.

The Nation in 1929

It was assuredly a time of prosperity for the rich: the number of millionaires, which reached 4,000 in 1914, had almost trebled by 1926, and the stock market was making new ones every year. But it was not only the rich who basked in the warmth of the late twenties. The Niagara of production testified to an unprecedented degree of national well-being, although—as we shall see in our next chapter—it was a well-being by no means enjoyed by everyone. In turn, the Niagara promoted that "democracy of things" we first noted in the mid-1850s. Fresh vegetables were now widely available, thanks to new techniques of storage and transport. The consumption of ice cream soared—up 45 percent just from 1919 to 1926. Automobiles, now colored in Versailles Violet and Florentine Cream rather than just funeral black, were owned by two households out of three. Rich and not-so-rich alike shaved with the Gillette Safety Razor, snapped pictures with their Kodaks, went to the movies (in December 1923 the movie attendance in Muncie, Indiana, was almost four-and-a-half times the population of the town), and shopped at Macy's, where "Goods suitable for millionaires" were available "at prices in reach of millions."[5]

Thus, if the technical achievement of the age of industrialization was hugely to augment the volume and to alter the composition of the nation's output, its social achievement was to bring about an era of self-conscious prosperity unlike any the country had known before. Especially among those who fared well, there was an acute sense of the American economy as a triumph of enterprise. There was only one problem: Although the national edifice of prosperity appeared to be built of granite, it turned out to be built on sand.

NOTES

[1] *The Age of Reform* (1955), p. 23.

[2] Quoted in Gilbert Osofsky, *Harlem: The Making of a Ghetto* (1965), pp. 135–36.

[3] Ray S. Baker and William E. Dodd (eds.), *The Public Papers of Woodrow Wilson* (1925), I, 640.

[4] Quoted in William Leuchtenburg, *The Perils of Prosperity* (1958), p. 202.

[5] From an 1887 Macy's advertisement, as quoted in Daniel Boorstin, *The Americans: The Democratic Experience* (1973), p. 113.

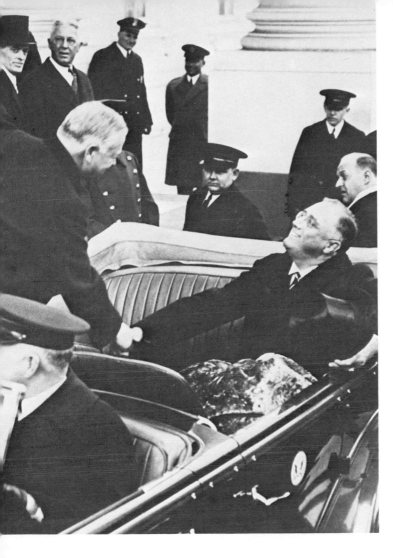

PART THREE

From Laissez Faire to Mixed Economy

The
Great
Depression

9

We turn now to a third aspect of the economic transformation of America. In our first section we concentrated mainly on the causes and the course of economic growth; in our second section we concentrated on the industrialization of the economy. Now we focus on the change in the mechanisms of the system itself. That is not to say, of course, that the subthemes of growth and industrialization will disappear—indeed, the problem of growth, or rather, of its sudden disappearance, will be prominent in the chapters immediately to follow. But the most striking aspect of the transforming process will lie elsewhere: in the gradual abandonment of the system of laissez faire and its replacement by a new "mixed" economic system.

Liberalism and Laissez Faire

Laissez faire means "leave alone." It is a phrase that we can trace back to the early eighteenth, perhaps even the late seventeenth, century, when the regulation-bound merchants of France replied to a government that asked what it could do for them: *"Laissez-nous faire"* (Leave us alone).

Laissez faire in its original version was merely a plea to be rid of the red tape that was throttling the emerging entrepreneurial energies of mercantile Europe. But under the intellectual guidance of Adam Smith, David Ricardo, and John Stuart Mill it became more than just a plea for deregulation. It was raised to the status of a genuine philosophy, combining the theory of a free-market economic system and the theory of a parliamentary democratic system into a larger view we call liberalism.

Laissez faire was thus the economic foundation for much of nineteenth-century thought. To be sure it was never pure laissez faire, in the sense of an absence of all government intervention into the economy. We have seen how crucial was the role played by government in shaping the course of economic development in America, from earliest colonial days through the late nineteenth century. That intervention continued into the twentieth century. The administrations of Theodore Roosevelt and Woodrow Wilson saw further extensions of government. Currency and credit and banking were subject to new regulations under the Federal Reserve Act (1913); trusts and mergers were subject to new scrutiny under the Clayton Antitrust Act (1914), and the Federal Trade Commission (1914); industries such as food and drug production became subject to new regulation under the Pure Food and Drug Act (1906).

Yet, with few exceptions, all these interventions by government were made with reluctance and were regarded as regrettable, albeit necessary, departures from the ideal of an ungoverned economic system. To put it differently, where intervention was inescapable, it was deemed best to hold it to a minimum; where governmental power was inescapable, it was believed best dispersed among the states rather than gathered into the federal structure; where sides had to be chosen in the economic process, it was presumed that the side of business would be the side favored by the authorities. "The chief business of the American people is business," said Calvin Coolidge, summing up the general view of a nation in which the pursuit of private money-making, benignly watched over by a business-minded government, was the unchallenged philosophy of the times.

It is easy to understand why such a philosophy was popular. It had its roots in the independence-minded past, in the Jeffersonian abhorrence of centralized power. It carried forward the glamorizing of business success provided by Social Darwinism. It went with the worship of business heroes such as Andrew Carnegie and Henry Ford. It accorded very well with the self-confident spirit of the times. And, above all, it seemed to work.

The Stock Market Boom

As we know, in the end it did not work. The chapter of economic history that opens with a flourish runs quickly into disaster. The philosophy that was without serious rival in 1929 would, within five years, be in retreat, and by the end of fifteen years, largely obsolete.

The reasons for that change provide the main narrative of this chapter and the two to follow. The causes are deep-rooted and lie in the actual breakdown of the mechanism that was celebrated by laissez faire. But we must not get ahead of ourselves. The breakdown was slow in coming, even slower in being recognized. The Great Depression was still a year or two off in 1929, and it would be preceded by the Great Crash. And the Great Crash was still nine months off, as 1929 opened, and was preceded by the Great Boom. Let us begin there, with a somewhat overdrawn, but vivid, account of that hectic time given to us by Frederick Lewis Allen:

> The rich man's chauffeur drove with his ears laid back to catch the news of an impending move in Bethlehem Steel: he held fifty shares himself on a twenty point margin.* The window cleaner at the broker's office paused to watch the ticker, for he was thinking of converting his laboriously accumulated savings into a few shares of Simmonds. [One reporter] told of a broker's valet who made nearly a quarter of a million in the market, of a trained nurse who cleaned up thirty thousand following the tips given her by grateful patients; and of a Wyoming cattleman, thirty miles from the nearest railroad, who bought or sold a thousand shares a day.[1]

Behind the Boom

Stocks were going up during the long boom of the 1920s for many reasons. One is that the profits of most corporations were rising. Between 1916 and 1925 the profits of large manufacturing companies totaled $730 million in an average year. From 1926 through 1929, their annual total profits jumped to an average of about $1,400

---

* A "margin" means that stock has been bought by borrowing from the bank or from the brokerage firm to cover the difference between the value of the shares and the amount of the down payment.

million. In 1929 profits were actually triple those of 1920. Hence one reason for buying stocks was the expectation that dividends would rise. And they did. From 1920 to 1929, dividends almost tripled.

A second reason was that banks and brokerage firms were encouraging people to buy stocks by lending vast sums to potential buyers. Loans from brokers to enable individuals to buy stocks—loans that were often equal to half the value of the purchase—soared from just over $1 billion in 1920 to $6 billion in 1928. Who could resist the chance to become as rich as Croesus when you could buy $1,000 worth of stock by putting up only $500 of your own, borrowing the rest from a brokerage firm or a bank? Hundreds of thousands of people *didn't* resist. A million and a half people were stockholders, a far larger number than ever before, and the number of shares traded on the New York Stock Exchange rose from 236 million in 1923 to 1.1 *billion* in 1928.

Finally, there was the allure of a seemingly foolproof method of getting rich. Many Americans were encouraged to join in the great stock market boom because they listened to the advice of trusted men. In 1928 John J. Raskob, a director of General Motors and chairman of the Democratic party, wrote an article for the *Ladies Home Journal* entitled "Everybody Ought to Be Rich." In it he said: "If a man saves $15 a week and invests in common stocks, at the end of twenty years he will have at least $80,000 and an income from investments of around $400 a month. He will be rich."

Raskob's arithmetic was perfectly correct. Suppose an ordinary citizen, earning a "middle" income of $2,000, managed to put $15 a week aside in 1921 and invested the resulting $780 in a group of seasoned securities. He would have fared as follows, if he had added $780 in each of the next years:

Value of Shares

1922	$1,092
1923	$1,909
1924	$2,809
1925	$4,800
1926	$6,900
1927	$8,800
1928	$16,000
1929	$21,000

In ten years his accumulated savings would have amounted to $780 × 10, or $7,800. All the rest of his wealth would have come from the rise in the price of stocks.

The Crash

Thus the growth in incomes that we traced in our earlier chapters was paralleled during the 1920s by a spectacular growth in wealth—alas, paper wealth. For on October 24, 1929, without any prior warning, the bottom suddenly dropped out of the market. The headlines in the *New York Times* for October 25 read:

WORST STOCK CRASH STEMMED BY BANKS; 12,894,650-SHARE DAY SWAMPS MARKET; LEADERS CONFER, FIND CONDITIONS SOUND

What was meant by the "crash" was that investors all over the country decided that the market was "too high" and placed orders to sell. But no one can sell a security—or any other item—at whatever price he or she wishes. The seller has to find a buyer. And if the buyers are nervous and pessimistic, the price at which they will agree to buy the stock may be much lower than the sellers expected.

What happened on the morning of October 24 was that buyers were only willing to buy stocks at prices far below the prices of the preceding day. Montgomery Ward, a favorite, had "opened" at a price of 83. (That is, the first transaction was a sale at $83 per share.) By midmorning it was being traded at 50. Goldman Sachs Trading Corporation, a speculative favorite, opened at 81 and dropped to 65. General Electric slid from 315 to 283. Some stocks could not be sold at all—there were simply no buyers to take them at any price.

By noon the roar of voices on the stock exchange floor had reached panic proportions, and a group of bankers met to issue reassuring statements that "conditions were sound." For a week the market rallied as buyers lifted up their courage and sellers lost their terrified impulse to sell. Then on October 29 came an even more devastating day. As the *New York Times* wrote about it the next morning:

STOCKS COLLAPSE IN 16,410,030-SHARE DAY

Stock prices virtually collapsed today, swept downward with gigantic trading losses in the most disastrous trading day in the stock market's history. Millions of dollars in open market values were wiped out as prices crumbled under the pressures of liquidation of securities that had to be sold at any price. . . .

Efforts to estimate yesterday's market losses in dollars are futile because of the vast number of securities . . . on which no calculations are possible. However, it was estimated that 880 issues, on the New York Stock Exchange, lost between $8,000,000,000 and $9,000,000,000 yesterday.

And October 29 was not the end. In 1932 Frank Vanderlip, former president of the National City Bank of New York, a leading financial institution, surveyed the wreckage in an article in the *Saturday Evening Post:*

> . . . The quoted value of all stocks listed on the New York Stock Exchange was, on September 1, 1929, $89,668,276,854. By July 1, 1932 the quoted value of all stocks had fallen to $15,633,479,577.
>
> Stockholders had lost $74,000,000,000. The figure is so large that not many minds can grasp it. It is $616 for every one of us in America. It is, roughly, three times what we spent fighting the World War. . . . In the bursting of the New York Stock Exchange bubble, the value of all stocks fell to 17 percent of their September 1, 1929 price. . . . Never before, in this country or anywhere else, has there been such a general loss in "security" values.[2]

In 1932 the United States Senate held a hearing on the fate of some of those stocks:

> SENATOR COUZENS: Did Goldman Sachs and Company organize the Goldman Sachs Trading Company?
>
> MR. SACHS: Yes, sir.
>
> SENATOR COUZENS: And it sold its stock to the public?
>
> MR. SACHS: A portion of it. The firm invested originally in 10 percent of the entire issue for the sum of $10,000,000.
>
> SENATOR COUZENS: And the other 90 percent was sold to the public?
>
> MR. SACHS: Yes, sir.
>
> SENATOR COUZENS: At what price?
>
> MR. SACHS: At 104 . . .
>
> SENATOR COUZENS: And what is the price of the stock now?
>
> MR. SACHS: Approximately 1¾.[3]

A run on a bank

Behind the Crash

What caused the crash? To this day we do not know what item of news, what rumor, what particular event may have started the collapse. Clearly there must have been an underlying nervousness among hundreds of thousands of stockholders, for the fall in prices soon fed upon itself. In addition, the collapse worsened because holders of stocks on margin—that is, on borrowed money—were forced to sell their securities to pay off their loans. Perhaps in the end we can only classify the Great Crash with other speculative busts that had happened elsewhere in history—land booms that came to nothing, crazes such as the tulip bulb speculative mania in seventeenth-century Holland, prior stock booms like the famous English South Sea "Bubble" of 1720.

What interests us is the impact of the crash on the economy. For as everyone knows, the crash ushered in something worse. Why did the collapse of stock prices—which everyone understood to be the result of a feverish speculation that was bound to burst sooner or later—trigger the much more dangerous and mystifying Great Depression?

Hidden Economic Problems

Looking back on that woeful chapter of our economic history we can find at least three reasons for the shakiness of our vaunted prosperity. Let us examine them before we turn to an analysis of the depression itself.

1. *The economy was extremely vulnerable to a crash.* The get-rich-quick philosophy of the 1920s was not limited only to the public. It also infected the business community. An orgy of financial manipulation, wild speculative ventures, and reckless practices made the decade of the 1920s reminiscent of the period of the robber barons.

More to the point, these practices resulted in pyramids of corporations, each holding the stock of others. The pyramids were very profitable as long as the corporations on the bottom stood firm. But when one of them slipped—when one company in a pyramid failed—it often brought down the heap with it. For example, the structure of a utility company controlled by a Chicago financier named Samuel Insull was so complex that it was said, in all seriousness, that no one, including Insull himself, could understand it. (Insull held 65 chairmanships, 85 directorships, and 7 presidencies of corporations.) One small part of the structure, Georgia Power & Light, was controlled by Seaboard Public Service Corporation, which was controlled by National Service Corporation, which was controlled by Middle West Utilities Corporation, which was controlled by Insull Utility Investments, which was controlled by Corporation Securities Company, which in turn was controlled by Insull Utility Investments. . . .

Thus despite endless assurances by businessmen that things were fundamentally sound, things were *not* fundamentally sound. Nowhere was this more true than in the banking industry. Banks were up to their ears in the very unsound business of lending money for security purchases; and when the market fell, the lending banks were grievously stricken. In addition, banks not only foisted all manner of unsound securities on the public but became convinced of the value of those very same investments and bought them themselves. Nor did the Federal Reserve Board use any direct controls,* such as raising the discount rate (the interest rate that it charges to member banks) to check the speculative mania of the times. And not least, the acquisitive mania of the twenties tempted banks into practices that hardly squared with "soundness." For instance, the First National Bank (one of the leading New York banks) paid $450,000 to the son of the president of Peru for his services in connection with a $50 million Peruvian loan the bank was about to make at a considerable profit. The services of the president's son, it should be added, consisted entirely of his agreement not to block the deal.

Hence one terrible consequence of the crash was that it toppled many banks whose failure in turn toppled other businesses. In the first six months of 1929, 346 banks failed. By 1932, 4,835 banks had closed their doors. When they did so, it meant that depositors or businesses could not redeem their savings or checking accounts. In the years from 1929 to 1933 over 9 million savings accounts were lost and countless businesses went bankrupt because they could not get their money out of the banks.

2. *There was trouble on the farms.* The crash brought down the fragile banking structure, but even without the stock market there was trouble brewing during the 1920s. The trouble was not in the cities or the big corporations, or among the suburbanites who danced the Charleston, but in rural America. Here lived 7 million out of America's 30 million families. They did not dance the Charleston because they had no radios on which to hear the music—less than 10 percent of America's farms had electricity. This meant that over 90 percent of the farms were entirely excluded from the market for refrigerators and electric appliances and even electric light.

Moreover, the average farm household was not only poor but was growing relatively poorer. In 1910 an average farmer's income had been about 40 percent of an average urban worker's income. By 1930 it had fallen to less than 30 percent. Moreover, each year more and more farm families lost their ability to maintain their own farms. Unable to meet the mortgage payments on their properties, they went into

---

* It should be noted that the Federal Reserve Board did not have control over margin requirements until 1934.

sharecropping or tenantry: by 1929 four out of every ten farmers were tenant farmers.

Perhaps what was most ironic in this rural tragedy was that it was caused in substantial part by the very success of the industrial portion of the nation. One of the results of industrialization, as we have already seen, was that farm tasks were increasingly mechanized. This gave rise to a flood of output from the farms—a flood that resulted in a drop in farm prices every bit as painful, though not quite so dramatic, as the drop in stock prices. For example, wheat sold for $1.45 a bushel in 1925 and slid to $1.03 in 1929 (it would go to 40 cents in 1931); cotton fell from 34 cents a pound to 16 cents. At those prices farmers could not make ends meet. A witness described the rural scene before a congressional committee in 1932:

> The roads of the West and the Southwest teem with hungry hitchhikers. The campfires of the homeless are seen along every railroad track. I saw men, women, and children walking over the hard roads. Most of them were tenant farmers who had lost their all in the late slump in wheat and cotton. Between Clarksville and Russellville, Arkansas, I picked up a family. The woman was hugging a dead chicken under a ragged coat. . . . She told me she had found it dead on the road, and then added in grim humor, 'They promised me a chicken in the pot, and now I got mine.'[4]

3. *There was a serious maldistribution of income.* Last, there was a weakness in the very heartland of prosperity—not in finance or farming, but in industry. This was the problem of wages and profits.

As we have seen, all through the 1920s output per worker had been rising in the manufacturing sector. A steady flow of technological improvements kept raising output even though employment was stationary or even falling in some industries. This obviously made it possible to pay higher wages to workers. Yet their earnings did not keep pace with their rising productivity. In mining, for example, where output per man rose by 43 percent between 1920 and 1929, yearly earnings *fell* from $1,700 to $1,481. In transportation and manufacturing, yearly earnings dropped from 1920 to 1922 and did not regain their 1920 level until 1929, although output per worker was up 50 percent over the period.

What happened to the gains from higher productivity? They showed up mainly as higher corporate profits—those booming profits that helped cause the stock market boom. Between 1923 and 1929, corporate profits rose 62 percent. Now we can see, however, that the boom in profits not only sparked the stock market rise but seriously undermined the prosperity of the country. For the profit boom signaled the fact that the achievements of the economy were very unevenly enjoyed.

At the top of the income pyramid, the boom created enormous prosperity, as the table below shows:

Percentage of Total Income Received by Top Groups		
	Top 1 Percent	*Top 5 Percent*
1919	12.2	24.3
1923	13.1	27.1
1929	18.9	33.5

Notice that the share of total income received by the richest families in the nation grew steadily larger as the twenties went on. And the not-so-rich? It follows that their share must have declined. According to a study made by the Brookings Institution, a leading research organization, an income of $2,000 would buy a family "basic necessities" in 1929. Yet that same study showed that in 1929 almost 60 percent of all American families received less than $2,000. Hence the contrast between the top and the bottom was extreme. In 1929, 15,000 families with incomes of $100,000 or more actually received as much income as 5 to 6 million families at the bottom.

The consequence was not just a matter for tongue-clucking. Income was being diverted away from ordinary families, who would have spent it for the products of mass industry, into the hands of the rich, who spent it for luxuries or who did not spend it at all.

In other words, the prosperity of the 1920s was a good deal less substantial than it appeared on the surface. A rickety financial structure brought havoc when the stock market collapsed. A declining farm sector created an undertow of falling incomes in the agricultural areas where a fourth of the nation lived. The boom in profits and the swelling of topmost incomes came at the expense of a much-needed encouragement to mass buying power. Thus the economy operated very unevenly, bringing real riches to a few but a false sense of widely shared well-being to the nation at large.

Desperation

THE GREAT DEPRESSION

It was an oddly invisible phenomenon, this Great Depression. If one observed closely, one might note that there were fewer people on the streets than in former years, that there were many untenanted shops, that beggars and panhandlers were much in evidence; one might see breadlines here and there, and 'Hoovervilles' in vacant lots at the edge of town (groups of tarpaper shacks inhabited by homeless people); railroad trains were shorter, with fewer Pullmans; and there were many factory chimneys out of which no smoke was coming. But otherwise there was little to see. Great numbers of people were sitting at home, trying to keep warm.[5]

However hard it was to see, the Great Depression was a vivid reality to virtually everyone. To begin with, unemployment soared beyond any previous experience. All through the long period of industrialization, recurrent periods of unemployment had plagued the economy, sometimes reaching as high as 10 percent of the work force. But those times of trial had always been brief and had always been followed by a resumption of growth, which brought with it job opportunities for almost everyone who wanted work.

The depression was different. The table below reveals its severity.

Labor Force and Unemployment, 1929–41 (numbers in millions)

| | | Unemployment | |
Year	Labor Force	Number	% of Labor Force
1929	49.2	1.6	3.2
1930	49.8	4.3	8.7
1931	50.4	8.0	15.9
1932	51.0	12.1	23.6
1933	51.6	12.8	24.9
1934	52.2	11.3	21.7
1935	52.9	10.6	20.1
1936	53.4	9.0	16.9
1937	54.0	7.7	14.3
1938	54.6	10.4	19.0
1939	55.2	9.5	17.2
1940	55.6	8.1	14.6
1941	55.9	5.6	9.9

SOURCE: United States Department of Commerce, *Historical Statistics of the United States* (1960), p. 70.

Nothing like this had ever happened before. For it was not only unemployment that the depression brought, but a total cessation of growth. In the nation as a whole, home-building came almost to a standstill—residential construction fell by 90 percent. Eighty-five thousand businesses failed, and production in those that survived was often reduced to half the volume of the 1920s. Wages reached levels that made sheer survival a problem: in Pennsylvania men were paid 5 cents an hour in sawmills; 7½ cents in general contracting. In Ohio the earnings of office workers were cut by a third, those of store clerks by nearly half. Thus, while the Great Crash had dashed American illusions about instant riches, the Great Depression threatened something much more fundamental. It brought into question the faith of Americans in the economic system itself. The system simply did not seem to work.

Political Paralysis

At first no one believed that. "We have now passed the worst," said President Hoover in May 1930. One year later he declared the depression to be "over." Meanwhile business spokesmen continued to assert that things were "fundamentally sound":

> Charles Schwab, Chairman of Bethlehem Steel, December 10, 1929: "Never before has American business been as firmly entrenched for prosperity as it is today."
>
> John Edgerton, President, National Association of Manufacturers, December 1929: "I can observe little on the horizon today to give us undue or great concern."
>
> James Farrell, President, United States Steel, January 1931: "The peak of the depression passed thirty days ago."[6]

But as the situation stubbornly refused to mend itself, sentiment began to change. Among the unemployed an ugly mood of frustration and anger was surfacing. In 1932 a small "army" of unemployed veterans converged on Washington to demand payment of a bonus promised them for their service in the First World War. Hoover refused to meet with them. Instead, the veterans were attacked with bayonets and tear gas, to the shock and dismay of the nation. In the farm states, representatives of banks who arrived to take possession of farms that could not keep up their mortgage payments were met by groups of unsmiling men carrying clubs. Representatives of farm groups warned the Hoover administration that the countryside was ripe for revolution.

Worst of all, however, was the inability of the business leaders to provide a recipe for renewed prosperity, save for "prudence" on the part of government. A Senate committee in 1932 spent two weeks listening to businessmen give the following advice:

> Bernard Baruch, financier and advisor to many presidents: "Balance budgets. Sacrifice for frugality and revenue. Tax—tax everybody for everything."

Jackson Reynolds, First National Bank: "I have [no remedy] and I do not believe anyone else has."

Myron C. Taylor, United States Steel: "I have no remedy in mind."

Nicholas Murray Butler, President of Columbia University: "Government economy and balanced budgets."[7]

Heeding the counsel of business leaders and the philosophy of laissez faire, the government under President Hoover believed that the economy would restore itself if it were left alone. Although his administration did more than any previous administration to revive the economy, Hoover felt that no radical steps were called for. His administration bought some agricultural surpluses to help bring farm prices up, and it began a modest program of public works, including the building of Boulder Dam (later renamed Hoover Dam) on the Colorado. Mainly, however, it tried to help business. In 1932 Hoover persuaded Congress to establish the Reconstruction Finance Corporation, which lent government money to banks, life insurance companies, railroads, and mortgage associations. Later that year the Home Loan Bank Act further aided financial institutions in danger of bankruptcy.

The Sins of Omission and Commission

All this did help somewhat. But what was striking was the administration's unwillingness to help the neediest—the unemployed. Before 1932 the federal government provided *no* funds for direct relief to the unemployed. Finally, in July of that year, the federal government began allocating relief money in the form of *loans* to the states. But by the end of 1932 the national government had released only $30 million for relief. Partly this was due to Hoover's philosophy of "rugged individualism." Partly it was due to the fact that the president could not bring himself to believe in the severity, or even the reality, of the plight of the unemployed. "No one is actually starving," he told reporters. "The hoboes, for example, are better fed than they have ever been. One hobo in New York got ten meals in one day."[8] Later, the president was actually to write about the many unemployed who eked out a living by selling apples on street corners: "Many persons left their jobs for the more profitable one of selling apples."

Inaction was the government's worst moral sin, but perhaps its greatest economic sin was in taking actions that unwittingly exacerbated the situation. Believing that the American business system was inherently sound and that the depression was a European import,

Louisville flood victims, 1937

Hoover signed the Smoot-Hawley Tariff Act of 1930, which raised tariff rates on imports to the highest levels in the country's history. This action had profound repercussions. By making it very difficult for foreign countries to sell their products to America, the tariff deprived European nations of a major source of revenue that would have enabled them to buy American goods (especially farm output) and to repay their war debts to the United States.

Nor did the government exercise its taxing and spending or monetary powers prudently. Arguing that a balanced budget was one of the major requirements for a nation's economic health, the government, in 1932, decreased its expenditures and actually enacted the largest tax *increase* up to that point in American history! Even more serious were the Federal Reserve Board's actions. During the speculative mania of the twenties, the monetary authorities could not bring themselves to check the unwise expansion of bank loans by raising the discount rate or by taking other measures. But when the depression came and the crying need was for banks to encourage business by lending them money for expansion, the Federal Reserve Board

—frightened about the possibility of inflation because gold was pouring in from Europe—suddenly tightened the monetary screws, *raising* interest rates and generally discouraging the financial community from helping its customers.

Yet, before we blame the Hoover administration out of hand for its undoubted mistakes, we must realize that most people did not understand how the depression could be cured—or why it did not cure itself. As time went on and the economy failed to recover, economists as well as businessmen felt baffled by events. The most frightening thing about the depression was that the nation was not only bankrupt in its affairs but bankrupt in its ideas.

THE ANATOMY OF THE DEPRESSION

What *was* the cause of the Great Depression? The answer was not clear for many years—indeed only in the last few decades has the mechanism of a "depression" become part of our general understanding. Much of our understanding derives from a book published in 1936, *The General Theory of Employment, Interest, and Money,* written by an English economist, John Maynard Keynes. Controversial at the time, Keynes' basic theories have by now become accepted by economists and governments all over the world. And like so many new theories that seem extraordinarily difficult at the time they are first pronounced, Keynes' essential ideas now appear very simple.

At the heart of Keynes' explanation of depression is a fundamental fact about a market economy: *the source of all its employment is spending.* Unless money is spent, money will not be received. Unless dollars are spent, neither businesses nor employees will get paid. Spending—*expenditure* is the more formal term—is the key to the generation of employment and income.

Who Does the Nation's Spending?

Keynes divides spenders into two groups: households and business firms. Households spend money for the goods and services they consume—consumer goods. These include food and clothing and automobiles and doctors' services and similar items. But consumers are not the only spenders in the economy. Business also spends money, not merely to keep its operations going, but to add to its plant and equipment, its capital wealth. We call this second kind of spending *investment*. A business invests when it is building a new factory, adding a wing to an existing establishment, piling up larger inventories to service its customers.

All that was familiar enough, even in the 1930s. But Keynes emphasizes a very important distinction between consumer spending and business spending. Consumer spending, he explains, is not usually marked by rapid changes (upward or downward), *unless consumers' incomes have previously changed upward or downward.* That is, households tend to spend a fairly steady proportion of their incomes. When their incomes fall—as in a depression—naturally they spend less. When their incomes rise, they spend more.

But it is different with business spending for investment. A business firm does not decide to build a new plant or to buy new equipment only because its *current* income is high. Indeed, we recall that Andrew Carnegie launched the great Thomson Steel Works even though there was a severe depression in 1873. Business spending for investment depends on businessmen's expectations of *future* sales. If a business firm expects to be able to sell more goods, it might spend money to enlarge its factory even though its current income is low. Vice versa, even if a business is highly prosperous, it might cut its investment spending if it feels that the future is not likely to continue as favorably as the past.

The Crucial Role of Investment

This gives us a first clue to the real meaning of the depression. *All depressions, or "recessions," or business slumps are brought about because the economy is not spending enough to create high levels of employment or income.* Usually the deficiency in spending stems from the fact that the business sector does not look to the future with confidence. It fears that the outlook is uncertain; it believes that risky investments should be avoided.

This is exactly what happened in the Great Depression. In 1929 the gross national product—the value of total output—was $104 billion.* In 1932 the gross national product (or GNP) had fallen to $56

---

* What is gross national product? *It is the market value of all the final goods and services produced by the economy in a year.* The word "final" means that the statisticians who compute GNP add up the value of all the "last" goods we produce but do not include the value of output that *goes into* those goods. Example: the statisticians count in GNP the market value of all the automobiles that are made, but not the value of the rubber, the steel, the paint, and the cotton cloth that various companies sell

billion. What caused the terrific collapse? One initiating reason was a collapse in investment spending, as the figures below show:

Investment Spending (billions of $)			
	Housing	*Other Construction*	*Plant & Equipment*
1929	3.6	5.1	5.9
1932	.6	1.2	1.6

The Multiplier Effect

Between 1929 and 1933, investment spending of all kinds shrank by 88 percent. One-third of all unemployment was directly generated by the shrinkage in output of industries that supplied capital goods. Unemployment then spread throughout the economy as a consequence of the cutback in investment spending. As workers were fired and lower incomes were paid out by construction firms and steel plants and other businesses making capital goods, employees were forced to cut back their spending for consumer goods. In turn, because they bought fewer consumer goods, firms that sold clothing, food, housewares, and so forth began to fire some of their workers, or to lower their wages. Thus the sharp drop in investment spending spread throughout the economy, creating a snowball effect as it went.

Indefinite Depression

Keynes' explanation of the mechanism of depression was very clear, and not too controversial. But buried in his analysis was a

---

to the auto-makers. The reason is that the value of these goods is *included* in the value of the finished car. In the same way, GNP includes the value of the clothes that are made, but not the value of the cloth, the thread, and the buttons that are included in the selling price of the finished garment.

What are "final" goods? There are four kinds. First there are all the domestically made *consumption goods* or services that households buy, such as autos and clothes. Second are the domestically produced *investment goods* that business buys, such as new buildings, machines, and additions to inventories. Third are the domestic goods or services that *government buys*—roads, public education, police, arms, and so forth. And fourth is the value of all *foreign goods* and services of all kinds bought by the nation, minus the value of all domestic production sold abroad. To recapitulate, then, *GNP is the total market value of the annual output of all domestic consumer output, all domestic investment output, all domestic public output, and all output sold abroad less foreign output imported into the country.*

deeper message that startled and shocked the business and academic worlds.

In part, the message was that *there was no automatic cure for a depression.* Only a resumption of spending—especially investment spending—would stop the snowball of depression. And there was no guarantee, no certainty, that investment would pick up. To be sure, for 150 years the business system had always resumed its pace as businessmen recovered their confidence, were fired up with new plans for expansion, or saw the profitable implications of new inventions. But there was nothing inevitable in this process. A depression could last indefinitely—or anyway, a very long time. Indeed, if business did not undertake enough investment projects, an economy could go on and on with large amounts of unemployment.

A New Role for Government

A second part of the message, mainly proposed by Keynes' growing body of supporters, was even more shocking. If business investment was an uncertain means of generating the volume of spending needed to bring full employment, then *why not use the government as a means of generating the needed spending?* Why not use the government to launch projects such as roads or dams, or to bolster household spending through such means as relief payments to the unemployed?

None of this sounds particularly revolutionary to us today. We are used to an enormous flow of government spending—for social security, space programs, arms, highways, welfare, housing, and on and on. But very little of that existed in the 1930s. In the 1970s, federal government expenditure of all kinds amounts to about 25 percent of our gross national product. In 1929 it amounted to less than 2 percent. Most of the main programs of government spending that we are accustomed to today did not exist at all then—we will begin to see their origins in our next chapter.

Moreover, the attitude of the business community was extremely hostile to the idea of government spending. Keynes' ideas were an affront to the philosophy of laissez faire. Most businessmen then thought that almost any form of government spending smacked dangerously of "socialism." Most of them did not understand that it was possible for government to play a positive role in creating the spending that propelled an economy forward. We have seen the parade of businessmen advocating that the government balance its budget. In those days nearly everyone thought of the government as a kind of large household which was properly guided by the same kind of prudent cautions that apply to a small household. Certainly no business leader conceived of the government as capable of increasing its spending power by borrowing the savings of the public in exactly the same way in which the business sector could increase *its* spending power by borrowing the savings of the public.

It would be a long time before "Keynesian" ideas about the means of curing a depression became accepted by everyone—indeed, not until the Second World War gave rise to enormous government expenditures (and unbalanced budgets) did the business community begin to understand the role that the Keynesians advocated for government. In the very different climate of the 1930s, Keynes' ideas were strange and threatening. Thus the New Deal's effort to put them into effect mainly succeeded only in frightening businessmen, who cut back their private investment spending as a consequence.

But all this brings us to our next chapter, in which we will trace the effect of the New Deal on the economy and on the economic philosophy of the times. We should be in a position now to understand the basic economic problem that Franklin Roosevelt faced. Let us see how he dealt with it.

NOTES

[1] *Only Yesterday* (Bantam ed., 1946), p. 349.

[2] Nov. 5, 1932, pp. 3–4.

[3] Quoted in John Kenneth Galbraith, *The Great Crash* (1955), pp. 69–70.

[4] David Shannon (ed.), *The Great Depression* (1960), p. 27.

[5] F. L. Allen, *The Big Change* (1952), p. 148.

[6] Arthur Schlesinger, Jr., *The Crisis of the Old Order* (1957), pp. 162–63, 177.

[7] Quoted in Schlesinger, *The Crisis of the Old Order*, pp. 457–58.

[8] Quoted in William Manchester, *The Glory and the Dream* (1974), p. 41.

The New Deal 10

On Election Day, 1932, Franklin D. Roosevelt won an overwhelming victory over Herbert Hoover. The popular vote, 22,800,000 to 15,750,000, and the electoral college vote, 472 to 59, tell only part of the story. In addition to carrying every state south and west of Pennsylvania, and capturing more counties than any previous candidate, the new president had taken from Hoover all but six of the forty states the ex-president had won in 1928. With the exception of the election of 1912, when the Republican party was split between Taft and Theodore Roosevelt, no Republican presidential candidate had ever been defeated so soundly.

THE HUNDRED DAYS

The nation had unequivocally declared its need for a new policy to deal with the depression. In the four months before Roosevelt took office the depression deepened and worsened. When inauguration day finally came, on March 4, 1933, the country was glued to its radio receivers to hear what the new president would say. What they heard was this:

> First of all, let me assert my firm belief that the only thing we have to fear is fear itself—nameless, unreasoning, unjustified terror. . . . I shall not evade the clear course of duty that [confronts] me. I shall ask the Congress . . . for broad Executive power to wage war against the emergency, as great as the power that would be given to me if we were in fact invaded by a foreign foe. . . . I pledge you, I pledge myself to a new deal for the American people.[1]

Roosevelt's clarion call was magnetic. "America hasn't been as happy in three years as they are today," wrote Will Rogers the next day. "No money, no banks, no work, no nothing, but they know they

FDR

got a man in there who is wise to Congress, wise to our so-called big men. The whole country is with him."[2] That weekend the new president received 450,000 messages confirming Rogers' opinion.

Financial Crisis

About few subjects have so many volumes been written as about the "New Deal"—those two words Roosevelt first uttered casually in his acceptance speech before the Democratic convention in Chicago in 1932. Not since Lincoln or Theodore Roosevelt had a personality so engaged the public. Millions of Americans hung pictures of Roosevelt in their living rooms and felt him to be a member of their families.

What the country desperately wanted from FDR was action—almost any action—rather than a continuation of Hoover's policy of waiting for the economy to cure itself. The public was not disappointed. The New Deal began with what historian Arthur Schlesinger, Jr., has called "a barrage of ideas and programs unlike anything known to American history." In the first dazzling "Hundred Days," March 9 to June 16, 1933, over fifteen major pieces of legislation were passed.

The most pressing problem that the president had to address himself to was the financial crisis, which had now reached a point of near panic, with more banks closing every day. Even before he convened Congress into emergency session, Roosevelt issued an executive order declaring a nationwide bank "holiday." Thereafter he instructed his first Secretary of the Treasury, William Woodin, to prepare an emergency banking bill within five days. When the special session of Congress convened on March 9, it gave its approval to actions Roosevelt had in fact already taken. The Emergency Banking Act gave the President unequivocal control over gold and currency movements, outlawed the hoarding of gold, sanctioned the issue of new Federal Reserve Bank notes, and established a procedure for reopening those banks that possessed liquid assets and for reorganizing those that did not.

The Emergency Banking Act represented a bold extension and assertion of government power. Curiously, the bill was written at lightning speed by conservative bankers and by Hoover's own Treasury officials and was then passed unanimously, *sight unseen,* by the House of Representatives! A few days later, some 60 million Americans turned on their radios to hear the first of Roosevelt's "fireside chats." In informal, fatherly tones, the president's voice conveyed a spirit of national purpose and demonstrated one of his many charismatic qualities—the power to persuade. After describing the complex banking structure in simple terms, he told the country that the banks would be safely opening in the twelve Federal Reserve Bank cities the next morning. They opened safely, because people believed Roosevelt and did not rush to withdraw their deposits. Indeed, by the end of the month net inflows of currency into banks amounted to $1.25 billion "Capitalism," a member of Roosevelt's "Brain Trust" later wrote, "was saved in eight days."[3]

Other Financial Legislation

Subsequent banking legislation established the Federal Deposit Insurance Corporation to guarantee bank deposits (up to $5,000 in those days; $40,000 today), divorced investment and commercial banking, and broadened the power of the Federal Reserve Board. These measures also had an immediate impact. People continued to deposit rather than withdraw money, and bank failures were sharply reduced.

In retrospect, the "obscure, unpretentious, unwanted Federal Deposit Insurance Corporation" (as John Kenneth Galbraith has described the measure, which was opposed by the American Bankers Association and endorsed only halfheartedly by the administration) may well have been the most important single piece of financial legislation passed by the Roosevelt administration. As Galbraith points out, for the first time an utterly reliable lender of last resort—the federal government itself—was squarely committed to the safety of bank accounts. No more powerful measure of financial or psychological endorsement was ever taken by the government.

Closely related to the reorganization of the banking structure was Roosevelt's determination to curb financial abuses, particularly in the securities market. Writing to Congress on March 29, 1933, he stated: "What we seek is a return to a clearer understanding of the ancient truth that those who manage banks, corporations, and other agencies handling or using other people's money are trustees acting for others."[4]

Within a year the country saw the birth of the Securities and Exchange Commission (the SEC) charged with broad powers to oversee the issuance of new securities, to insist on the divulgence of full information regarding new issues, and to establish an agency to maintain a watchful eye over the operation of that great gambling casino, the stock exchange. It would be too much to say that the Banking Act, the

Federal Deposit Insurance Corporation, and the SEC cured American finance of all its problems or prevented financial misdeeds in the future. But with these acts, and the Public Utility Holding Company Act that prohibited the old pyramiding of utility companies, the New Deal effectively removed the worst elements of the financial crisis that was threatening to undermine the system itself.

Unemployment

The New Deal was not so successful in combating unemployment. For one thing, Roosevelt was himself a strong believer in balanced budgets for government, and therefore he shrank from the full application of a Keynesian remedy of all-out government spending, whatever the effect on the deficit. We will go into this in more detail later in this chapter. But despite the inhibitions imposed by a genuine desire to achieve budget economies, the New Deal did attack the problem of unemployment and human suffering far more vigorously than its predecessor.

On April 5, 1933, Roosevelt created the Civilian Conservation Corps to provide jobs in reforestation and conservation projects for young men between the ages of eighteen and twenty-five. Wearing their forest-green CCC uniforms, over 2½ million youths planted 200 million trees, not only beautifying the land but establishing windbreaks to prevent the erosion that had devastated many farm lands.

Then, in May, Roosevelt signed into being the Federal Emergency Relief Administration, headed by Harry Hopkins, a confidant and trusted adviser. The FERA had $500 million to allocate to state and local relief agencies, but Hopkins was convinced that jobs, not money, were the prime requisite to restore confidence. Hopkins persuaded the President to sponsor the Civil Works Administration, a federally sponsored program to employ people in building roads, schools, playgrounds, airports, or to teach. Before Roosevelt finally disbanded the CWA because of its mounting costs, it had given work to over 4 million people and had channeled some $950 million into the economy. Then, in 1935, Hopkins was put in charge of another alphabet agency—the WPA (Works Progress Administration). By 1943 this agency had employed 8½ million people and had spent a total of $11 billion.

In a nation that had not yet heard of Keynes and that was still wedded to the ideas of laissez faire, all this was a radical departure indeed. Yet few voices were raised in protest. For the country knew,

WPA

as did Roosevelt, that the alternative to these experiments in government employment was the risk of an interminable depression with massive unemployment. No one dared run that risk.

Industry and Labor

One of Roosevelt's pet proposals for ending the demoralization of the economy was the National Industrial Recovery Act. The NRA was a curious mixture of things, designed to please many constituencies. It contained the authorization, for example, for the Public Works Administration (with a budget of $3.3 billion), a works project that supplemented the WPA. It contained a clause specifically prohibiting interference with attempts to unionize. It outlawed much child labor. It established a precedent for the government regulation of minimum wages and hours. Not least, it allowed business to do legally what it had sought in vain to do through pools, trusts, and collusion—namely, to establish industry-wide prices, and codes of fair practice.

The NRA did not achieve all its objectives by any means, and its use of government powers to protect labor on the one hand and to legalize "trusts" on the other offended many people. Though it was greeted with much initial enthusiasm, there was a general sigh of relief when the act was finally declared unconstitutional by the Supreme Court in 1935. But by then the NRA had served its purpose of restoring orderly markets in many areas, and its specific reforms were soon continued under new legislation aimed at establishing minimum wages and hours in certain industries, at abolishing child labor, and most important, at protecting the rights of labor. (According to James MacGregor Burns, the passage of the Wagner Act in 1935, which assured the right of unions to organize and to bargain collectively, was "the most radical legislation passed during the New Deal.")[5]

Agriculture

The NRA had something for business and something for labor. But the Roosevelt program for farm relief was incorporated in another major piece of legislation. This was the AAA—the Agricultural Adjustment Act of 1933. The AAA went much further than Hoover's efforts to help the farmer through the government purchase of some surplus crops. It aimed to break the vicious circle of farm poverty by making it possible for farmers to do collectively what they could not do individually—to limit their production so that the price of their products would rise.

The program was intended to work through compulsory restrictions on the production of designated corps, together with government subsidies for staple commodities such as wheat, cotton, and pork. However, since crops were already growing when the law was enacted, Secretary of Agriculture Henry A. Wallace felt it necessary to tell farmers to destroy their produce in the field. Thus, while millions of Americans were still hungry, cotton planters received $100 million for plowing under 10 million acres of growing crops, and farmers were paid to kill 6 million baby pigs and 200,000 pregnant sows! Yet, if the program revealed an appalling lack of imagination, it did succeed in its overall objectives. More than 30 million acres were taken out of cultivation, and farm prices rose from depression lows to more normal levels. By 1936 the farm sector had doubled its income, and there was no more talk of revolution brewing in Ohio.

Soon thereafter a much more imaginative program made up for the government's failure to deal more sensibly with the problem of farm surpluses. This was its effort to bring economic growth to a backwater region through the establishment of a federal power-generating system, the Tennessee Valley Authority. During the First World War the government had built a hydroelectric plant at Muscle Shoals, Alabama, to provide power for the manufacture of synthetic nitrate explosives. Although farmers and other interest groups succeeded after the war in warding off plans to hand these facilities over to private enterprise, they failed in their efforts to have the site come under federal control. Now Roosevelt hoped to turn one of the country's most underdeveloped areas into an experimental laboratory for extensive social planning. The TVA constructed dams and powerhouses, established programs for flood control, soil conservation, and reforestation, and produced electricity and fertilizer. Moreover the TVA became a "yardstick" that enabled the government to influence the rates charged by private power companies.

Together with the power generated by the TVA, one other New Deal action dramatically altered the course of the farmer's life—the Rural Electrification Administration of 1935. One statistic sums up its accomplishment. Before 1935, nine out of every ten farms had no electricity; by 1950, nine out of ten had electric light.

Social Security

We have not yet discussed what is perhaps the most important single measure that the New Deal passed: Social Security. After signing the measure on August 15, 1935, Roosevelt remarked: "If the Senate and the House of Representatives in this long and arduous session had done nothing more than pass this bill, the session would be regarded as historic for all time."[6]

Essentially, the Social Security Act established a national system of old-age insurance. Once workers reached the age of sixty-five they would receive retirement benefits paid for by taxes on their wages and their employers' payrolls. Payment would, up to a point, vary with the amount each individual earned. The act also created a federal-state system of unemployment insurance and provided for federal-state joint assistance to the destitute, to the handicapped, and to dependent mothers and children.

Not all Americans approved of this unparalleled legislation. "Never in the history of the world," said conservative Congressman John Taber, "has any measure been brought in here so insidiously designed

TVA

as to prevent business recovery, to enslave workers, and to prevent any possibility of the employers providing work for the people." Congressman Daniel Reed agreed: "The lash of the dictator will be felt and 25 million free American citizens will for the first time submit themselves to the fingerprint test."[7]

These were not isolated criticisms, nor did they match the more strident invective that was hurled at Roosevelt. Many businessmen regarded the president as a "traitor to his class," and the reforms of the New Deal, far from being welcomed by them, were bitterly resisted and interpreted as the entering wedge of socialism. In 1934 some of these arch-conservative businessmen formed the American Liberty League, around which anti–New Dealers from both parties coalesced.

The innovations of the New Deal were also regarded suspiciously by another conservative element in society—the nation's courts. One after another of the major New Deal efforts, such as the Agricultural Adjustment Act and the National Industrial Recovery Act, were declared unconstitutional by a Supreme Court that viewed with alarm the efforts of the federal government to use the powers of the Constitution to regulate and restrain economic life. Even some of the most liberal justices felt that Roosevelt exceeded the proper bounds of executive power. Not until the Eisenhower years in the 1950s was the new role of the government finally accepted as a necessary element in a highly organized industrial system, rather than as a threat to that system.

The New Deal in Perspective

Can we sum up the economic accomplishments of the New Deal as a whole? Two general conclusions become apparent through the string of laws and new agencies. First, *the New Deal was an effort to make the system work in certain areas in which it had failed.* The stock market crash, the farm disaster, the bank failures, massive unemployment—these were not merely localized or transient failures that could be safely left to the dynamic forces of the economy to cure. The public had waited too long to believe that things would straighten out by themselves. What was needed was a new assurance that serious problems affecting the livelihood and lives of millions of wage-earners would not be allowed to fester unheeded. If the economy did not function reliably by itself, the public wanted the government to make it work.

That is what the New Deal tried to do, though not always with success. For all the accusations of "socialism" that were hurled against it, the New Deal was essentially conservative in its intent. As evidenced by the authorship of the emergency banking legislation, it sought not to replace the business system with another totally different system but to amend the business system to make it succeed.

Second, *the New Deal was an effort to create a new relation between government and citizenry in economic life.* The belief that prevailed throughout the years of American economic growth had been that the best guardian for each able-bodied citizen was himself. This was indeed an integral part of the philosophy of laissez faire. When Herbert Hoover spoke of "the American system of rugged individualism" and deplored agencies for relief and for the provision of a retirement income, he was speaking not just as an individual whose view of the economy inclined him in a conservative direction, but as a true spokesman of a philosophy endorsed by large numbers of the business community.

What Hoover and the business community failed to realize was that the basis for a system of rugged individualism had been eroded by the very success of the industrial growth of the economy. In 1890, for example, twice as many Americans lived in rural areas as in urban ones. When growth slackened in the industrial centers and unemployment grew, at least some affected families could move in with their relatives on the farm. In the 1930s, as we have seen, the proportion of rural and urban dwellers had swung the other way. Almost 60 percent of the nation lived in urban areas; so it was no longer possible for a recession affecting large numbers of workers to be cushioned by a reliance on country cousins. The workable basis for rugged individualism had gone with the industrialization and urbanization of the country. The New Deal was not an effort to make people dependent on government for security in case of economic trouble. It was a response to a situation in which no other solution was possible.

SUCCESS AND FAILURE

We have looked into some of the major reform movements of the New Deal—some marked by considerable success, some by much less. But we have not yet considered a matter we glimpsed when we discussed the causes of the depression. This was the effort to renew growth, not merely by repairing the weaknesses of the nation's financial and farm sectors, but by using the government as a means of spending to supplement the laggard expenditure of private investment.

Government Spending

Certainly the idea was very far from Roosevelt's mind when he took office at the very bottom of the depression. Campaigning for the presidency, he urged "balanced budgets," just like everyone else, and the idea of a large and aggressive program of public spending as a way of swelling the nation's output was as foreign to him as it was to the most conservative of the nation's businessmen. What was different about Roosevelt and the New Deal, in its early days, was a sense of the human urgency of the situation. We have seen that Herbert Hoover was able to speak of the unemployed shivering at wintry street corners with their little piles of apples for sale as having *chosen* their economic condition. In contrast, Roosevelt and his advisers saw the unemployed as the victims of an economic disaster for which they were not responsible and over which they had no control. Hence they responded to the immediate situation by hastily throwing together the collection of emergency programs that we have seen.

Of course this necessitated the spending of money by the government. Federal Emergency Relief increased from $6 million in 1933 to $115 million in 1935. Expenditures by the Civilian Conservation Corps began in 1933 at $141 million and grew to $332 million in two years. The Civil Works Administration spent $215 million in the first year of Roosevelt's term and more than double that the next year. These are all very small numbers to us, who are used to billions and tens of billions rather than mere millions, but they were very large numbers in a day when the total military expenditures of the government were less than $700 million in a normal year. Do not forget, either, that in the 1930s gross national product was less than $100 billion, whereas today it is over $1.5 *trillion.*

As a result of these emergency measures, total government spending rose. In 1932, the last year of the Hoover administration, the federal government spent $4.6 billion for all purposes—education, highways, national defense, postal services, relief, and so forth. By 1935 the total was up to $6.5 billion; by 1936, $8.4 billion—an unprecedented sum. Helped along by this "pump-priming," business began to spend more too—spending for business investment rose from $0.9 billion in 1932 to $11 billion in 1937. Consumer spending rose as well, supported by the new dollars flowing into households: consumers spent $46 billion in 1933 and $67 billion in 1937.

Disappointing Results

On the face of it, then, it would seem that the effort to restore growth was a success. Real gross national product had fallen to a low of $74 billion in 1933—off by one-fourth from the high of 1929. By 1937 it was back to $109 billion. Unemployment, which had reached the dreadful total of almost 13 million men and women in 1933, was down to 7.7 million by 1937.

Yet it is clear, at second look, that the program was at best only a partial success. For despite the recovery under the impetus of federal spending, gross national product in 1937 was still only 5 percent above its peak in 1929—instead of really growing, the economy was only catching up (and was far below the trend of the past). And although 7.7 million unemployed was a good deal less serious than 13 million, it still meant that 14 percent of the labor force was unable to find work, compared with only 3 percent in 1929.

Chart 1 below shows us what was happening with government spending and GNP:

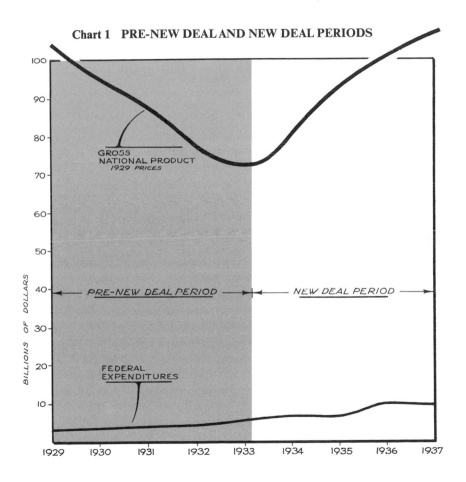

Chart 1   PRE-NEW DEAL AND NEW DEAL PERIODS

Notice how government spending rose, pushing up GNP but hardly bringing it above the level of 1929 prosperity.

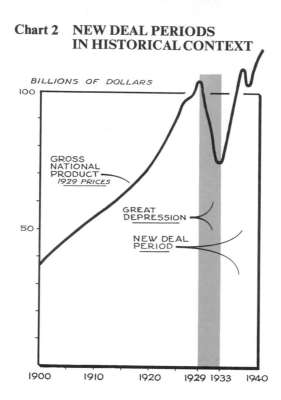

Chart 2 NEW DEAL PERIODS IN HISTORICAL CONTEXT

BILLIONS OF DOLLARS

100

GROSS NATIONAL PRODUCT
1929 PRICES

GREAT DEPRESSION

50

NEW DEAL PERIOD

1900   1910   1920   1929 1933   1940

Chart 2 shows the problem even more clearly, for now we place the New Deal period in a longer-range historical context.

The second chart shows the long, irregular upward slope of growth prior to the Great Depression, the subsequent collapse, and then the recovery following on the New Deal. Note that by 1937 the economy had not yet reached the "trend line" established by the pre–New Deal period.

The Doldrums

Why was the economy in 1937 barely above the level of 1929? Why had not the bold new program of the New Deal quickly brought the country back onto the long "growth path" of the past?

If we had been able to visit Washington or the main industrial centers of the country in 1937, the answer we would have heard was that the government was doing "too much." James Farley, chairman of the Democratic party, warned Roosevelt that "The one criticism which is being constantly hammered home and which seems to be having the most effect is the charge that the President and his Administration are carrying on an orgy of public spending. . . ."[8]

Farley's opinion was widely held. After resigning as Roosevelt's director of the budget because he believed that the president was spending too much, Lewis Douglas wrote the president: "I hope, and hope most fervently, that you will evidence a real determination to bring the budget into actual balance, for upon this, I think, hangs not only your place in history but conceivably the immediate fate of western civilization."[9] Ironically, Roosevelt himself worried that he was spending too much money. In 1937, when the economy seemed on the way toward a modest recovery (as we can see from Chart 2), he slashed spending, sharply cut the rolls of the WPA, and turned off the "pump-priming" expenditures of the PWA.

The result was disconcerting. Government expenditures fell by a billion dollars—but gross national product fell by $5 billion! Out of the blue, another selling wave hit the stock market, which dropped a staggering 40 percent. Worst of all, unemployment jumped from 7.7 million to over 10 million.

There was very little choice as to what to do next. The PWA was hurriedly given additional funds; government spending increased by over $1 billion; unemployment slowly fell to 9.4 million in 1939, then to 8 million in 1940. The country resumed its sluggish recovery. In 1939, gross national product went up to $111 billion—just above the 1937 level—and finally, in 1940, it climbed to $121 billion, surpassing by a mere 16 percent the level of 1929.

Stagnation and Fear

What *was* the trouble? No one was very sure at the time. One much-discussed thesis was that the American economy had entered a period of long-run stagnation. Economic growth in the past, it was argued, had stemmed mainly from two sources—population growth and technological improvements. Both of these were powerful stimuli for business investment: population growth offering new markets for housing and consumer goods in general, and technology opening new areas for capital investment. The problem of the late 1930s, it was said, resulted in large part from an undoubted slowing down of population. Most demographers thought that the United States would soon have a stationary population. This meant that the entire burden of growth would be thrust on the shoulders of technology. And no new industry-building technology comparable to the automobile industry seemed on the horizon. To the "stagnationists," the only remedy was to accept government spending as a permanent ingredient in the total economy.

The stagnation theorists were wrong about the future trend of population and wrong about the prospects for technology. But they were not wrong about the permanent addition of government spending to the economic system. The trouble was, however, that virtually no businessmen were able to envisage or understand such a change from the ideals of a laissez faire society.

Thus, looking back, we can see that much of the stagnation was in fact caused by the *belief* that the New Deal was doing "too much." Frightened by the policies of an activist, anti-laissez-faire administration, the business community never gained enough confidence to bring its own spending for investment purposes up to the levels of the 1920s. In 1929, businesses had poured $16 billion into new equipment, new plants, and home and office building. In 1937, the best year of the early New Deal, private investment was only $11.7 billion (and it fell to half that the following year).

Thus the critics were not entirely wrong when they blamed the doldrums on the policies of the New Deal, with its "dangerous" spending proclivities. But the critics were right only because the business community was so alarmed by New Deal spending that business spending for investment never regained its pre-1929 momentum.

The Dilemma of the Government

Indeed, from our present-day perspective, we can see a quite different reason for the failure of the New Deal spending program. *The New Deal did not spend nearly enough!* Precisely because business did not spend predepression amounts for investment, the full-scale application of Keynesian policies would have meant that the government should have spent twice or even three times as much as it did, financing its spending by borrowing money from the public in exchange for government bonds.

But that truly bold policy was quite impossible in a period when even the modest measures of the New Deal were enough to inspire fears of "socialism" and when government borrowing was not seen as an alternative to private investment borrowing but as a reckless and dangerous policy. Thus the New Dealers were caught in a trap. They were unable to spend enough to restore the full momentum of growth, but they were also unable to cut back their spending programs without sending the economy into a tailspin.

The War

No one knows how this dilemma of policy might have eventually been resolved, for suddenly events took a dramatic change that provided a decisive demonstration of the power of government spending. In 1939 war broke out in Europe; in December 1941 the Japanese bombed Pearl Harbor. Suddenly the nation found itself in a position of peril before which all quarrels about economic policy seemed trivial. The clear necessity, to which all agreed, was to mount a gigantic war effort—to build an armada for the sea, and another for the air, and simultaneously to equip a vast army for the land. All this required the expenditure of stupendous sums, and no one worried about the fact that only government could raise those sums by taxing and borrowing. Again Keynes was correct, for in 1940 he wrote: "It seems politically impossible for a capitalistic democracy to organize expenditure on the scale necessary to make the grand experiment which would prove my case—except in war conditions."[10]

Thus government spending skyrocketed—in the first six months of 1942 the government placed over $100 billion in contracts. GNP boomed. And unemployment quickly fell almost to zero:

	Federal Purchases ($ billions)	GNP ($ billions)	Unemployment (millions)
The Effects of War Spending (current prices)			
1940	6.2	100.6	8.1
1941	19.9	125.8	5.6
1942	52.0	159.1	2.7
1943	81.2	192.5	1.1
1944	89.0	211.4	.7
1945	74.8	312.6	1.0

To be sure, with the outpouring of military spending there was some inflation—consumer prices were about 28 percent higher in 1945 than they had been in 1940.* But even if we adjust the GNP figures for this inflationary influence, there is no doubt that growth was fully resumed. Chart 3 shows us the dip caused by the cutback in

---

*Price ceilings imposed by the government helped prevent much greater wartime inflation.

Chart 3 THE 1938 SLUMP

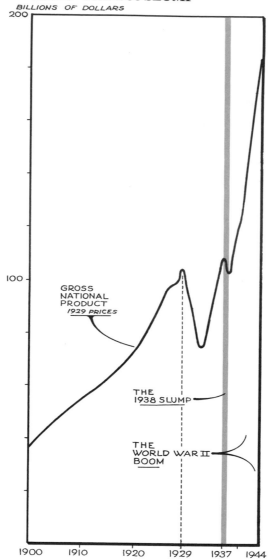

BILLIONS OF DOLLARS
200

GROSS
NATIONAL
PRODUCT
1929 PRICES

100

THE
1938 SLUMP

THE
WORLD WAR II
BOOM

1900   1910   1920   1929   1937   1944

spending in 1937, and then the great surge that followed with the
onset of spending during the war. (The figures have eliminated inflation in a manner we will discuss in Chapter 11.)

Many volumes have been written about the Second World War.
Most of us study the war as a heroic chapter in the defense of democracy, or as a great contest between rival political systems. Yet, if we
think back on Chapter 1, we will recall that history can be "read"

from many angles, bringing into focus themes that give it special meaning for different purposes.

As students of economic history, we "read" the chapter of the Second World War in an unusual light, just as we read the history of the Civil War in an unaccustomed way. From our perspective, it is the burst of economic growth brought about by war spending that provides the main lesson. It shows that government spending can indeed play a decisive role in creating economic expansion, just as private investment spending did in the past. This lesson has had profound consequences for our time. For if government spending for war purposes can bring about economic expansion, why should we not use government spending to bring about economic expansion for peacetime purposes? As we will see, this is a question that has deeply influenced thinking about the problem of growth in today's economy.

NOTES

[1] *The Public Papers and Addresses of Franklin D. Roosevelt*, II (1938), 11ff.

[2] *How We Elect Our Presidents* (1952), p. 141.

[3] Raymond Moley, *After Seven Years* (1939), p. 155.

[4] *Public Papers and Addresses*, II, 93–94.

[5] *Roosevelt: The Lion and the Fox* (1956), p. 218.

[6] *Public Papers and Addresses*, IV (1938), 325.

[7] Quoted in Arthur Schlesinger, Jr., *The Coming of the New Deal* (1958), p. 311.

[8] Quoted in Arthur Schlesinger, Jr., *The Politics of Upheaval* (1960), p. 621.

[9] Quoted in William Leuchtenburg, *Franklin D. Roosevelt and the New Deal* (1963), p. 91.

[10] Quoted in Richard Hofstadter, *The Age of Reform* (1955), p. 309.

The Mixed Economy   11

The war was over in 1945, and the nation waited anxiously to see what would happen once war spending stopped. From 1945 to 1946, federal expenditures fell by over $50 billion, from $83 billion to $31 billion. Gross national product declined from $214 billion to $211 billion. And unemployment doubled, from one million to two million.

POSTWAR GROWTH

President Truman was worried about the future of the economy, especially about inflation. The rationing of scarce goods, such as gasoline, had ended in 1945, and Congress passed a bill cutting taxes by some $6 billion. Consumers had piled up savings of $150 billion during the war, and Truman feared, quite correctly, that those savings could give rise to an inflationary binge of household spending before the economy had reconverted to consumer-goods production.

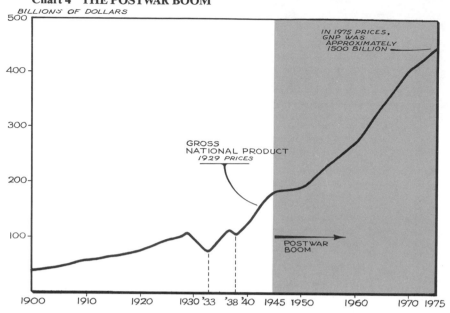

Chart 4 THE POSTWAR BOOM

BILLIONS OF DOLLARS

IN 1975 PRICES, GNP WAS APPROXIMATELY 1500 BILLION

GROSS NATIONAL PRODUCT 1929 PRICES

POSTWAR BOOM

We will return to the problem of inflation. But even more worrisome to Truman was the prospect that the stagnation of the late 1930s might resume once the spending spree was over. Here, happily, he was wrong. For despite the dislocations associated with the end of the war, and the gloomy predictions of many forecasters, the economic ship of state forged full speed ahead. By 1947, as GNP rose to $234 billion, it seemed likely that the country would avoid a recession. By 1950, with GNP nearing $300 billion, it was clear that the economy had left the doldrums and was caught up again in a powerful current of growth along the historic trajectory of the past. We see this in Chart 4, where the figures are somewhat lower because we have eliminated inflation.

What accounted for the upward surge? One cause was that Americans did indeed lose no time in spending their war savings, on household goods and durable goods alike. This household buying made up for much of the slump in war spending. A second reason, which we will examine in greater detail later, is that renewed business confidence sparked a boom in private investment spending. And a third reason is that total government spending did not decline as precipitously as expected. Federal expenditure did fall for two years. But thereafter, government spending began to rise again, spearheaded by state and local outlays for schools and roads, then augmented by a jump in federal spending with the onset of the Korean War in 1950.

The statistics of postwar growth are dizzying. By 1960, GNP had reached $500 billion. In 1971 it passed the trillion-dollar mark. Before 1980, despite the recession of 1973–75, it is virtually certain to reach $2 trillion. Hence this is a good place to interrupt our narrative and inquire into this major indicator of growth. Exactly what does a trillion-dollar GNP mean?

The Meaning of $1,000,000,000,000

We can best answer the question by comparing the trillion-dollar GNP of 1971 with two other GNPs. In 1929, GNP was $104 billion—for simplicity's sake, let us round that off to an even $100 billion. In 1865, when the sixty years of massive industrialization began, GNP was (in very rough numbers) $10 billion. Thus our question involves a comparison of these benchmark years. Does a trillion-dollar GNP mean that the United States was ten times richer in 1971 than in 1929? A hundred times richer than in 1865?

Americans may live a great deal better today than in 1865, and they certainly live a great deal differently; but no one would claim that they are a hundred times richer. It's even hard to know what we might mean by being a hundred times richer: Would we eat a hundred times as much food per person? How, then, shall we compare a $10 billion GNP in 1865 with a $1 trillion GNP a little more than a century later?

Per Capita GNP

The first difference is evident: population. As we know, gross national product measures the value of our annual total final output. But in 1865 there were 36 million Americans; in 1929, 121 million; in 1971, 207 million. Therefore, to find what a trillion-dollar GNP "means," the first requirement is to try to reduce it to GNP per person, or *per capita*. The table below shows the result:

	Approximate GNP ($ billions)	Population (millions)	GNP Per Capita ($)
	Total and Per Capita GNP		
1865	10	36	278
1929	100	121	826
1971	1,000	207	4,830

This immediately reduces the problem to more manageable size. GNP per capita in 1971 was not ten times, but only about six times bigger than in 1929; not a hundred times, but about seventeen times bigger than in 1865.

Applying a Price Index

We are now ready to allow for a second difference: inflation. The best price index we have tells us that prices fell from 1865 to 1929 by about 25 percent—that a dollar in 1929 bought about 25 percent more goods and services than a dollar in 1865. Between 1929 and 1971, on the other hand, the index shows that prices roughly trip-

Prices in 1932

led—that a dollar in 1971 bought only a third as much as a dollar in 1929.

With these data, we can gain a better grasp of what growth actually was from one date to the next. If we divide per capita GNP by our price index, we will be able to compare one period to another as if there had been no change in prices. As the statistician would put it, we would then compare "real" GNPs per capita—that is, per capita GNPs expressed in dollars of equal purchasing power.

Real GNP Per Capita					
	Per Capita GNP *(current dollars)*		*Price Index*		*Real GNP Per Capita*
1865	$ 278	÷	100 (× 100)	=	$ 278
1929	$ 826	÷	75 "	=	$1,101
1971	$4,830	÷	225 "	=	$2,147

Real GNP Per Capita

The table above shows us that real GNP per capita in 1929 was about four times as high as in 1865. It shows that real GNP per capita in 1971 was roughly double the level of 1929, and about eight times as high as in 1865.

Working with price indexes is the only way that we can "deflate" GNP statistics—that is, wring the inflation out of numbers such as the huge trillion-dollar sums of the 1970s. As we can see, price indexes reduce the difference in growth by a large amount. Real growth per capita since 1865 is less than half the growth that shows up in the figures before we correct for inflation. From 1929 to 1971, the real percentage growth in GNP per capita is 194 percent, not the 584 percent that the uncorrected figures show.

Income Distribution

The figures still do not give us all the information we need to compare one period with another, for they do not show how incomes were distributed in the two periods. Did the gap between rich and poor increase or diminish as average real incomes roughly doubled from 1929 to the present? The next table shows that there was a significantly more equal sharing of incomes in 1971 than in 1929:

Distribution of Family Income (Before Taxes)		
	(percent of all income)	
	1929	*1971*
Lowest 40 percent of families	12.5	17.4
Next 40 percent	33.1	41.1
Top 20 percent	54.4	41.6
Top 5 percent	30.0	14.4

Experts in income-distribution statistics warn us that these comparisons can be deceptive, especially at the top of the income pyramid. As taxes rise—and they rose steeply over the period—high-income receivers use such means as capital gains to receive wealth that is not technically classified as "income." Nonetheless there is general agreement that a substantial movement toward equality occurred between 1929 and 1971, and that the share of income going to the topmost group declined significantly.

THE DECLINE OF LAISSEZ FAIRE

We shall shortly examine the question of what may have caused our powerful and persistent inflation. But first we must return to our narrative of economic growth and transformation. For when we look behind the nation's escape from the doldrums of the 1930s, one central development stands out: *The business community had begun to see the government as a supporter of and stimulant for economic expansion.*

The figures for the beginning of the postwar boom reveal this new attitude. We see on page 215 that as public spending rose after its immediate postwar dip, *private investment spending also rose.* It dipped in 1949, but it rose again with government spending in 1951.

This suggests that a change had come over the business community. Perhaps as a result of the boom caused by spending during the Second World War, perhaps because the business estimate of Roosevelt's policies was already mellowing, perhaps because the work of Keynes was becoming standard fare in colleges and business

Public Spending and Private Investment (in billions)		
	Government Spending (federal, state, and local)	Business Investment
1945	$83	$10
1946	31	28
1947	28	32
1948	35	43
1949	40	33
1950	39	50
1951	61	56

schools—for whatever reason, the suspicions and fears of the business world had largely vanished. As the prestigious Rockefeller Panel Reports stated in 1958:

> Public expenditures in support of growth are an essential part of our economy. Far from being a hindrance to progress, they provide the environment within which our economy moves forward.[1]

The change was not merely a growing understanding and acceptance of government spending. A whole new philosophy of a "mixed" economy was slowly replacing that of laissez faire. In the mixed economy the government was recognized by all sectors, including business, as being charged with the responsibility for maintaining the forward motion of the system. The government was expected to spend heavily when there was a slack in the economy and to curtail its expenditures when the private sector was buoyant.

In addition, the government was generally conceded to be the appropriate agency for safeguarding the welfare of its citizens. Individual men and women were no longer urged to provide economic security for themselves solely by private saving. Everyone recognized that that was no longer realistic. Nor was the support of the poor entrusted to acts of private philanthropy. A "welfare" state was now approved by all as a necessary complement to American society. Welfare expenditures—for social security, unemployment compensation, health assistance, even for a minimum of guaranteed incomes—were regarded by business as a source of economic strength, not economic weakness.

The Changing Role of Government

To be sure, the idea of a mixed economy did not emerge overnight or without resistance. In retrospect, we can see that it began with the passage, under President Truman, of the Employment Act of 1946, which committed the federal government to the promotion of "maximum" employment through fiscal and monetary means.

The Employment Act marked a new stage in the evolution of government's role in the economy. Originally, as we have seen, the government was a *promoter* of business, underwriting "internal improvements," granting land to railroads, and helping infant industries to take root. A second stage was the emergence of the government as a *regulator* of the economy, using its powers to assure the orderly working of individual markets or industries. (Witness the emergence of the ICC and the antitrust policies of the late nineteenth century.) With the Employment Act came a third stage. The government now took on the function of *guarantor*, taking as its prime objective the maintenance of socially acceptable rates of growth and levels of employment.

The transition of the national government from promoter, to regulator, to guarantor of economic growth gained further support under President Eisenhower and a conservative Republican Congress. "If I do anything," Eisenhower said after his first inaugural, "it's going to be less government and not more government."[2] Yet the exigencies of the time forced him to abandon many of his ideas and to extend many of the "welfare" provisions of the New Deal. By the time Eisenhower left office in 1961, his administration had incurred an overall deficit of $18.2 billion, the highest deficit incurred in peacetime years up to that point. Under Eisenhower, moreover, social security benefits were extended to an additional 10 million Americans, and a vast new Department of Health, Education and Welfare had been created.

More Intervention

The idea of a mixed economy became still more explicit under John F. Kennedy, to whom it was a foregone conclusion that government intervention in the economy was a necessity. Under his presidency, the government entered into economic affairs much more freely than it had under Eisenhower. Wage guidelines were initiated to help dampen the wage-price spiral of inflation. Minimum wages were further increased and social security extended. Assistance was provided for regional development of the backwater areas of the country.

But Kennedy's greatest departure from traditional economic policy took place in January 1963. The economy was hesitating on the verge of what seemed to be a potentially serious recession, with rising unemployment levels. Urged on by his advisers, Kennedy proposed a bold step. He asked Congress to reduce taxes by $10 billion *without reducing government spending*. That is, he asked Congress deliberately to incur a government deficit, using the government's borrowing powers to finance its spending. The result, he explained, would be a stimulus to the economy, because consumers would have more money to spend. As GNP rose, government tax revenues would also rise, and in the end the budget would be balanced at a higher level of GNP than if there had been no tax cut to stimulate total output.*

Kennedy's proposal to incur a deliberate government deficit produced a furor, and the tax cut was not actually passed until Lyndon Johnson assumed the presidency after Kennedy's death. By that time the idea had begun to win the approval of much of the business community; today the federal government does not hesitate to stimulate the economy by incurring deficits on a much larger scale than Kennedy had dared to suggest. In his budget for 1972, for example, President Nixon projected a deficit of almost $40 billion to ward off a depression of potentially dangerous proportions.

Johnson extended the idea of the mixed economy in other directions. His program for a Great Society brought new departures for government, including direct aid to the nation's elementary and secondary public schools and a far-reaching program of Medicare. And to cap the general movement toward a mixed economic system, President Nixon, a staunch conservative, intervened in the economy on an unprecedented scale when he froze all wages, salaries, rents, and prices for a ninety-day period in 1971 and then initiated a succession of "phases" of wage and price controls to curb inflation.

---

* The question of government deficits is a complicated one, better covered in an economics course than in a survey of economic growth. A key aspect of the problem lies in the "internal" character of government debts. By internal, we mean that a government debt is usually held by its own citizens. Because government has the power to tax, it can always raise the necessary funds to pay off its bonds when they come due, or to pay interest on them. By way of contrast, a corporation, no matter how large, has no way of forcing people to buy its products so that it can pay back its debts. The power to tax is what makes government debts entirely different from private debts. That is why it is said, quite correctly, that a government debt, held by its own citizens, is a debt that a nation owes to itself.

The Commitment to Growth

We cannot review here all the legislation that has gone into the creation of a new relation of government to the economy. But one central theme emerges with clarity: *The government has become committed to the maintenance of economic growth and stability as a major aim of its overall policy.* This is by no means a development that we find only in the United States. Indeed, if we look at other advanced industrial countries, we find that our mixed economy is very similar to theirs. If anything, the amount of government spending in GNP is smaller in the United States than in many nations abroad:

Government Spending as Percent of GNP, 1972

France	37
West Germany	38
Italy	40
United Kingdom	40
United States	34

Does this mean that our economy is now free from the dangers that killed the prosperity of the 1920s?

We know from the experience of the mid-1970s that it does not. We can still have stock market collapses, although the regulation of margins and bank loans for the purchase of securities makes the effects of a "crash" less dangerous than in 1929. We can still have business and banking failures, although the insurance of bank deposits virtually removes the individual disasters that such failures caused in the past. We can still have heavy unemployment, too, although the existence of unemployment insurance helps to mitigate that social evil.

Thus many of the elements of serious depressions are still to be found in the economy. What has changed is a passive attitude that allows these elements to exert a snowballing effect. The spiral of falling income, spreading from business to household and back to business, is no longer permitted to run its course unchecked. The result is that we can still expect economic reverses, but not an economic rout.

America Compared to Europe

Finally, we should not exaggerate the degree to which the possibilities of a mixed economy have been accepted or realized in the

American economy. As with all changes in ideas and ideologies, the old persists along with the new. This is particularly the case in the United States, where the traditions of rugged individualism and Social Darwinism were accepted in a much more fervent, even semireligious, way than was the case in Europe. As a result, the embrace of a mixed system has been much easier to achieve in Europe, and its use for social as well as economic goals has been pressed much more boldly. In 1971, for example, when unemployment was reaching 6 percent in this country, the level of unemployment in West Germany was 0.7 percent, in France 2.1 percent, in Denmark 1.1 percent. Unemployment subsequently rose to 10 percent here, but it never rose to such terrible heights abroad.

Again, a good part of the "mix" in the mixed American economy has been arms expenditure. About a third of all U.S. federal spending since 1950 has been for arms. In the period 1965–75, $600 billion was spent for weapons, only $6 billion for federal housing. Had the international situation permitted a drastic cut in arms, could the American system have accepted a wholly reversed proportion of social and military spending? Probably not. Certainly there exists a new economic structure in the United States—a structure committed to a much greater degree of publicly guaranteed economic guidance and welfare than in 1929. But we know that lingering ideas of laissez faire limit the reach of the mixed economy in its American version.

PROBLEMS OF A MIXED ECONOMY

All this makes it clear that the evolution of a new economic mechanism has by no means solved the problems of economic growth and transformation. Indeed, it suggests that the advent of the mixed economy brings problems of its own—problems endemic to the new public-private economic structure, just as the old (and, as we have seen, not yet wholly rejected) system of laissez faire brought its own problems. Let us now examine some of the issues that seem to inhere within the mixed system.

Inflation

We have already touched on one of those issues. It is the steady, apparently irreversible, rise in prices that has eroded the well-being of consumers since the days of the Truman administration.

The arms economy

Of course, inflation is not a wholly new experience for the United States or for other Western societies. Throughout history, every war has been marked by an upward movement of prices. During the Civil War, for example, prices almost doubled; and they more than doubled in the First World War. During the Second World War, despite the presence of price controls, the price level rose by 50 percent.

But the inflation since 1945 has been of a different kind. First, much of it took place in peacetime—before and after the Korean and Vietnam wars as well as during them. Second, it is an inflation that persisted during periods of recession, when prices ordinarily would have fallen or at least stabilized. And last, it is an inflation that has been experienced by all nations of the world, not just by the United States. Indeed, during 1973 and 1974, when the United States was suffering "double digit" inflation—inflation of more than 10 percent a year—in many countries of Europe and in Japan inflation had reached rates of 20 percent a year and more.

What is the source of this inflationary phenomenon? There is no clear answer. Unlike the case of depressions, where Keynes' ideas about an inadequacy of spending give us a simple way of grasping the kernel of a complex issue, we have no theory of inflation that explains its persistence or its powerful momentum.

We do, of course, have some knowledge of why prices have risen so insistently. There has been an expansion of the supply of money that has raced ahead of the supply of goods. There has been a tremendous diversion of United States production into war-related goods, as a consequence of the Vietnam War, coupled with a failure to tax away war-related incomes and profits. In addition, a series of disasters has affected various products. Food supplies became scarce in 1973 following a year of poor weather around the globe, and agricultural prices soared. Oil supplies became tight after the oil embargo in 1973, and oil prices quadrupled. Highly concentrated industries pushed for high profits rather than for high volume. These events certainly contributed to the rise in prices.

The Roots of Inflation

Yet none of these explanations seems quite adequate to explain the inflation that has lasted so long and has affected so many nations, including those without large military budgets. But there is one plausible hypothesis to which we should pay attention, because it is directly connected with the developments we have studied in this chapter. It is that the underlying cause of the malady may be the spread of the mixed economy itself. In the combination of growth-mindedness and welfare-mindedness we may have a basic change in outlook and behavior that spells the difference between relative price stability and chronic inflation.

Why should a mixed economy give rise to inflation? One reason is that the assurance of growth means that business enterprises no longer anticipate a bust for every boom. Convinced that depressions are a "thing of the past," corporations can pursue their policies of expansion much more confidently than in the old days. Thus they break the old rhythm of the business cycle, which interrupted growth from time to time and caused inflated prices to turn downward.

Related to this development is the change in the power of labor in mixed economies. No longer is labor limited in its power to seek wage raises by the relatively weak ability of workers to carry on a strike. Large union treasuries, unemployment compensation, and a back-stop of welfare benefits make the staying power of a striking union far greater than in the past. This may explain why the percentage of GNP going to wages has increased in every modern capitalist society, as well as why wages have generally risen faster than productivity in those societies.

That inflation is a product of a mixed economy is only a hypothesis, not a clearly established fact. Perhaps inflation will wane as mysteriously as it appeared. But there is nothing yet to indicate that it will. Rather, it seems likely that the combined pressures of business spending and government spending, and the enhanced bargaining power of labor, will make an inflationary tendency an integral part of any mixed economy that strives for high levels of employment and welfare. If this is the case, we will have to devise measures to deal with inflation as we have had to devise means of coping with depression. In all likelihood those measures will entail a still greater degree of government intervention into the economy, very possibly along the lines of permanent wage and price controls. This is a matter that we cannot decide at the moment. The decision will be a major item on the political agenda of the years to come.

The Multinational Corporation

A second aspect of the mixed economy brings us back to a familiar subject—the rise and role of giant enterprise. We have seen that J. P. Morgan capitalized United States Steel at $1.4 billion in 1901. At that time it was the biggest industrial corporation in the United States. In the mid-1970s, United States Steel's assets were valued at

The corporation goes abroad

$8.1 billion,* but it was no longer even among the top ten industrial corporations. By then the biggest industrial corporation—Exxon—had assets worth $45 billion.

These figures reintroduce the problem of business concentration, which we last examined in Chapter 6. The basic thrust we saw then is still highly visible. In the late 1940s the biggest *two hundred* industrial corporations in the nation owned about half of the total assets of all manufacturing corporations. By the mid-1970s the biggest *one hundred* corporations owned half of all manufacturing assets. "Some of these corporations," wrote A. A. Berle, an astute observer of the trend toward concentration, "can be thought of only in somewhat the way we have heretofore thought of nations."[3]

Has this continued trend toward bigness and concentration of power been a product of the mixed economy? That does not seem to be the case. The trend began, as we know, in the days of laissez faire. The problem of what to do about the giant corporation is still very much unresolved, but it is not new.

* Prices in 1971 were roughly five times as high as in 1901. Thus the *real* increase in the value of U.S. Steel assets was very small: from $1.4 billion in 1901 to $1.6 billion ($8.1 billion ÷ 5) in 1971.

What *is* new is the rise of the *multinational corporation*. Multinationals are not merely giant companies. They are corporations that consider the entire world, not just the United States, as their market. Among the top 100 U.S. industrial companies, 62 have branches in six or more countries. The total value of their plants and equipment located outside the United States is well in excess of $100 billion.

The multinationals remind us of a tendency toward international expansion that began in the mid-nineteenth century. We have already traced the growth pattern of successful corporations that brought them first up to, and then beyond, the shores of their national market. The Singer Sewing Machine Company, with its great plant in Scotland in 1897, was thus the precursor of companies like Pepsico, which now produces its famous drink in 114 countries, or General Motors or Ford or IBM, which produce their products or components in literally scores of nations. Just to make the phenomenon concrete, consider the following table:*

GNPs of Various Countries, Compared with Sales of Selected Multinational Corporations (Billions of 1971 Dollars)

Netherlands	$39.4	Royal Dutch/Shell	$12.7
Belgium	31.7	Unilever	11.5
General Motors	28.3	Greece	10.8
Switzerland	26.3	General Electric	9.4
Exxon	18.7	IBM	8.3
Denmark	18.2	Mobil	8.2
Austria	17.8	Chrysler	8.0
Ford	16.4	Texaco	7.5
Norway	15.6	Portugal	7.3

* Warning: corporate sales are not the same as GNPs. The table vastly overstates the importance of the multinationals with respect to manpower; for example, GM employs fewer than 1 million persons, whereas Greece has a population of 9 million. On the other hand, the table understates the economic strength of corporations: GM can borrow a great deal more easily than Greece, and it controls all its receipts, whereas the government of Greece gets only taxes from its GNP. Nevertheless the table makes it clear that Berle's comparison was not wholly fanciful.

We should add that multinationals are by no means just American firms. They exist in every Western country and in Japan as well. As an example, Nestlé, the chocolate firm, is a vast Swiss enterprise. But 95 percent of its business is conducted outside Switzerland. By and large, multinationalism is as advanced in Europe and Japan as it is here.

Imperialism

The multinationals remind us of a question that we first raised in Chapter 5. To what extent has our economic growth depended on the penetration of foreign markets by American enterprise? Is multinationalism simply the latest form of a very old pattern of imperialism?

There is no question that foreign markets have contributed to our growth. Historians disagree only on the extent, not the fact, that exports or foreign production have assisted our economic expansion, and that access to cheap raw materials abroad has accelerated our industrial development. This search for foreign markets and raw materials is still a very noticeable aspect of the capitalist system— here and elsewhere.

But we should at least note one change that the modern multinationals have brought. They are less concerned than the corporations of the 1890s or 1920s with exploiting the economies of the poorer, underdeveloped economies, and more interested in tapping the economies of other rich business societies. Imperialism in the nineteenth century meant the domination by corporations of weak producers of raw materials, such as the banana republics, or the corporate penetration of weak markets, such as Standard Oil's famous sales campaign: "Oil for the lamps of China." Today, the nations that produce the raw materials are imposing ever-tighter conditions on the corporations that utilize those materials, and a number of the old international companies have been seized and nationalized. Even more to the point, the multinationals are no longer primarily interested in selling oil for the lamps of China; they want to sell computers for the industries of Europe and Japan. They have concentrated their main marketing thrust on other capitalist economies with advanced technology and high purchasing power. Although they continue to exercise great influence on many of the economies of the Third World, in the long historical view that influence seems to be waning, not increasing.

Multinationals and the Mixed Economy

But from the point of view of our interest in the mixed economy, the rise of the multinationals poses another problem. For the essence of the mixed economy is a greater degree of government control over, or responsibility for, many aspects of that economy. And yet the multinationals, by choosing either to keep their profits abroad or to send them home, can play hob with the policies of their government on the foreign exchange market. By building plants overseas rather than at home, they can create jobs for foreign nationals rather than for domestic workers. Indeed, some enthusiasts see the multinational as an ultimate successor to the nation-state itself—a truly international entity, no longer bound by old-fashioned political borders but pursuing its program of production and distribution on a global scale, almost indifferent to the wishes of the various nations in whose territories it may locate a portion of its activities.

Thus, at the very time when the mixed economy has begun to strike a new balance between business and government, business has upset that balance by leaping over the borders of national sovereignty. It is unlikely that corporations will ever outmode the state, for the pull of national identity and political sovereignty seems much stronger than that of company identity or economic efficiency. Yet there is no doubt that the multinationals present new challenges to the idea of a mixed economy. We can do no more than identify the problem today. It too will have to be added to tomorrow's agenda of political business.

The Drift Toward Planning

The rise of the multinational gives us one further insight into the mixed economy. For the multinational represents an extension on a hitherto unimagined scale of a trend that we first saw in the late nineteenth century with David McCallum's treelike table of organization. This is the effort to *plan* the flow of production and distribution over which the corporation presides. In essence, the multinational is an attempt to organize a coherent structure of business activity on an international rather than a national scale.

This extension of corporate planning is a prime element in the mixed economy of our times. We tend to think of the mixed system as primarily one of augmented governmental authority over economic activity. That is certainly one aspect of the system. But it is paralleled by the growth of authority within the world of private production. As John Kenneth Galbraith has pointed out, large-scale business more and more tries to look ahead, to reduce the uncertainties of the marketplace, to arrange long-term contracts with its labor force and its suppliers. Although no business is large enough to control the environment in which it operates—not even government is powerful enough to do that!—its efforts can best be understood as an attempt to plan its growth, rather than to move haphazardly or opportunistically ahead, as did the small firms of the nineteenth century.

Within the government sector too, planning seems to be the direction in which things are moving. The planning need not resemble that of the great centralized monolith of the Soviet Union. Planning can take many forms, concentrating on particular areas such as energy or transportation, or extending its concerns to wider issues such as inflation. But assuredly the growth of the mixed economy has replaced the ideal of laissez faire with that of consciously directed economic movement. Under laissez faire, social movement was subject to the collective actions of business firms and the wholly unforeseeable evolution of technology. Under a mixed economy those prime movers are still at work, but nations are more and more determined to exert their political will over the shape of things that business and technology produce. Thus the political side of society—its collective decision-making—takes on added importance, and the purely economic side—the workings of the market mechanism—begins to recede as a dominant force.

In 1914 Walter Lippmann, the most thoughtful of all conservative commentators on American affairs, wrote a book titled *Drift and Mastery*. As we have seen, the history of nineteenth-century America was not just "drift" but growth; and the record of the mixed economy by no means yet demonstrates "mastery" over economic affairs. Nonetheless, the emergence of a mixed economy is an assertion of our *intention* to master our destiny. Much of the rest of this book will be an effort to take the measure of that challenge.

NOTES

[1] *Prospect for America,* p. 279.
[2] Quoted in Herbert Parmet, *Eisenhower* (1972), p. 174.
[3] *Economic Power and the Free Society* (1957), p. 15.

PART FOUR

Growth and Its Limitations

The Failures of Growth

12

GROWTH AND WELL-BEING

In the chapters behind us we have looked at various aspects of our economic transformation, stressing in turn growth, mechanization and industrialization, and systemic change. Now, in this final section, we are about to consider a final aspect of that transformation—one that brings together those subthemes into a new perspective: the *limitations of growth*.

The word *limitations* has two meanings, both of which apply here. The first has to do with our *physical capacity* for continued growth—with the question of whether or not expansion can continue. That is a matter of very grave importance from the point of view of our transformation, for the impending end to growth—and there *is* such an impending end—carries the likelihood of substantial institutional change.

But before we can inquire into that problem we must look at the second meaning of the word *limitations*. This has to do with the restricted abilities of our changing, enlarging, industrializing system to satisfy our personal and social needs. Here *limitations* refers to the *failures and disappointments of our economic experience.*

Money and Happiness

The second, psychological, meaning of limitations raises a fundamental question—a question seemingly so simple and self-evident that we might at first dismiss it as foolish. The question is whether wealth, the chief result of economic growth, brings contentment, well-being, happiness. The very thought smacks a little of a pious sermon. But we can approach the matter objectively, and the results are surprising.

Between 1946 and 1970 eleven surveys have been conducted in the United States on the correlation of income and happiness. In each one, public opinion poll-takers asked a representative sample of citizens: "Are you happy?" After each answer was recorded—"yes," "no," "fairly happy"—the income of the respondent was ascertained. Thereupon a simple statistical test was run to match the percentage of reported "happiness" against the level of income of the respondent.[1]

The immediate results are much as we would expect. Invariably the surveys revealed that "happiness" was reported by a significantly larger proportion of rich than poor people.* From this finding, we would expect to discover a systematic change in the eleven surveys with the passing of time. Over the quarter-century of the inquiries, as a result of economic growth, the absolute incomes of all members of American society had risen. Families at the bottom of the scale in 1970 earned incomes that were the equivalent of families in the middle brackets in 1946. In other words, all families were standing on an economic escalator, rising together as economic growth increased income at every level.

Therefore, as money incomes rose, for all families, we would expect

---

* A statistician would properly ask whether the cause-effect relationship might not run from happiness to wealth, not from wealth to happiness. That is, happier people might make more money *because* they were happy. To test against this, the poll-takers inquired into the reasons for unhappiness. Three main reasons were reported: personal problems, ill-health, and lack of money. Since wealth would eliminate the third reason and would help cope with the second, there is good reason to think that money was the cause, not the effect, of happiness.

The well-stuffed life

the proportion of persons reporting "happiness" to increase and the proportion of those reporting unhappiness to decrease. *But that is not what we find.* Despite the rise in incomes at all levels, the percentage of happy and unhappy people has remained the same over the twenty-five years of the surveys.

Why this failure of money to bring happiness? The main reason, according to Richard Easterlin, an economist who has examined the data, is that the concepts of "rich" and "poor" are not determined by the absolute number of dollars one receives, but by the relative position a family occupies along the income scale. A "poor" family in America may receive a dollar income that would make it a rich family in some other country, but that does not lessen its feeling of deprivation and poverty at home. Visitors to America from underdeveloped lands marvel at first at the cars and TV antennas in the slums and cannot believe that slumdwellers are not rich. Soon, however, they learn that the *feeling* of poverty is not determined by what a family possesses so much as by what *other* families possess. Therefore, the very fact that all families ride upward together on the escalator serves to maintain the feeling of relative poverty among those who are at the lower end. Increases in everyone's money income, it follows, do not bring happiness.

Growing Entitlements

Another reason why the results of economic growth do not enhance our feeling of happiness is that our sense of "entitlements" rises along with our actual achievements. The benefits of higher incomes are at first sharply experienced and keenly enjoyed—when we get a raise in pay, or move into a bigger home, or buy an automobile. Then our enjoyment fades as we become accustomed to our new advantages and assume that they are normal and necessary. Have not our parents told us that we were lucky to be born when we were, instead of in the hard times they knew when they were our age? Do any of us feel lucky?

These same sobering considerations apply to the results of economic growth that appear as new products. Our grandparents may have experienced a thrill when they installed their first telephone. It soon became a necessary nuisance. So, too, our parents may have acutely experienced the pleasures of their first car or TV set. They have long since forgotten that moment.

Growth thus cancels out the gains of new wealth by raising our threshold of expectations. Moreover, there is no reason to regard this ever-rising sense of entitlement as a moral failure on our part. As members of the human collectivity we are all sharers in the advances that humankind has made and continues to make. We do not celebrate in our daily lives the taming of fire or the domestication of animals or the invention of writing. Yet these milestones of economic growth assuredly brought enormous increases in well-being in their day.

The Real Gains from Growth

These reflections make us recognize that the economic transformation we have witnessed must not be confused with a long upward march of well-being. We know that in terms of real income we are twice as "rich" as our parents and eight times as well endowed with purchasing power as our antecedents in 1865; but we must resist the conclusion that we are twice as well off, much less eight times so.

Of course there have been improvements. Some of them are susceptible to exact measure, such as the increase in longevity, the gradual conquest of various diseases, the increased space per person in our houses, the richer diet, the more varied possibilities for spending our incomes.

Yet when we begin to look carefully into these changes we can see that many of them must be carefully weighed before we can conclude that they represent absolute increases in well-being. The rise in life expectancy is, of course, a gain, but it is accompanied by the ills of old age. The space per person in our dwellings is larger, but the space outside our dwellings is much smaller. And then, is it a gain or a loss when our increased living space reflects the fact that older people are no longer permitted to reside with their grown-up children, but are sent off to villages of "senior citizens" or to the neglect of old people's homes?

So, too, we eat more and more varied foods, but our diet is often less nutritious and delicious than the food of the farm. We enjoy spending our larger incomes, but we suffer the inconveniences that accompany our larger material possessions. We travel at high speeds and encounter the annoyance of traffic jams. We reside in houses with all modern conveniences and are at the mercy of a blackout, a recalcitrant plumber, a balky appliance. We have the convenience of the telephone and also its maddening insistence. We have larger incomes and ever more insistent blandishments on how to spend them—who could have imagined that manufacturers would one day croon the virtues of their wares over national television? And then, in some ways, growth has brought actual deteriorations in life: smogs, pollution dangers, and other risks that we will discuss in the following sections of this chapter.

The attempt to come to grips with the real gains from growth produces some valuable lessons. No one doubts the usefulness of GNP statistics as a general measure of our expanding collective capacity to cope with nature. Growth has meant enormous additions to our ability to wrest food and material from the planet. No one who has seen the cruelty that poverty can bring to an underdeveloped nation would shrug off the gains of economic development as illusory or worthless.

Nonetheless there is a human scale to these matters. At some point along the path of social enrichment, the undeniable gains that wealth can bring begin to mix with dubious results that wealth also brings. As we proceed from grinding poverty toward affluence, the net gains from growth become less. Perhaps at some point the ill effects of affluence—the careless disregard of production, the false estimation of our personal worth as a reflection of our assets—may even outweigh the benefits of economic riches. The Greek legend of Midas and the Biblical estimate of the rich man's chances of entering heaven testify to a deep-seated psychological and moral wariness of riches. They alert us to the feelings of ambivalence and even distaste that surround wealth along with our admiration and hunger for it. All of this suggests deep reasons why the quest for wealth has brought results that have so often disappointed us.

GROWTH AND SOCIAL NEGLECT

Now we must turn from the personal, psychological aspects of wealth to its collective, social uses. Another reason that growth has seemed a mixed blessing is that we have not used it to produce social gains.

Poverty Again

Take the problem of poverty once more. In 1975 the government defined poverty to be an income below about $5,500 for a nonfarm family of four. In that year almost 25 million persons were "poor" by this official definition, and twice that number—50 million—were "near poor"—that is, they had incomes at least 25 percent above the poverty line but below the $14,000 estimated to be necessary for an acceptable standard of life for an urban family of four. Why had economic growth not eradicated this statistically defined poverty?

The answer is by no means simple. We should begin by stressing that economic growth *has* eliminated a considerable amount of officially defined poverty. The percentage of households designated as "poor" or "near poor" in 1975 was considerably below the corresponding percentage only fifteen years ago. In 1959, 22 percent of all households fell below the official poverty line. In 1975 that percentage had been cut nearly in half, even though the poverty line itself had been adjusted upward to take inflation into account. Thus a first answer to our question is that economic growth has eliminated some poverty by raising the incomes of those at the bottom of the income heap.

But this is only a partial answer. For we already know that poverty is not a matter that can be measured in dollars and cents alone. Poverty is a social condition, not just an economic fact. For example, a family of four living in a slum may receive enough from unemploy-

The culture of poverty

ment insurance, welfare, or occasional jobs to bring it near to, or even above, the official poverty line of $5,500. Nonetheless, a family living in the slums cannot easily escape the condition that we call poverty.

The Culture of Poverty

For life in the slums is mean, hard, dangerous. "One of the most fully documented facts about crime," we read in the report of a Presidential Commission on Law Enforcement, "is that the common serious crimes that worry people most—murder, forcible rape, robbery, aggravated assault, and burglary—happen most often in the slums of large cities."[2] Housing is also scarcer and more expensive in the slums; in Chicago, for example, blacks living in ghettos typically pay about $20 a month more for housing than their white counterparts in the city. Even prices are higher, despite the fact that incomes are lower. A Federal Trade Commission report reveals that slum-dwellers pay up to $250 for TV sets that sell for $130 in better-class (and better credit-rated) neighborhoods.

Unemployment too is rife in the slums. In the 1970s, the unemployment rate in poor urban neighborhoods was 60 percent higher than in the country at large. Among some groups, such as black teenagers, it reached levels that dwarfed the worst experience of the Great Depression—40 percent of black teenagers looking for work were unable to find it.

Hence economic growth will not cure the social condition of poverty unless it also alleviates the "culture of poverty." But economic growth has failed to do this. A survey in 1960 showed that 15.6 million dwellings out of 58 million occupied dwelling units in the United States were either dilapidated or located in fast-deteriorating city neighborhoods. Since then, in places such as Newark, Detroit, the South Bronx, St. Louis, the extent and conditions of the slum have become much worse.

Market-guided Growth

Why have the slums proliferated despite economic growth? The main reason is that growth has been guided by the pull of the market-place. We have expanded our output and upgraded our products wherever there was purchasing power to command the needed resources. That is why our growth has been strongest in luxury goods for the new affluent middle classes, and in weaponry. But there is no market pull for the goods needed to improve slums. If we are to change conditions in the slums, the productive power of our economic growth must be directed by nonmarket means into low-cost housing, better police protection, cleaner streets. The only means to accomplish this purpose is the government. Where there is no pull of market demand, growth can be achieved only by taking resources away from the marketplace and using them for social—that is, non-market—purposes.

And that we have not been willing to do. Surely the extent of the slums would be far less, and poverty would be greatly reduced, had we spent $600 billion on public housing rather than $6 billion. As one commentator has observed, "The American middle class knows that poverty could be eliminated, if only we will it; they simply do not will it."[3]

Why do we not will it? We are faced again with a problem that finds its roots in American attitudes. We have seen that other capitalist nations have succeeded in reducing unemployment far below U.S. levels. So, too, many of those nations have done far more than we to eradicate slums. You will not find the conditions that prevail in almost every city in America in any city in Holland, Sweden, Norway, Denmark, Austria, or West Germany. Much of the social neglect that has perpetuated poverty in the face of economic growth is therefore the consequence of American political, social, and even moral attitudes and institutions. All this suggests that, until we change the political and social constraints that guide our economic activities, poverty will continue in America despite further economic growth.

Worse, our willingness to improve the conditions of the slums may have *declined* as a result of economic growth itself. For growth has pumped higher incomes mainly into the hands of the great body of middle- and upper-middle-class citizens, most of whom have now moved out of the central cities or the worst neighborhoods into the prosperous suburbs. Any taxes paid by middle-class suburban citizens for the remedy of the slums are not enjoyed by themselves, but by others—often blacks or other ethnic minorities. There is a real danger, then, that the dynamics of income distribution in a market system lessens the willingness to put money into social repair. If this is true, we can expect the disease of poverty to continue in America, despite further economic growth.

The Irrelevance of Growth

One reason, then, why economic growth has not brought the amelioration we might have expected of it has simply been the failure of American society to use growth in ways that might have yielded greater social returns. But that is not the only reason. Another cause is that there are certain problems that economic growth does not seem to affect at all.

Take the problem of crime. We would certainly imagine that the rise of general purchasing power would reduce crime, especially property crime, because the members of a richer society would be less inclined to steal. But it has not. Between 1960 and 1972, violent

The throwaway economy

crimes per 100,000 population rose from 160 to 397; property crimes from 947 to 2,431.

Why have property crime and violent crime risen despite economic growth? Part of the reason is certainly connected with the worsening of the city ghetto, where so much crime takes place. Another part, however, seems to be a change in public attitudes. Department stores, for example, report marked increases in pilfering rates among all age and ethnic groups. This appears to be the consequence of a tendency to excuse pilfering as a mere "rip-off" of no importance rather than as an actual "crime."

Are such attitudes associated with economic growth? Is it possible that the relentless whetting of our appetite for goods through advertising or the gargantuan waste associated with throwaway packaging and "disposable" products lessens our respect for goods, even for wealth itself? We really do not know. The fact is that we understand very little about the causes of crime or its relation to the economic environment. Probably it is safest to conclude that economic growth, as such, has no effect one way or the other on crime—just as it seems to have no connection with the morality of political behavior, or the state of the arts, or the advent of war. Thus we must put the growth of riches into its proper perspective when we are considering the condition of social life. Economic growth is a major force for social change, but beyond a certain point it is not necessarily a force for social betterment.

THE DANGERS OF GROWTH

So far our investigation has warned us against easy expectations about the gains that economic improvement can bring. Now we need a last critical view, more sobering than anything we have said so far. We need to consider the possibility that economic growth can bring something far worse than disappointments. It can bring dangers that will profoundly influence the nature of our economic transformation in the future.

Exponential Growth

The reason for our wariness of growth has to do with its exponential character. For when we speak of economic growth we do not mean that we add a fixed amount—say $10 billion—to our productive capacity each year. We mean that our productive capacity increases by a certain *percentage* each year. Thus our economic capacity grows like interest in a bank, faster and faster. The graph below shows the terrific acceleration of all exponential growth patterns.

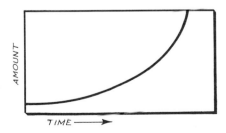

This acceleration is illustrated by a famous parable called the Lilypad Problem. A farmer has a fishpond in which there is a lily pad. The pad is very small, but each day it doubles in size. If it keeps on growing, in a year it will completely cover the pond and choke off all life. The farmer decides to cut it back when it covers half the pond. What day will that be? The 364th day of the year. *The farmer has one day to save the pond.*

All exponential curves shoot upward as time goes on. This is because we *double* the previous amount for each successive period of time. For example, if population grows at the rate of 3 percent a year, here is what happens to population sizes at thirty-year intervals.

World Population
(at 3 percent growth rate)

1970	3.5 billion
2000	7.0 billion
2030	14.0 billion
2060	28.0 billion
2090	56.0 billion

Economic magnitudes also grow at exponential rates. Real gross national product has grown at a rate of about 1.8 percent per capita for the past century, doubling about every thirty-nine years. Total industrial output has grown at approximately 6 percent a year, doubling roughly every twelve years.*

The dangers posed by this exponential property of growth are self-evident. The ravenous appetite of an exponentially expanding economy threatens to exhaust our resources; an exponentially expanding volume of the pollution associated with industrial production threatens to damage the environment beyond repair. The danger of growth is thus that we will outrun the life-carrying capacity of the planet and that growth will terminate in a disaster of terrible proportions.

S-Curves

Are these fears justified? There is both an easy and a difficult answer. The easy answer is that exponential growth, by its very nature, cannot go on indefinitely. This is because no exponential process can continue without becoming "infinitely" large. It has been calculated, for example, that if Adam and Eve had doubled their

---

* There is a valid rule of thumb for growth rates. If you know the *rate* at which something is growing, you can find out how many years it will take to double by dividing the growth rate into the number 70. For instance, a savings account at 5 percent will double in fourteen years (70 ÷ 5 = 14).

numbers every 25 years over the last 4,000 years, human population would have long ago solidly filled the entire solar system. A little closer to home, if we continue to increase our present use of mineral resources by only 3 percent, in 1,000 years we will need a volume of minerals larger than the earth!

Hence we know that exponential growth cannot go on forever. Justus von Liebig, a nineteenth-century chemist, formulated a "law of the minimum" stating that exponential processes must halt when they surpass the lowest threshold of the various supporting elements of the environment. Amoebas, for instance, will cease their exponential growth when they overreach the food supply of their nutrient culture, or when their excretions poison that culture. Thus, in actuality, all social growth processes follow "S-curves" rather than curves that shoot upward at near-vertical slopes, because sooner or later the von Liebig minimums are approached and usually the process of growth tapers off before the barrier is reached.

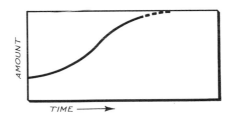

Time Spans

That answer is easy, however, because it does not tell us *how soon* growth will have to begin to level off. The difficult answer tries to predict how much longer we can keep on growing, at present rates, without encountering shortages of minerals, foodstuffs, or energy, or without poisoning our atmosphere or soil or water.

That answer is difficult because so much depends on advances in technology. For example, in 1972 the Club of Rome, an international research organization, published *The Limits to Growth*, the first major warning about the dangers of exponential growth. The study presented the following table showing how many years we can keep on growing at existing growth rates before we run out of estimated reserves of certain critical resources:

Years of Resource Availability at Present Growth Rates

Aluminum	31
Coal	111
Copper	21
Iron	93
Lead	21
Petroleum	20
Tin	15

SOURCE: Donella L. Meadows et al., *The Limits to Growth* (1974), pp. 56–57.

Resources and Technology

This table indicates that our growth curve would have to level off within a few decades because we would then exhaust the basic raw materials needed to sustain a continuously expanding economy. Fortunately, the table does not take technology into account. And technology may totally alter our dependence on given materials or may vastly increase our supplies of those materials. For example, today our "reserves" of iron ore consist mainly of beds of a material called taconite. Fifty years ago, when we were still mining the rich Mesabi Range, we did not even count taconite as a source of iron! So, too, fifty years ago, it was assumed we would run out of oil in twenty years. Twenty years later we had *more* oil reserves than we started with because the technology of oil discovery had improved so dramatically.

Therefore we cannot predict when we will run out of particular resources, because technology is continually expanding the kinds of resources that we can use. Oceans and rocks, for example, contain gigantic supplies of virtually all elements, including minerals, in "trace" amounts; if we can develop the technological means of refining sea water or granite, we will have no mineral resource problem for hundreds of years.

Moreover, as we begin to draw heavily on the reserves of a particular mineral or resource, its price will rise. Hence buyers will naturally purchase smaller quantities of it, and business firms will redouble their efforts to find less expensive substitutes. In this way the market system itself cushions the consequences of a resource shortage and acts as a kind of feedback mechanism to convert dangerous exponential use-curves of particular items into S-curves.

Nonetheless the market pressures that encourage the development of substitutes, and the technological "fixes" that promise gigantic quantities of potential resources, only postpone, they do not remove, the limits to growth. Ultimately the market can do no more than divert demand toward our most plentiful and least expensive resources, such as sea water or common granite. Thereafter we must depend entirely on the capacity of science and technology to make these common materials usable for economic purposes.

We cannot blandly assume that technology will solve these problems. We do not yet have the technology we need to "make" resources out of sea water or rock. We do not know whether or when such a technology will be developed. We are not sure that we have enough energy, in the form of oil, coal, or uranium, to process enormous volumes of water or rock. We have not yet developed a technology that would enable us to utilize solar energy efficiently.

The Pollution Threat

In other words, we live in a condition of uncertainty. And that uncertainty is compounded because of the second risk that exponential growth poses—the risk of polluting the environment so severely that life itself is endangered.

This is not just an imaginary possibility. On more than one occasion in the past few years, residents of Los Angeles and St. Louis were warned by local health authorities against any form of exercise because deep breathing was dangerous. Scientists have discovered that certain widely used chemical fertilizers lower the long-term fertility of the soil. We do not know how to dispose of nuclear wastes in complete safety; yet, at present growth rates, by the year 2000 there will be, at any one time, some 3,000 six-ton trucks loaded with dangerous radioactive wastes in transit to burial sites. And some scientists fear that the growing generation of heat from industrial processes may alter the climate patterns of the earth or change global temperatures, with potentially catastrophic effects, within another century.

These warnings about pollution, however, are also subject to the same consideration that affects warnings about resource use. For all, or nearly all, of these dangers can be greatly reduced by technology. There is little doubt that we can produce goods with much less adverse impact on the environment than we do now. But, as with resource technology, no one can tell us how rapidly the appropriate technological "fixes" can be found. Today, for example, we do not yet have a really clean, economical way of making steel or paper or elec-

Global pollution; above, Japan; below, West Germany

tricity. We do not even have an electric automobile, the first obvious step in lowering the pollution that assails our eyes and noses in any city.

A Timetable for Growth

Hence it is very difficult to give dependable answers to the question of how long we can go on growing. All that we can say is that we cannot continue very much longer—perhaps no more than two or three decades with existing techniques that depend on scarce raw materials such as oil or that generate dangerous gaseous or liquid by-products. That is why all industrialized nations are beginning to change their attitudes toward growth. Until very recently, the view of the United States, the European nations, and Japan was that the more growth the better. Indeed, nations boasted of their growth rates; and Japan, growing at over 10 percent a year—doubling its GNP every seven years!—was the economic wonder of the world.

Today governments, especially in the industrialized West, are eyeing growth more cautiously. Japan has deliberately undertaken policies to lower its growth rate by more than 25 percent, partly to lessen its dependence on raw materials such as petroleum, partly to lessen the pollution that has made it necessary for Tokyo citizens to wear air-filter masks on really bad days. In our own country, the Arab oil embargo produced long lines at gas pumps and brought home the need for a policy of energy conservation and research, and pictures of a dying Lake Erie made believable the warnings that America was changing from an affluent into an effluent society.

A sharp debate divides experts as to how much longer growth can safely continue. Some feel that technology will permit us to continue along the growth path of the past century for a very long time. Others feel that we are too near the margin of danger and that technology must be used, not to sustain growth, but to help us become a "stationary" economy.

If the problem were somehow confined to the industrial countries alone, there is no doubt that *controlled* growth—growth that minimized the use of scarce resources and avoided as much pollution as possible—could continue for at least the remainder of this century and well into the next. But the problem becomes more pressing because the underdeveloped countries will be adding their demands for resources (and their contribution to pollution) to the demands of the rich nations. It seems plausible that by the midpoint of the next century growth will be pressing dangerously on the resources, energy supplies, and ecological safety margins of the earth. A reasonable guess is that growth will have to be near zero—perhaps even negative—a century from now.

This is, of course, only a guess. But one thing has become clear even to the most ardent advocates of growth: Growth is a dangerous process as well as a beneficial one. No one today ignores the costs of growth or urges growth without careful controls. As Kenneth Boulding, a noted economist, has put it, we are leaving the era in which we thought of ourselves as living in a wide-open, expansive "cowboy economy" and entering a new era in which we begin to see ourselves living in a fragile, self-contained "spaceship economy."[4]

NOTES

[1] Richard Easterlin, "Does Money Bring Happiness?" *The Public Interest* (Winter 1973).

[2] *The Challenge of Crime in a Free Society: A Report by the President's Commission on Law Enforcement and Administration of Justice* (1967), p. 35.

[3] Adam Walinsky, *New Republic* (July 4, 1965), p. 15.

[4] "The Economics of the Coming Spaceship Earth," in Henry Jarrett (ed.), *Environmental Quality in a Growing Economy* (1966).

The
Transformation
Ahead

13

We have looked into the long-term problems of growth, with special attention to the dangers inherent in a continuation of exponential expansion. But we have not yet considered one last and most important issue. This is the challenge posed to the vitality of capitalism itself by the impending end of growth.

Capitalism in Transition

For surely, expansion has been the main impelling force behind our economic history. It was the thrust of growth that brought giant enterprise, big labor, and big government into being. It was growth that sparked the ceaseless introduction of new technology. Above all, it was economic growth that provided the necessary setting for the successful search for profit, the central motivation of the market system.

Moreover, growth has provided us not only with a tremendous

stimulus but with an indispensable safety valve. All through the economic transformation of the American economy we have witnessed a struggle among the participants, above all between labor and capital, for larger shares in the output of the economy. One cannot give larger *shares* to everyone, but one can give larger *pieces*, especially if the output "pie" becomes steadily larger.

This is what growth has provided, and this is what the absence of growth would remove. If growth comes to a halt, the search for "more" that is so deep a part of our culture and our economic mechanism cannot mean more-for-everyone. "More" can then be gained only by one group, if others take less.

Thus an impending end to growth has a profound significance for the future. The end of growth also means the onset of a period in which tension over income shares must necessarily rise. Can capitalism withstand such an exacerbation of internal strain, such a tugging and pulling, such a stimulus to its never wholly absent class animosities?

The Long-term Future

This seems a proper place for me to step in front of the curtain of textbook anonymity and to speak in my own voice. For this question cannot be answered solely by a recourse to the facts we have gathered. Necessarily the answer reflects private interpretations, and it is important that this mingling of subjective feeling and objective finding be made explicit.

I base my own answer on the premise that planning will be the central political and economic necessity of *all* economic systems over the coming generations. This is a conclusion to which our analysis has already led us, when we considered the growing need to assure the smooth operation of giant corporations within a mixed economy. But this trend takes on enormous added importance when the need for control and direction involves not merely the profitable working of the system, or the avoidance of the "normal" problems of a complex economic system, but the very safety and continuity of the human enterprise itself.

This new impetus to planning derives from the explosive character of economic processes in contemporary industrial societies. As we have seen, industrial life requires the ever more voracious consumption of mineral and other resources, and spews forth ever more gigantic quantities of wastes and noxious by-products and heat.

Growth in our time has become a process whose termination will be lethal unless it is curbed and redirected.

And so it *will* be curbed and redirected, by ever more rigorous scrutiny, monitoring, and prohibition. Wasteful methods will be replaced by conserving methods; wasteful habits by frugal ones. Dangerous processes and products will be at first discouraged, then outlawed. The composition as well as the volume of output will be examined with an eye to its compatibility with human safety, and the division of the social product will be determined by standards that minimize the strains within society.

None of this will take place tomorrow. Fortunately, it need not. We have a generation, perhaps even two or three generations, in which to make our peace with nature. But the peace must be made, and the only means by which that can be done is through the extension of deliberate control over the freewheeling economic process. There is no escape from the conclusion that planning must extend further and penetrate deeper into economic life as the dangers of an environmental catastrophe draw closer.

Economic Planning and Liberty

Will this increasing need for planning mean a loss of our democratic prerogatives, even a risk of dictatorship? It would be foolish to deny that such a possibility exists. Indeed, it is likely that as Spaceship Earth becomes less of a metaphor and more of an experienced reality, its inhabitants will have to submit to a much greater degree of social discipline than they are accustomed to today.

Yet, in the short-term future—the next few decades—I see no reason to believe that planning must entail a reduction in the right to form and join parties of our choice, to speak our minds freely, to assemble and protest peacefully. Indeed, it may well be that political freedom would be more seriously threatened if we did not plan, and if, as a consequence, our economy was suddenly forced to adapt to economic or environmental pressures without warning or foresight. If we *do* plan, we may be able to make the transition to a more regulated, safety-conscious, slow-growing society with little or no political curtailment. That depends, I believe, on the differing social and political attributes of different societies. Some capitalist societies may well make the transition easily; others may not. Needless to say, the same applies to the ability of different socialist societies to cope with the identical problems that will affect their own economic futures.

Beyond Capitalism

But I have not yet addressed myself to the question of the significance of the end of growth for our economic system. Here I must state bluntly that I believe the coming transformation will indeed take us beyond capitalism. I suspect the societies that will inherit the earth a century or so from now will not depend very largely on the market mechanism or on private property, that their acquisitive spirit will be less in evidence and certainly less celebrated, and that the prevailing social order will be as different from contemporary capitalism as contemporary capitalism is from our colonial beginnings.

What might such a system be like? I imagine that it will be much more collective and much less private; much more state-centered and much less corporation-centered; much more traditional or even religiously oriented, and much less restless or materialistically inclined.

All this is, of course, sheerly personal speculation. But I think that we can perhaps find some clues to the future from our study of the past. For it must be clear that America's economic transformation is not complete. Even without the threat of environmental danger, the course of economic evolution is unfinished. We have learned how to apply prodigies of skill to the production of goods, but not to the enhancement of that central human experience, work. We have learned how to increase the volume of output, but not how to distribute it equitably. We have overcome some of the malfunctions of a highly complex economy, but have hardly begun to consider remedies for others no less serious. Our economic transformation has been a mixture of exhilaration and disappointment, achievement and failure, intense concentration and carelessness.

Hence the lines of the continuing transformation can be seen in the unfinished trajectory of our history. In a new stable, "stationary" economic milieu, mechanization must give way to a more humanistic approach to work and to the use of machinery in life. The mixed economy must yield to an economy of smaller scale, more responsive to individual aspirations and to public needs. The mindless celebration of change, novelty, discovery must make place for a new estimation of preservation, tradition, rediscovery.

When I say "must," I do not mean that all this is preordained. It is a possibility, not an inevitability. Whether we will achieve these goals in the next stage of our economic transformation cannot be blandly predicted. This is because the transformation itself is not a mechanical process but a dynamic working-out of history in which there are always margins for success and failure, options for wise and foolish choices, alternative variations on a main theme. We look into the future, not to discern what must be, but to catch a glimpse of destinations to which we can bend our energies during our lifetime.

Suggestions for Further Reading

Preface: Economic Transformation as a Theme of History

Three useful introductions to the problem of economic development are Robert L. Heilbroner, *The Great Ascent* * (1963); Benjamin Higgins, *Economic Development* * (1968); and Charles K. Wilber (ed.), *The Political Economy of Development and Underdevelopment* * (1973), a collection of essays, often very critical.

PART ONE   The Momentum of Growth

Only a handful of scholars have attempted to write general overviews of this period. Two of the most useful volumes are Stuart Bruchey's *The Roots of American Economic Growth, 1607–1860* * (1965), and Douglass C. North's *The Economic Growth of the United States, 1790–1860* * (1961), an analytical study which stresses the role of commerce as a vehicle for economic growth. There is a wealth of useful information in Curtis P. Nettels' *The Emergence of a National Economy* * (1962), a detailed account of the years 1775–1815.

Transportation

The best general account of developments in transportation is George Rogers Taylor, *The Transportation Revolution, 1815–1860* * (1951). Other useful studies include L. C. Hunter, *Steamboats on the Western Rivers* (1949), a classic work; R. E. Shaw, *Erie Water West: A History of the Erie Canal* (1966); and Carter Goodrich (ed.), *Canals and American Economic Development* (1961). Two complex econometric studies that try to measure the impact of the railroad on American economic development are Robert W. Fogel, *Railroads and American Economic Growth* * (1964), and Albert Fishlow, *American Railroads and the Transformation of the Antebellum Economy* (1965).

---

* Available in a paperback edition.

Labor

For labor in early America see Richard B. Morris, *Government and Labor in Early America** (1946). The best general account of labor in the manufacturing sector is N. J. Ware, *The Industrial Worker, 1840–1860** (1924). On the life of the early New England textile operatives see Caroline Ware, *The Early New England Cotton Manufacture* (1931), and Hannah Josephson, *The Golden Threads* (1949). Important specialized studies include G. S. Gibb, *The Saco-Lowell Shops* (1950); and W. A. Sullivan, *The Industrial Worker in Pennsylvania* (1955).

Technology

Nathan Rosenberg's *Technology and American Economic Growth** (1972) is an excellent general statement. Important technological changes are summarized in H. J. Habakkuk, *American and British Technology in the Nineteenth Century** (1962). There are two excellent biographies of Eli Whitney: Allan Nevins and Jeannette Mirsky, *The World of Eli Whitney** (1952), and Constance McLaughlin Green, *Eli Whitney and the Birth of American Technology** (1956).

The Civil War Era

There are a number of useful essays, including the important T. C. Cochran article, in Ralph Andreano (ed.), *The Economic Impact of the American Civil War** (2nd ed., 1967). For a discussion of economic developments and the coming of the Civil War see Allan Nevins' magisterial *The Ordeal of the Union* (1947). L. M. Hacker, *The Triumph of American Capitalism** (1940), and E. D. Fite, *Social and Industrial Conditions in the North During the Civil War* (1910), are also useful.

For slavery and its effect on the economic development of the South see A. H. Conrad and J. R. Meyer, *The Economics of Slavery* (1964); Eugene Genovese, *The Political Economy of Slavery** (1965); Harold Woodman (ed.), *Slavery and the Southern Economy** (1966); and R. W. Fogel and S. L. Engerman, *Time on the Cross** (1974), a controversial econometric study. Fogel and Engerman's findings are challenged in Paul David et al., *Reckoning with Slavery** (1976).

PART TWO   Industrialization Takes Command

Two well-written introductions to the period are John A. Garraty, *The New Commonwealth** (1968), and R. H. Wiebe, *The Search for Order** (1967). Important general studies of industrialization include E. C. Kirkland, *Industry Comes of Age** (1961); Allan Nevins, *The Emergence of Modern America** (1927); T. C. Cochran and William Miller, *The Age of Enterprise** (1942); and Glenn Porter, *The Rise of Big Business, 1860–1910** (1973). *The Transformation of the American Economy, 1865–1914* (1971), by Robert Higgs, is a good account of economic changes. Rendigs Fels' *American Business Cycles, 1865–1897* (1959) is a very specialized study.

Business Leaders

Business leaders and business ideology are discussed in Matthew Josephson, *The Robber Barons** (1934); E. C. Kirkland, *Dream and Thought in the Business Community** (1956); and William Miller (ed.), *Men in Business** (1962).

Other important works on intellectual currents include Richard Hofstadter, *Social Darwinism in American Thought** (1955); Sidney Fine, *Laissez Faire and the General Welfare State** (1956); and R. G. McCloskey, *American Conservatism in the Age of Enterprise** (1951).

Technology and Steel

For a brilliant introduction to the Industrial Revolution and steel production see David Landes, *Unbound Prometheus** (1969). Other useful works on technology include W. P. Strassman, *Risk and Technological Innovation* (1959), and E. E. Morison, *From Knowhow to Nowhere* (1974). *Iron and Steel in the Nineteenth Century* (1964), by Peter Temin, is an econometric study. J. F. Wall's *Andrew Carnegie* (1970) is both a definitive biography and an excellent account of the industry that Carnegie dominated.

Big Business

Although it is very detailed, Alfred D. Chandler's *Strategy and Structure** (1962) is the best introduction to business expansion in these years. See also S. P. Hays, *The Response to Industrialism, 1885–1914** (1957), and K. E. Boulding, *The Organization Revolution** (1953). There are several excellent studies on the growth of particular industries. See, for example, Allan Nevins, *A Study in Power: John D. Rockefeller, Industrialist and Philanthropist* (1953); R. W. and M. E. Hidy, *Pioneering in Big Business, 1882–1911: History of the Standard Oil Company* (1955); Allan Nevins and F. E. Hill, *Ford* (1954–57); H. F. Williamson and A. R. Daum, *The American Petroleum Industry* (1959); H. C. Passer, *The Electrical Manufacturers, 1875–1900* (1953); and Matthew Josephson, *Edison** (1959).

On business consolidation see G. H. Evans, Jr., *Business Incorporations in the United States, 1800–1943* (1948), and Ralph Nelson, *Merger Movements in American Industry* (1959). For the federal government's response to these trends see Hans B. Thorelli, *The Federal Antitrust Policy* (1955), and William Letwin, *Law and Economic Policy in America: The Evolution of the Sherman Antitrust Act* (1965).

Labor

For a sampling of the important testimony taken by the Senate Committee on Education and Labor in 1883 see John A. Garraty (ed.), *Labor and Capital in the Gilded Age** (1968). The Knights of Labor are discussed in N. J. Ware, *The Labor Movement in the United States, 1860–1895** (1929). The AFL is the subject of Philip Taft's *The AFL in the Time of Gompers* (1957). For women at work consult Robert Smuts, *Women and Work in America** (2nd ed., 1971). Other valuable monographs include Charlotte Erickson, *American Industry* *and European Immigration, 1860–1885* (1957); G. N. Grob, *Workers and Utopia** (1961); David Brody, *Steelworkers in America** (1960); and Melvyn Dubofsky, *Industrialism and the American Worker, 1865–1920** (1975). On the Homestead strike see Leon Wolff, *Lockout** (1965). A brilliant general analysis of labor from a Marxist point of view is presented in Harry Braverman's *Labor and Monopoly Capital** (1974).

Work and Life

Sigfried Giedion's *Mechanization Takes Command** (1948) is a rambling but useful work. The standardization of work is the subject of F. W. Taylor, *The Principles of Scientific Management** (1911), and C. R. Walker and R. H. Guest, *The Man on the Assembly Line* (1956).

Urbanization

Two excellent introductions to the topic are Sam Bass Warner's *The Urban Wilderness** (1972), and Blake McKelvey's *The Urbanization of America* (1963). For slums and tenements see Robert Bremner, *From the Depths** (1956), and Roy Lubove, *The Progressives and the Slums* (1962). On Harlem see Gilbert Osofsky, *Harlem: The Making of a Ghetto** (1965). See also Allan H. Spear's *Black Chicago: The Making of a Negro Ghetto, 1890–1920** (1967).

PART THREE   From Laissez Faire to Mixed Economy

Useful introductions to the social, political, and economic trends of the 1920s include F. L. Allen, *Only Yesterday** (1931); J. W. Prothro, *The Dollar Decade: Business Ideas in the 1920's* (1954); William Leuchtenburg, *The Perils of Prosperity** (1958); and Paul Carter, *The Twenties in America** (1968).

The Great Crash and the Great Depression

For the stock market collapse see John Kenneth Galbraith, *The Great Crash** (1955), and Robert Sobel, *The Great Bull Market: Wall Street in the 1920's** (1968). On the Great Depression consult Charles P. Kindleberger, *The World in Depression, 1929–1939** (1973); L. V. Chandler, *America's Greatest Depression** (1970); Broadus Mitchell, *Depression Decade** (1947); A. U. Romasco, *The Poverty of Abundance** (1965); and Caroline Bird, *The Invisible Scar** (1966), a narrative history. The activities of the Federal Reserve Board are the subject of two technical studies, Milton Friedman and A. J. Schwartz, *The Great Contraction, 1929–1933** (1965), and Peter Temin, *Did Monetary Forces Cause the Great Depression?* (1976).

The New Deal

William Leuchtenburg's *Franklin D. Roosevelt and the New Deal** (1963) is the best single-volume study, but see also Arthur Schlesinger's excellent *The Age of Roosevelt** (1957–), and J. M. Burns' *Roosevelt: The Lion and the Fox** (1956), which contains an analysis of Roosevelt as an economist.

Keynes

Two useful guides to Keynes are Alvin Hansen, *A Guide to Keynes** (1953), and Robert Lekachman, *The Age of Keynes** (1966).

The Mixed Economy

The emergence of the mixed economy is traced in Harley Vatter, *The United States Economy in the 1950's** (1963); John Kenneth Galbraith, *American Capitalism** (1952); Editors of *Fortune, America in the Sixties* (1960); and S. E. Harris, *Economics of the Kennedy Years* (1964).

Multinationals

Mira Wilkins, *The Emergence of Multinational Enterprise: American Business Abroad from the Colonial Era to 1914* (1970), is an important scholarly work. See also Richard Barnet and Ronald Müller, *Global Reach** (1974). For a general criticism of American diplomacy see W. A. Williams, *The Tragedy of American Diplomacy** (2nd rev. ed., 1972).

PART FOUR   Growth and Its Limitations

For a sobering look at the problems and prospects for capitalism see R. L. Heilbroner, *Business Civilization in Decline** (1976). The growth of planning in the private sector is covered in John Kenneth Galbraith's *The New Industrial State** (rev. ed., 1972).

Growth and Well-Being

Useful articles on the economic growth controversy are presented in W. A. Johnson and John Hardesty (eds.), *Economic Growth vs. The Environment** (1971), and Andrew Weintraub, Eli Schwartz, and J. Richard Aronson (eds.), *The Economic Growth Controversy** (1974). Other important works in this area include Barry Commoner, *The Closing Circle** (1971), and R. L. Heilbroner, *An Inquiry into the Human Prospect** (1974). For an opposing view see Peter Passell and Leonard Ross, *The Retreat from Riches: Affluence and Its Enemies** (1973).

PICTURE CREDITS

Index